D0058475

"*Taste Berries for Teens* is a very person
to take to your room and shut the doo
It's also a book you'll want to share w
slip a copy of a particular story to rem
the light." Enjoy it. Let it soothe your h
give rise to unending possibilities for your life."

Senator Carol Roessler
Wisconsin State Senate

"Keeping up with the demands of my school life, coping with the highs
and lows of how I'm feeling about my friends—or a particular guy, trying to figure out what I'm going to do with my life . . . it's a lot. *Taste
Berries for Teens* is a great book to help you sort yourself out."

Rachel Burres, 17

"These stories offer keen insight into those human qualities that make
our society a better place to live. Very inspirational."

Terry N. Trieweiler
Montana Supreme Court Justice

"These stories show the turmoil that is the stuff of being a young person
in today's world, and shed light on the many ways young people are
sorting it out and, in the process, making a real difference. This is a book
you will definitely want to read. Interesting, informative, useful, funny,
thought provoking."

Cathy Schmachtenberger
Books Are Fun

"The stories in *Taste Berries for Teens* are so personal, I felt like I was
reading about my own life. It's very reassuring and very helpful to know
that I'm not alone in how I feel and what I find important. I think this
book should be required reading in schools."

Chiana McCulky, 16

"Amidst the turmoil and adventure of being a teenager in today's
times, this book is a tremendous breath of fresh air. Today's times offer
teenagers unlimited possibilities and unlimited choices. This is both
good and bad news. A nice feature of *Taste Berries for Teens* is that it
can help young people make better and informed choices, because
they see the outcomes of other options they might have chosen. Give
a copy of this book to a teen you know who is struggling with his life,
and to one who is already on track toward worthwhile goals—so that
he stays there."

Robert Ray
president, Drake University
three-term former governor, State of Iowa

"*Taste Berries for Teens* is a clone of my heart! In one story it's like, 'Yes! That's exactly how I feel: I can jump from the highest mountain without a parachute because I am invincible!' The next story is like, 'Yes! That's how I feel, too: I have no energy to scale the mountain, but who cares? I don't even want to get out of bed.' There are so many conflicts within me, and yet, this book helps me feel normal. It's so nice to know that other teens feel the ups and downs like I do. Reading this book gives me hope: I'm normal after all!"

Heather White, 14

"Being a teenager can be lonely because you get used to talking to yourself. Pretty soon, either you think you're pretty great or pretty crazy. It's nice to have a sounding board, a measuring stick, a barometer. That's what this book is."

Brad Charles, 15

"My story is in chapter 8!"

Steve Smith
astronaut and veteran of two space flights,
over three hundred Earth orbits and three space walks

"What a marvelous book! I was inspired by the kindness and generosity from so many of the teens reporting on things they had done. I am truly impressed by the dreams they have for the world. It is also evident that by using their talents, today's teens can—and will—change the world!"

Ronald Glosser
vice chairman of the board, *Guideposts*

"We sometimes forget what it's like to be a teenager—there is such an abundance of good times, and of bad. *Taste Berries for Teens* has found a way to bottle these up together, and in keeping with the effects of a taste berry, make the bad tolerable. Read this remarkable book. It's a prescriptive on how to use the stage of adolescence to instill values, meaning and direction in our young people."

Janice Williams
AmeriCorps–21st Century Scholars

"This book will be one of the most favorite ones you own, and the reason is because it will inspire you to think deeply about what you would like to do in life and 'who' you wish to become, and to decide what's the best way to get there. You'll read about other teens and learn how they are asking and addressing issues relevant to teens living in a new era, faced with wonderful and spectacular challenges. An absolutely phenomenal resource!"

Lauren Gartland
Building Champions

Taste Berries™
for Teens

INSPIRATIONAL SHORT STORIES AND ENCOURAGEMENT ON LIFE, LOVE, FRIENDSHIP AND TOUGH ISSUES

With contributions from teens for teens

Bettie B. Youngs, Ph.D., Ed.D.

author of *Values from the Heartland, Gifts of the Heart* and *Taste-Berry™ Tales*

Jennifer Leigh Youngs

Health Communications, Inc.
Deerfield Beach, Florida

www.hci-online.com

We would like to acknowledge the following publishers and individuals for permission to reprint the following material. (Note: The stories that were penned anonymously, that are public domain or were previously unpublished stories written by Bettie B. Youngs or Jennifer Leigh Youngs are not included in this listing. Also not included in this listing but credited within the text are those stories contributed or based upon comments by teens.)

The Paintbrush by Lee Ezell, adapted from *You and Self-Esteem: A Book for Young People.* ©1996 Bettie B. Youngs. Reprinted with permission.

The Dragon in My Drawer!, How Big Is Your Splash?, Did I Pass Your Test for Friends?, Hidden Beneath the Folded Things, I'll Be in the Bleachers, Time Cannot Erase Our Love Affair, When I Bite My Tongue, and *A Capacity to Mend,* by Elmer Adrian. Reprinted with permission.

Always *Your Friend, Unconditional Love* and *Your Long-Term Address,* by George E. Young. Reprinted with permission.

(continued on page 341)

Library of Congress Cataloging-in-Publication Data

Youngs, Bettie B., date.
    Taste berries for teens: inspirational short stories and encouragement on life, love, friendship and tough issues: with contributions from teens for teens/Bettie B. Youngs, Jennifer Leigh Youngs.
        p. cm.
    ISBN 1-55874-669-2 (trade paper)
    1. Teenagers—Conduct of life.   I. Youngs, Jennifer Leigh, date.   II Title.
BJ1661.Y69 1999
248.8'3—dc21   98-55375
                                                                                              CIP

©1999 Bettie B. Youngs and Jennifer Leigh Youngs
ISBN 1-55874-669-2 trade paper

Publisher: Health Communications, Inc.
            3201 S. W. 15th Street
            Deerfield Beach, Florida 33442-8190

Cover illustration and design by Andrea Perrine Brower

To teens everywhere:
May we honor and protect your *ideals*,
value your *wisdom*, learn from your *experiences*,
and point you in the direction of your *calling*.

Also by Bettie B. Youngs

Taste-Berry Tales: Stories to Lift the Spirit, Fill the Heart and Feed the Soul (Health Communications, Inc.)

Gifts of the Heart: Stories That Celebrate Life's Defining Moments (Health Communications, Inc.)

Values from the Heartland (Health Communications, Inc.)

Stress & Your Child: Helping Kids Cope with the Strains & Pressures of Life (Random House)

Safeguarding Your Teenager from the Dragons of Life: A Guide to the Adolescent Years (Health Communications, Inc.)

How to Develop Self-Esteem in Your Child: 6 Vital Ingredients (Macmillan/Ballantine)

Self-Esteem for Educators: It's Job Criteria #1 (Jalmar Press)

Keeping Our Children Safe: A Guide to Emotional, Physical, Intellectual and Spiritual Wellness (John Knox/Westminster Press)

You and Self-Esteem: A Book for Young People (Jalmar Press)

Developing Self-Esteem in Your Students: A K-12 Curriculum (Jalmar Press)

Getting Back Together: Repairing Love (Adams Media Corp.)

Is Your Net-Working? A Complete Guide to Building Contacts and Career Visibility (John Wiley)

Managing Your Response to Stress: A Guide for Administrators (Jalmar Press)

Also by Jennifer Leigh Youngs

A Stress-Management Guide for Young People (Learning Tools Press)

Goal-Setting Skills for Young Adults, coauthor (Learning Tools Press)

Problem-Solving Skills for Children, coauthor (Learning Tools Press)

Contents

PART 4: THE RIGHT STUFF: ATTITUDES FOR LIFE
SUCCESS—BECOMING A PERSON OF ...

PART 6: GIVING, SHARING, MAKING A DIFFERENCE

Acknowledgments

We would like to thank some of the people who were "taste berries" in the development of this book.

To our publisher, Peter Vegso, and the entire staff of Health Communications, Inc. In particular, to the editorial staff—most especially Lisa Drucker, Matthew Diener, Christine Belleris and Erica Orloff—a very special thanks. Not only are they fun to work with, but their encouragement and support on a project of this undertaking is so important. Another special thank-you to Andrea Perrine Brower, who designed the cover of this book, as well as the gorgeous covers of three of Bettie's other books: *Values from the Heartland, Gifts of the Heart* and *Taste-Berry Tales*. And, to Tina Moreno, Cathy Jones and Maria Rios of our staff, for their professionalism and generous support, a most heartfelt thanks. Finally, with much gratitude and respect, we offer a very "taste-berry" thanks to all the teens who worked so diligently on this book with us, proving once again that teens see so clearly from the "eyes of the heart."

We each would like to individually thank some very special people for their support and encouragement while we worked on this book.

Bettie

I'd like to thank some very delicious and important "taste berries" in my life. First and foremost, I must return a heart full of love to my coauthor and daughter, Jennifer Leigh Youngs. Jennifer has always been a special soul mate of mine, and doing this book together taught me—for the second time—the true meaning of the words "labor of love"! To my anchors in all times:

the wisest and most loving woman I have ever known—and the first line of defense on my behalf—my mother Arlene; and one of my best friends—a staunch confidant and wise and very loved old sage—my father Everett. Also, an ever-standing thank-you to my brothers and sisters, and brothers- and sisters-in-law—all of whom are dear to me and so giving of friendship. I never take you for granted. And, to a "perfectly good Texas boy," my husband David. Always, always he is a "taste berry"!

Jennifer

I would like to give glory to God. Walking with him has transformed my life with countless blessings and even a few small miracles. Many times throughout my destiny there was only one set of footprints, always reminding me to look up. And, I'd like to thank my parents for loving me as they do. Growing up isn't easy, and I'm sure there were times when they wondered what spaceship dropped me off! Thank you for seeing me through all the tough times and for all the support and unconditional love—and for the conditional love as well. Thank you for having my best interest at heart—always, I know that I am loved! I am lucky to have you both, a fact that becomes clearer to me with each passing year.

To you, Dad (Dic Youngs), thanks for being my friend and protector. Even though as a teen I didn't appreciate your telling my dates that they'd "better have my daughter home on time" (and then reminding them that you could use the baseball bat that sat in the corner), I so appreciate that part of your heart that loves me enough to oversee that I am safe in the world. You will always be my hero and I will always "go to bat" for you. You have shown me what to look for in a "good guy": integrity, honesty, loyalty, friendship, humor—and a great voice! And, Dad, thanks for that tone of voice and that look in your eyes when you say, "That's my girl!" It's been worth more than you know.

To my mother (Bettie Youngs), who has taught me the value of loving myself, and helped me find the courage to forgive the parts of me that I don't accept and helped me come to believe that, in the end, it is the brightness of the light within that counts. There was a time when I didn't want to be like you, and a time when I feared that I wouldn't be. You have helped me "see" the person I am, and you have modeled the woman I hope to become. Thanks for loving me as you do: it shows in everything you do—like giving me the opportunity to coauthor this book. Working together has been so much fun, so fulfilling, so cherished.

Thanks to my dear friend Tawny Pearl Flippen—best friends always. And, to Turtle, Frog, White Light. And, to Ron Young, whose heart ventures past the surface and into the spirit, "seeing" the good in everyone—as you say, "Life is good." And, to the friends I didn't mention—you know who you are and how much I value your friendship. You are true "taste berries" and you make my life sweeter.

Preface

I had just completed *Taste-Berry Tales*, a book of short stories for adult readers highlighting some of the many wonderful ways people make a difference in the lives of others. After a number of people had read the book, many suggested that it would be a wonderful idea to do a book specifically for young people, highlighting some of the many things teens do to become caring, responsible people, and ways they make a difference in the lives of others—and in the world. Having been a classroom educator, and experiencing firsthand the parenting of an adolescent myself—and having had so many of her friends constantly in my home—I knew so well that teenagers greatly contribute to the betterment of others, and their perspective on life and living is a valued one. Though I was very interested in doing a book for teens, I had other pressing matters and a heavy travel schedule. In short, it hadn't reached my "Must Do" list.

But the idea refused to go away and, curiously, it insisted on having voice—a persistent one. That voice increased in volume during Christmas when I received a holiday letter from my friend, Colleen Morey, a program administrator in Connecticut. In her letter, Colleen described an experience she'd had with a group of young people, many of whom were jaded, and had pretty much given up on life, so much so that some of them called themselves "losers." To enlist their enthusiasm (and so that they would learn to use the computer), Colleen linked her students up with another group of young people—living in Bogotá, Colombia!

In "talking" and sharing with each other, Colleen's students learned that the kids in Bogotá were living in an orphanage and had never once so much as received a present or gift from anyone in their entire lives. The American teenagers were surprised—and empathetic. It was unthinkable to them to be without the basics—CDs, several pairs of shoes, clothes they liked and had chosen for themselves, a room of their own and foods they liked (staples like pizza, hamburgers and french fries). Colleen's students decided to do something to change the plight of their newfound friends.

So they began collecting boxes upon boxes of clothing, books, CDs (very big on their list!), medical supplies and other things they felt these young people should have. Several months and some fifty-plus boxes later, Colleen's students were ready to send these items to their friends in Bogotá. This presented a new challenge: How would they afford to send the many boxes to Bogotá?

At the same moment this challenge presented itself, out of the blue, Leeanne Hansen (Colleen's former college friend) called Colleen to say she'd been thinking about her and wanted to renew their friendship. Having lost track of where Colleen was living, Leeanne had called Colleen's parents for her phone number. The two friends talked by phone and discussed the possibility of getting together. "How about tomorrow?" Leeanne suggested. "It just so happens I am on my way to the East Coast, and as luck would have it, I'll be in the very city where you now live."

The two former friends and schoolmates, who had not seen or spoken with each other for nearly ten years, were reunited and had the chance to catch up on all that was going on in their lives. You can only imagine their intrigue when Colleen told Leeanne of her current work, including the challenge to help her students find a way to transport the items they had collected for the children in Bogotá, Colombia—especially since Leeanne was coordinator for Airline Ambassadors (founded by her friend Nancy Rivard), a volunteer group that provides humanitarian assistance to children around the world. Wouldn't you know it, with the return of Leeanne into Colleen's life came the resolution of the problem of how to deliver the boxes to Bogotá. During Christmas break, Colleen and Leeanne delivered the boxes, courtesy of Airline Ambassadors!

When I read Colleen's Christmas letter, I was so moved by it that I called her to learn more about it and to tell her that she must share her story. "What incredible timing," Colleen declared. "This past week my students have created a new goal: Ever more fired up by their efforts, they want to share their story with others, hoping that other young people around the world will be inspired to do similar things. In fact, they'd like to solicit students from other schools—maybe even from around the world—but we don't know how to get the word out."

"Your timing is perfect," I said. "I can help you. What a coincidence that I'm writing a book for young people, one that will be published in a number of foreign countries. . . ." And so this book made it to my "To Do" list. No sooner had I added it to my list than my daughter called and said, "Mom, I'm working with teens around the country and I'd like to share the things I've learned with teens—so let's do a book. . . ."

Coincidences? Maybe. But perhaps even more is going on than meets the eye—like, synchronicity. Synchronicity is a word used to describe a meaningful coincidence of two or more events where something other than the probability of chance is involved. The overall effect leaves us with the feeling that the sequence of events has to be more than coincidence. And that's exactly what happened here. As if orchestrated by divine intervention, each person who needed to carry out the next necessary step appeared when needed. If we watch closely, and most especially if we are looking for it, we will find that synchronicities happen in our lives quite frequently, like in the creation of *Taste Berries for Teens.*

Introduction

Why *Taste Berries for Teens*? A taste berry is a glorious little fruit that convinces the taste buds that all food—even food that is distasteful—is delicious. The bright little berry has been used by aboriginal tribes around the world for countless years to make the sometimes necessary eating of bitter roots—and grubs—tolerable. On some days, we could all use a taste berry!

The good news is that people can be "taste berries" to each other. Has someone said a kind word or done some deed that made a victory more satisfying, a joy sweeter, a broken heart less painful? If so, that person was acting as a taste berry. When we help others—such as by being a great friend—we sweeten life's joys and ease the bitterness of its disappointments and losses. For example, in the story "The Shirt Off His Back," when a little boy asked Toby Long for the shirt off his own back, Toby felt he couldn't give it up. Later, Toby was filled with such remorse that he organized a huge project and collected thousands of T-shirts to send to kids in need. But being a taste berry doesn't have to mean acting on such a grand scale. Taste berries use the events of daily life to help others, and to make the lives of others happier. In "My Stand-In Brother," Curt Lindholm describes how his friend Stephen was his taste berry, giving him strength and support as Curt went through the pain of losing his little brother.

Teens know plenty about being taste berries. From sending a thank-you note to earning merit badges; from helping a friend sort out feelings during a time of personal turmoil to supporting a friend through her parents' divorce; from helping each other with homework to deciding what each wants to do after high school and beyond; from rescuing a lizard to serving the homeless in soup kitchens and building Habitat Homes throughout the world—teens are taste berries to others. And, as a result, they are changing the world.

This book is organized into seven parts, with stories and comments from teens within each part. Each chapter focuses on a theme, which is presented in the chapter's opening by means of a lead-in story or parable. This is followed by a section called "A Word from the Authors," which previews the chapter coming up—giving a glimpse of the highlights of some of its other stories, as well as clarifying the chapter's theme for teens. After this section, there are the comments from teens, edited first by teens for content, then by the authors. We asked teens nationwide to send us their stories, as well as to read and rate each other's stories. Young people from the ages of twelve to twenty from across the United States read and critiqued individual stories, and commented or shared a story or example of their own. In some cases, we worked within schools and got to meet many teens firsthand.

The stories and comments we received represent the personal opinions of the teens who shared them. (Keep in mind that this was a diverse group—both male and female—of varying ages and backgrounds.) As such, they do not necessarily reflect our own opinions, nor are we suggesting that the reader should necessarily agree with them. Nor do the stories in this book represent the full range and scope of the many issues that today's teens face. We'd also like to stress that many of the situations described would be tough for any of us to handle—no one expects teens to go it alone. In this book you'll meet other teens who are dealing with tough challenges and you'll learn how they are working through them. Although some of these teens figured out what to do on their own, others needed to turn to friends, family and professionals to give them a hand.

Teens can find themselves sorting out things that seem overwhelming—whether it's because they are feeling like they don't "measure up," are facing serious and life-changing issues, are handling day-to-day stresses and strains, or are dealing with a combination of any of these. If you are facing struggles that seem overwhelming, rather than suffer alone or resort to doing things that are self-destructive, we urge you to confide in an adult you trust. This is especially true in the cases of physical or sexual abuse, suicidal feelings, eating disorders, depression, pregnancy and/or using drugs or alcohol. Remember that parents, teachers and other professionals—such as school nurses or counselors— were once teens (and many are now the parents of teens) and know what it feels like to be unsure of oneself, to have fears and anxieties about coping with life in general. Because adults *remember*, we feel honored to help young people find healthy, supportive ways to deal with their lives. Trust that adults have the best interest of teens at heart and want to help you make the best possible choices when dealing with whatever is going on in your life. If in the past you had an unpleasant or painful experience because an adult seemed aloof to your needs—or even broke your trust—it can be helpful to remember that, fortunately, adults unsympathetic to helping teens are the exception, not the rule.

During those times when everything in your life seems bleak, it's important to give yourself permission to be extra good to yourself—that means resting and eating properly, exercising to stay fit and release tension, and being patient with yourself. You'll find that if you take care of yourself, and reach out to those you know will offer friendship, understanding and guidance, you will be able to use a difficult experience to help you learn to develop healthy responses for coping with life's challenges. If you're uncertain where to go for counseling, turn to an adult (whether a parent, teacher, school guidance counselor or clergyman) whom you feel you can trust to direct you to the proper place. Also, many schools provide peer crisis counseling, which offers teens valuable support. Learning how to cope effectively can help you become a happy person and develop compassion for others. This is how to become a greater taste berry to yourself and to others.

We look forward to your—our readers'—letters and comments. We welcome hearing which of these stories touched you and which ones you liked best. We'd also love to hear about the taste berries in your lives—or how you've learned to be better taste berries in the lives of others. We're working on *Taste Berries for Teens II*, so if you have stories you'd like to submit for consideration, please send them to us at:

Taste Berries for Teens II
c/o Tina Moreno
3060 Racetrack View Drive
Del Mar, CA 92014

"Taste Berries" *to you!*

Part 1

Self-Worth

*Our life is like a piece of paper
on which every passerby leaves a mark.*

—Ancient Chinese Proverb

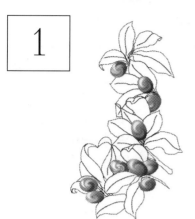

1

Who I (Really) Am

Every artist dips his brush into his own soul, and paints his own nature into his picture—as he does in living his life.

—Henry Ward Beecher

THE PAINTBRUSH

I keep my paintbrush with me, wherever I may go,
In case I need to cover up, so the real me doesn't show.
I'm so afraid to show you me; afraid of what you'll do,
I'm afraid you'll laugh or say mean things; afraid I might lose you.
I'd like to remove all the layers, to show you the real, true me,
But I want you to try to understand; I need you to like what you
   see.
So if you'll be patient and close your eyes, I'll remove the coats
   real slow,
Please understand how much it hurts, to let the real me show.
Now that my coats are all stripped off, I feel naked, bare and
   cold,

And if you still find me pleasing, you are my friend, pure as
    gold.
I need to save my paintbrush though, and hold it in my hand,
I need to keep it handy in case someone doesn't understand.
So please protect me, my dear friend, and thanks for loving me
    true,
And please let me keep my paintbrush with me, until I love me,
    too.

A Word from the Authors

Each of us longs to "be ourselves." And yet, we seek the
approval of others: "Do you think I'm okay?" "Do you accept me
as I am?" "Do you like the way I look?" "Do you approve of how
I act?" "Do you like me?" "Will you be my friend?" We want the
answers to each of these questions to be a wholehearted "Yes!"
When others like us and accept us, we feel worthy—like we're a
terrific person. But even though we may want to feel liked and
accepted by others, we may not always get a positive response—
some people may not think as much of us as we would like.
Sometimes this doesn't bother us, but most of the time, especially if their approval is important to us, it's only natural to feel
rejected, hurt or left out.

All of us are vulnerable to the scrutiny of others. Why are we
so sensitive to their review of us? We want them to accept and
approve of who we are at our inner level, not just for what they
see of us at the surface. What we really want is for others to like
and accept us for *who* we are—*as* we are. But what if they don't
like what they see? The fear of being rejected is at the heart of
the struggle between hiding and revealing ourselves—and can
cause teens to feel as though even the people closest to them
don't really understand them very well.

Almost all of the teens we heard from said that in order to win
favor and friendship from others, they had to "play into" or

portray an image they believe someone else holds of them, rather than "be themselves." It's a coat of paint teens aren't all that happy about wearing: The price-tag for being "someone else" comes at a loss of true identity. Sometimes the loss includes self-respect and self-esteem—your own. The good news is, while you are willing to do *some* things to gain acceptance, there's a limit—and then you begin to feel uncomfortable about it. Feeling uneasy about covering up who you are in order to be liked by someone else is a healthy feeling. You are *you*—and that is who you are supposed to be. You shouldn't have to become someone you're not.

As we read the stories for this unit, my daughter and I talked at length about how easy it is for the image we hold of ourselves to be influenced or colored by others. "When you're a teenager, you get pulled in a lot of different directions, especially when you're trying to meet the expectations of different people—all of whom are important to you," Jennifer commented. "There's a fine line between going along, doing the things others want you to do, and being true to yourself—listening to your own voice and preferences, acting on what you believe, and doing what's important and best for *you*."

"Give me an example," I prompted.

"Well, let's take the image I had of myself as an athlete in high school, more specifically, as a pitcher on my school softball team," she responded. "Just before I'd wind up to throw a pitch, I'd look up in the bleachers and see your smiling face, confident I'd strike out the batter. You'd reinforce it by shouting, 'You can do it, Jen!' Meanwhile I was thinking, 'I just hope this pitch goes somewhere in the direction of the plate and not a half-mile over the batter's head and out of the ballpark entirely!' I wasn't nearly as certain as you were of my pitching skills. Then I'd look over at Dad who had reminded me—on more than one occasion— 'Jen, you're better at soccer. That's your best chance for a scholarship. That's where you should be concentrating your time.' All the while, I was wishing I could concentrate on my first love—tennis.

"Once a friend of mine asked me if my favorite sport was softball, soccer or tennis. 'Softball,' I answered. But I thought about it for a minute and knew softball *wasn't* my favorite sport. My answer was based on the gratification I felt having you at my games, and your enthusiasm about my playing softball. On the way home from the games, whether our team won or lost, you thought I played well. In your eyes, I could do no wrong. It was a very good feeling.

"Correcting myself, I said to my friend, 'Actually, I prefer soccer.' But once again, I realized that there were conditions around my playing soccer that made me continue to play it. A couple of times a week, and sometimes on the weekends, Dad spent time with me, teaching me soccer tricks. And, he came to practically every soccer game and once, after one of the games, he told me I was 'the most powerful athlete on the team.' You see, having you and Dad attend my games was the biggest appeal of my playing softball and soccer. It was your presence and approval, not the sport itself, that kept me playing these sports. Now tennis—that was my favorite sport when it came to playing for the fun of it."

"But you received a letter in softball and soccer—because you were so good at them," I reminded her.

"Well, you guys were at practically all the games!" Jennifer said, laughing. "It was just great to look in the bleachers and see one or both of my parents there. Whenever I saw you, that was my favorite game, and my favorite sport."

"So why didn't you play on the tennis team, then?" I asked, bewildered that as a parent, living with her as closely I did, I hadn't picked up on how *she* really felt about each of these sports at the time.

"Simple," she said. "I did play tennis for a while, but the tennis games were mostly held out of town. Since our team took the bus, you and Dad weren't able to come."

I must have looked forlorn, because Jennifer added, "Don't feel bad, Mom. I'll bet there are very few kids who sit at the piano when they're first learning to play, saying, 'I'm practicing for the next half-hour without complaining because I see myself as a great pianist, the next Beethoven.' More likely they're saying, 'I'm practicing because in thirty minutes, I'll get a hug, a bowl of ice cream, time with my friends, an hour of television—and avoid being in trouble with my mom (or dad) for not practicing!'

"And by the way, you two (parents) weren't the only conflicting voices that I had to deal with. There were expectations of friends and coaches. For example, in the dugout was my best friend—also a pitcher—who each game prodded, 'Jennifer, work it so that in the fourth inning I can come in and relieve you!' Which meant, of course, that I was to deliberately pitch a succession of 'balls' and not strikes, so the coach would send me to the dugout and her to the mound. Then there was the coach who said, 'Just do your best'—right before he promised that if we had a good game, he'd take the team out for pizza. Now I had to deal with the question, 'What should I do—am I a good best friend, or a determined pitcher?' So you see, being pulled in so many directions by so many people—all of whom you genuinely want to please—makes having a paintbrush seem like a necessity!"

Perhaps that's what made "The Paintbrush" such a popular piece with teens! We received so many poignant and heartfelt letters from teens everywhere who said "The Paintbrush" described their feelings to a "T," that we felt obliged to make it the first selection in this book! Teens everywhere said, "being a teenager is tough stuff"—one of the biggest reasons being that parents, teachers and even your friends see you differently than you see yourself. In the following stories in this chapter, you'll learn that the struggle to gain acceptance, to be liked and considered worthy without having to be someone else—without having to "cover up"—is a challenge for both girls and boys, whether you are thirteen or eighteen—or ninety! "The Dragon in

My Drawer!" was written just this past year by your friend, ninety-year-old Elmer Adrian, who admitted, "The image others see is not the authentic me."

Hmmm, maybe it's a view everyone shares throughout their lives!

Like paint, the views teens shared about being your "authentic self" came in various shades, too. Some of you wanted a paintbrush to cover up, such as sixteen-year-old Shaun Martin, who confessed he needed one "until the *real me* . . . will stay around long enough for me to get used to." Being a teen means constantly growing and changing in many ways. Sometimes many layers of paint were needed for more than camouflage—they were needed as protection. This was true for fourteen-year-old Mia Templett, who tells us *why* each day she paints a smile on her face, and for thirteen-year-old Alana Ballen, recently diagnosed with bipolar disorder. As we suggested in the introduction to this book, when facing problems of so serious a nature, we urge any teen to turn to a trusted adult for help and guidance. Hopefully, as a result of receiving such support, both Mia and Alana can look forward to lighter colors—and brighter days. And many teens, like sixteen-year-old Rebecca Holbrook, thought that perhaps adults, too, cover up their real selves, as she feels her mother does because her mom's "life didn't really turn out the way she wanted."

Other teens were tired of needing a paintbrush and wanted to lay theirs down, to stop being someone else's shade of friend, as did fifteen-year-old Marie Benton. So enthralled that she'd been chosen to do a school project with the all-popular Heather Winslow, Marie found herself shamelessly parading up and down the library, mimicking Heather—even though she knew her actions were suspect! It's nice to see that Marie, like so many teens, is developing the courage to act in ways that feel right to *her*.

While some of you learn lessons firsthand, some learn them

by watching others, like fifteen-year-old Chelsey Collinsdale, whose sister told conflicting stories about wanting a pager to wear to school. As Chelsey tells us, "You have to decide how willing you are to sacrifice your true self in order to have others like you." Still, other teenagers, like sixteen-year-old Chad Dalton, said, "My true color comes out when I'm with *real* friends," and tells us what "color" it takes to be considered his friend. And Eric Chadwick, seventeen, discovered that when it came to the beautiful girl he wanted to date, it was he, and not the girl, who had done the painting! Perhaps Christina's rudeness was her paintbrush—maybe this beautiful girl didn't *feel* all that beautiful. This is a good reason *not* to judge a book by its cover, whether the cover looks appealing or unappealing.

All in all, you said you want to be true to your own color—the self you know better than anyone else does. You want to do as legend Elton John did; he found a newer, wiser, healthier self after getting a fresh look at who he was beneath the layers of paint he had added over the years to meet the expectations of others. You proclaimed what singer-songwriter Stevie Nicks declared: "This is who I really am—and who I want to be."

There is one thing all teens do agree on though: You may, on occasion, wear a coat of paint, but beneath its surface is a self you deeply love and honor. And would like the rest of us to love and honor, too.

Until then, you ask for understanding in keeping your paintbrush handy until you've learned the art of balancing the need for acceptance without sacrificing your own sense of self. In the meantime, please don't give up on the rest of us, who, like your friend ninety-year-old Elmer Adrian, are trying to find the courage to put our paintbrush down, too!

Will the Real Me Please Stand Up!

Lately I've started to wonder what it means when people say, "Just be yourself!" It's a dumb thing to say to me right now because most of the time *I'm* not sure *who* I am! How can I be? I'm constantly changing. I mean, I look and sound totally different than I did just three months ago. Then I had a decent complexion; now it's oily and zit-ridden. Three months ago, my voice sounded like a normal human being's; now it fluctuates between squeaky one day and deep the next—like I'm echoing into a big drum or something. And some of my body parts look like they don't belong with the other parts. I started working out last year, so I was really buffed. But I've grown five inches in the last six months, so I'm gangly and look completely out of proportion. I'm happy about getting taller, except that now my muscles don't look as big and my head looks as if it's sitting on a tall skinny post.

I used to have no problem getting girls to come up and talk with me. Now I've lost confidence that they find me attractive. I worry that if by chance a girl should get interested, it'll only be a matter of time before she'll be turned off by my skin breaking out so much, or laugh when my voice does its squeak-and-croak act.

It's not just my body that has changed—*everything* has. I've always thought of myself as a regular guy; but now, from one day to the next, my emotions are all over the place. One day I feel up, the next down. Some days I think, "Hey, I'm really quite smart," and others, "I'm as dumb as a rock!" One week I'm sure what I want to do with my life, the next, I'm totally unsure. I'm a wreck! Really, I just want the real me to please stand up and stay around long enough for me to get used to him.

Oh yeah, I need a paintbrush for sure!

Shaun Martin, 16

"Ladies and Gentlemen, Mr. Elton John"

"It's never too late to be what you might have been."

—George Eliot

Legendary singer, songwriter Elton John is very open about his before and after days of drugs and alcohol use, specifically how it has changed the way he sees himself. He likes what he sees. "My life has changed radically . . . because I've given up drugs and drinking," [*Good Housekeeping*, Feb. 1998, p. 29] the famous piano-man says. He credits going into rehab for what he calls his "second chance in life," [*Good Housekeeping*, Feb. 1998, p. 30] saying he not only feels like a different person, but *is* different. "When I got sober, my tastes completely changed," the Grammy award-winner admits, [*Interview*, Jan. 1998, vol. 28, p. 58] "as did my priorities." He considers his new drug-free life a very positive change, one that holds a new lease on life. "I'm so much more creative now," he says. "And my best creativity is yet to come!" [*People Weekly*, Dec. 29, 1997, vol. 48, p. 64] The superstar is quite convinced that the "new self" he's discovered in being drug free is also the key to his coping better with life. For example, in discussing "Candle in the Wind 1997" (the biggest-selling record in the history of recorded music), a song he wrote to memorialize his friend, Princess Diana of Wales who died from her injuries in a car accident, he says, "If this had happened when I was using drugs, I would never have been able to cope . . ."

It sounds like Elton John has discovered not only a "new and improved" Elton John, but laid claim to an even better "taste berry!"

Bettie B. Youngs

Are You Going to Get a Pager?

I don't "suck up" to others as much as I used to, mostly because of watching how obvious it is to others when someone does suck up. In fact, I've learned quite a bit about paintbrushes lately—from my sister, of all people. My older sister is acting like a yo-yo, being one person around her family, and then like someone completely different when she's with her friends. I realized from watching her that I've done that sometimes, too. When she's with her friends, my sister acts and says things practically the opposite of the way she really is.

I think my sister works way too hard to fit in with her friends. She agrees with them even when they say things that are totally stupid or definitely wrong, or completely opposite of what she believes. Like last week, for example, my sister and I were talking about how many of our friends have pagers. I told her I wanted one. My sister said she thought it was dumb that kids in junior high and high school had them, especially wearing the pager to school, since most of your friends are at school anyway. As she said, "Why would they page you when they could see you in the halls and in class?" I agreed with her. I mean, it's not like your parents are going to page you when you're in class!

But the next day after school, when two of her friends came over to our house, my sister told her friends she thought wearing a pager to school was totally cool and she couldn't wait to get one. When I reminded her that just the evening before she thought a pager was a dumb idea, she stared at me—and if looks could kill, I'd be dead! "You're such a pest!" she snapped, "Why don't you get lost!"

Usually my sister and I get along really well and are good friends. She wouldn't have said that to me if she wasn't trying to impress her friends.

When her friends left, I asked her if she really had changed her mind about wanting a pager to wear to school. "No," she said. "But both of my friends have pagers and wear them to school, so I didn't want to tell them that I thought it was a dumb idea."

"Well, if you do get a pager," I told her, "that is, if Mom and Dad even allow you to get one, you know they'd make you pay for it out of your allowance."

"I know," she said. "And besides, I have an answering machine. That works just as well."

So you see, my sister just told her friends what she thought they wanted to hear. I couldn't figure out why my sister wimped out! Personally, I don't want to work that hard to have friends. I mean, what would be so terrible about my sister believing one thing about kids having pagers and her friends believing something different? Besides, when your friends know where you stand in terms of how you feel or what you think is cool or uncool, they respect you. At least show respect for yourself by sticking up for what you believe in. And even if they don't agree with you, good friends will think you're cool for being true to yourself. That's just the way it is. I think that if your friends don't like that you think a little different than they do, then maybe you shouldn't want them as friends. And, you should consider the loss of friendship their loss, not yours.

I'm not saying that it doesn't bother me when someone doesn't like me or doesn't want to be my friend because I won't go along with everything they say or do. It's just that sometimes you have to "count the cost" as my mother says, and take a stance about how willing you are to sacrifice your opinion of things just to have others like you. Besides, it's a lot of work to keep up a front that isn't really who you are. To me, when you do that it's like painting a coat over the shade you really are.

Chelsey Collinsdale, 15

The Most Beautiful Girl . . .

We don't always see others the way they are, but rather, as we want them to be. I thought Christina Thomas was the most beautiful girl I had ever seen. It took me a long time to get up the courage to ask her out. Finally, I did. When she accepted, I thought I was the luckiest guy in the world. The feeling was short-lived.

The first couple of times I went out with Christina, I was so nervous (and happy to be with her) that I pretty much just agreed with whatever she said. But as I began to relax around her, I saw a person who was very different from what I had imagined.

I was surprised to discover Christina wasn't very respectful of other people. She was always saying mean things about them, always putting them down. And she was rude to people for no reason.

I only went out with Christina for five weeks.

Now I see the real Christina. I know what Christina Thomas is really like, and I don't think she is nearly as pretty as I thought at first.

I think it's possible to wear two coats of paint, one on the outside and one on the inside. The coat of paint Christina has on the outside is awesome, the one on the inside isn't as impressive. Seeing her beauty, I thought she must "be" beautiful, but I've learned that people aren't always what they appear to be. But I doubt that Christina Thomas was ever any different with me than she was with others.

I think that maybe it wasn't Christina who had the paintbrush. I was the one who had painted Christina in a "color" she was not.

Eric Chadwick, 17

Stevie Nicks—On Stevie Nicks

I missed out on a bunch of my really great years because I was so seriously into using drugs. But I'm so far away from that now. I'm really into caring for myself now in every way. As a result, I feel almost like I'm another person. And I'm very sure I don't want to be "her" again.

I genuinely like the person I am now; *this* is who I want to be. This is who I really am. [*People* magazine, Jan. 19, 1998.]

Stevie Nicks, Songwriter/Singer, Fleetwood Mac

The Dragon in My Drawer!

Sometimes when I'm a bit uptight
from doing everything just right,
I have a room, my own retreat
where I can kick my shoes off of my feet.

My desk is cluttered and piled high,
even the curtains are awry.
When I look at this untidy mess,
"Yes!" I shout. I like it, I do confess.

There are things tossed on the floor,
a dragon's in my dresser drawer.
He guards the clothes not folded right
and warns, "Hands off or I shall bite!"

Then, before I leave my room, I comb my hair
and straighten out the things I wear.
But I'll tell you what—that prim and proper image others see
is not the authentic me!

Elmer Adrian, 90

Heather's Clone

At times, I cover up the "real me" by acting in ways I think the other person wants or expects me to, rather than acting on who I really am. I did it just yesterday.

I woke up yesterday feeling sort of "blah"—feeling kind of sick, but not sick enough to stay home. I would have preferred to stay in bed, but I went to school anyway since I didn't want to fall behind in my homework and have to do extra over the weekend. I got up late, showered, got dressed in a hurry, ran my fingers through my hair and rushed out the door. Needless to say, I didn't look my best.

Luckily, my first-period teacher didn't have anything ambitious in mind for us. Our class mostly worked on individual assignments at our own desks. I was not so lucky in my second-period class. The teacher, Mrs. Whetherill, took our class to the library and assigned us to work in pairs on a research project. I was paired with Heather Winslow!

Heather is one of *the* most popular girls at school. Some people might call her selective; others might call her uppity. And preppy. Since I'm just one of the average kids at school, Heather smiles when she sees me, but that's about it. It's not like I'm someone she'd consider hanging around with.

Like everyone else, I'd do almost anything to be her friend (or even to be seen with her). And that's pretty much what I did yesterday!

Heather is a perky sort of person, so even though I wasn't feeling all that well, I put on my I've-got-a-great-personality-and-attitude act. I tried to perk up and be Heather's clone—so she wouldn't mind getting stuck with me for the project. But my transformation didn't end there! The teacher allowed us to walk around the library to get the different reference books we needed for our assigned projects. The two books Heather and I needed were easy to find. But even though we had all the reference books we needed for the project, that didn't stop Heather from pretending we needed others. Heather walked back and forth across the entire length of the library several times—to be seen, of course. I was so happy to be seen with Heather Winslow that I followed her on these aimless jaunts, no doubt looking conspicuous since Heather is more experienced in this sort of thing than I am. I never was quite sure when to appear busy looking for books, or, once I'd attracted attention to myself, when to smile at everyone since it was obvious I had distracted them into noticing me. Heather, of course, had it figured out: She did both.

But I didn't just stop at being Heather's shadow, either! I also tried to sound like her!

Heather giggles all the time. It's a sort of a high-pitched, peculiar sound, one she uses more for getting attention than anything else. So as she walked around searching for bogus reference books, Heather giggled loudly enough to get the attention of other students as she walked by them. And so did I! I mimicked Heather's giggle even though I'm not someone who normally giggles at every little thing. I'm sure that I sounded totally ridiculous, since they'd never heard these strange, quirky little sounds coming from my mouth before. I hadn't either!

At the time, it was fun. Since I was with Heather, *everyone* looked at us. The problem was, because I didn't feel all that great in the morning, I hadn't bothered to put on anything nicer than jeans, an old sweatshirt and my ratty pair of tennis shoes. My hair looked absolutely awful; it was having a bad day, too. Nevertheless, here I was giggling and parading around, drawing attention to myself. I'm sure I looked as ridiculous as I sounded.

Being seen with Heather and getting as much attention as she was (or at least more than I was used to) felt good—yesterday, that is. Today I'd describe my feelings about my behavior in the library more as embarrassed than anything else. I know my classmates knew I was showing off, and even worse, I know I

was. It's just that sometimes—even when you know you're acting like a dweeb—it's hard not to get caught up in someone
else's behavior. Especially when you're with someone like
Heather, who has a way of making you feel like you're obligated
to go along with whatever she's doing or saying. It's like the
chameleon going along with the colors in its surroundings.

Sometimes I feel like a chameleon, changing my colors when
I'm around different kinds of people. When I'm not feeling super
secure with myself, I tend to act more or less intelligent, athletic
or pretty than I really am. To try to blend in with whoever I'm
with, I cover up the "real me" by acting in ways I think the other
person wants me to. That's what happened when I got paired up
with Heather.

Sometimes you have to do what your friends expect of you
because if you don't, you won't have any friends. I know I followed Heather around and tried to be her clone in order to
be liked by her. But, you know what, it didn't work. The next
day Heather acted like she didn't know me! All that work for
nothing!

At least I'm aware of what I did—not that it's much of a consolation. I do want to be more true to myself and not have to
paint myself over to be someone else's "color." What I'd really
like is for Heather to think I'm so cool she'll follow me around
and want to be my clone! Now that's a color I'd like to see.

Marie Benton, 15

The Mask She Wears

Reading "The Paintbrush" made me feel sad for my mother. She works very hard at two jobs and is usually so tired. She has zero social life. Still, she tries to sound upbeat and positive—way more than she really feels. I think her life didn't really turn out the way she wanted, and that she hides a lot of disappointments. I know she doesn't like either one of her jobs. And she doesn't like the house we live in. It needs painting and new carpet and a lot of repairs, things we can't afford to do right now. Mom says we should get a newer, smaller place, but a newer, smaller house can't really fix things because the real problem is that Mom doesn't want to live in this town any longer. She and my father divorced last year, and my mother would like to move back near her parents. But I really like the school I go to and I like my friends. When my mother was my age, her father's company transferred him to a different city. She had to leave her friends behind and complete high school in a whole new area. Mom said it was a terrible experience for her. She told me that she doesn't want me to have to go through the same thing. So we're going to stay here until I finish high school. I like that idea, but I know it's tough on my mother, one more compromise she's making. Even though Mom acts like it's okay with her, I know it isn't. It must not be much fun to be her.

I appreciate all the things my mother does for me. I know she works hard at trying to make the best of our situation. I'm trying to do my part, too. I'm trying to complain less about the things I want but know we can't really afford, such as a phone of my own. And I'm trying to be a little more understanding and patient with my mom when she's stressed out.

I guess that sometimes adults have to be someone other than who they'd prefer to be. Sometimes adults paint on a mask, too.

Rebecca Holbrook, 16

Quiet and Shy—Not!

I know there are times when my parents and teachers—even some of my friends—see me differently than I *really* am. They think I'm quiet and shy, really smart but not very cool. What they don't know is that's who I am when I am with them, but it's not who I *really* am. The *real* me comes out when I'm around guys who are more like me—like Tom Henderson and Graham Barry. Tom and Graham bring out the best in me, the real me.

I met Tom and Graham at a *Young Scientist* contest last year. Tom is from Orem, Utah, and Graham is from Ontario, California. The three of us were among the five finalists in a national competition for *Promising New Scientists*. As soon as the three of us met, we really hit it off. As we talked about the conference, we discovered that all three of us were interested in laser space debris mitigation, which is the study of the prevention of space garbage damaging satellites and the new space station. It was great to meet other people my age who actually knew what I was talking about. When I talk about "space garbage," most of the kids at my school just say, "Oh, you mean like asteroid-type things? I played a video game about that once."

Luckily, we met each other on the first day of the conference, so we were able to spend a lot of time together for the entire three days. We ate all our meals together, went to each others' event showings, and went out and saw a little of the city together. Then when we'd get back, even though it was late, we'd talk until 2:00 or 3:00 A.M. It was great! We talked about everything from the best schools to go to, what degrees to get, the kind of jobs we want, and even the names of the best people in each field. We want to study with the pioneers. Both Tom and I want to study with Dr. Claude Phipps from Santa Fe, New Mexico. He's the inventor of ORION, a space debris mitigation company that developed a laser that knocks down space garbage before it does any damage to expensive space vehicles. Some of the space garbage travels at over one thousand miles per second! Although you can't track something as small as a grain of sand, it can still do some real damage. Graham wants to study under Jim Cronin, the physics Nobel Laureate from the University of Chicago.

Even though the three of us don't get a chance to see each other very often, we're still the best of friends. We're always sending articles and newspaper clippings to each other, and sometimes we'll send a copy of a class paper we think the other would find interesting. And we call each other a couple of times a month. That may not sound like a lot of time together, but even so, Tom and Graham are better friends of mine than any of the kids I see every day at school. And they know me better than any of the kids at school know me. The three of us just really understand each other and where we're coming from.

I have more fun with them than anyone else. When I get a phone call or email from either Tom or Graham, it's the best feeling—a real high. I always feel happy and in a good mood, even when I'm working through a problem, when I talk with Tom and Graham. It's like this other person in me wakes up. With them, I'm my "real shade."

Chad Dalton, 16

About the Smile I Wear . . .

Everyone I know has dreams and plans to do something wonderful. I only have one simple goal: to make it through each day. I'm hoping and praying it's going to get easier.

My mother and stepfather separated seven months ago. My mother still loves him and wants to get back together with him. What she doesn't know is that my stepfather was sexually abusing me. It started last year and continued until the day he left.

I know I have to tell my mother about it, but right now I don't think she can handle it. So when the phone rings late at night, I wake up panicking, hoping it's not him and hoping my mother doesn't ask him to come back. She's heartbroken that he's left. My heart was broken when he was here—and so relieved when he left. Now my heart will survive. Maybe. I'm so angry. Once I was so happy.

I am filled with shame and guilt. My shame keeps me sworn to secrecy. Guilt makes me feel alone. Other students may see me as shy; they have no idea what I hide.

I walk around with a smile on my face because if I don't, I'll walk around looking as sad as I feel. Then I'd cry out loud instead of silently on the inside.

I know that eventually the days will be easier to face. I'm looking forward to that time. Until then, I tell my heart to hide the hurt away. So when I get dressed each day, I paint a smile on my face. It helps me convince myself that I'll be okay. My smile is a coat of paint to get others to be kind to me, to see the me that one day I'm hoping to see again, too.

Mia Templett, 14

My Bipolar Disorder

So many things about being a teenager are tough. One of them is making sense of being told "be yourself," when the other part of that message—even though it's silent—is "as long as you're beautiful, cheerful and thin." Everyone wants you to be perfect in every way. I know a lot of kids who "cover up" because it's so impossible to be like we're supposed to be.

I've had a lot of trouble being perfect, especially with the "thin" part. Even though the bathroom scale said I wasn't overweight, the pounds just didn't seem to sit in the right places. When I looked in the mirror, I was anything but beautiful or perfect. The more I tried to change my body, the less cheerful I felt. I said to my mom, "I'm so fat while all the girls at school are so skinny!"

"You're not at all fat," she said. "Besides, you don't have to be the same as all the girls at school. Just like every flower is beautiful in its own way, being an individual bloom is wonderful for people, too." But I knew better. It would be just great to live in a world where you were liked and considered pretty because being an individual bloom was okay. Instead, you have to be a perfect flower or you aren't going to be selected as good enough for a corsage—to fit in with everyone else.

Actually, I've had *a lot* of trouble with trying to be a perfect flower. So, I'd cover up with my trusty "paintbrush" so nobody could tell how depressed I was. It can hurt to show people how you really are when you're sure they won't like what they see. My friends, and even some of my classmates, said I was the class clown, always up and on and funny. At the time, it seemed like a good way to prove I was cheerful. But it's a lot of work to always be up and on, funny and witty. I got so tired of it, and then I reached a point where I wasn't able to pretend that I was cheerful anymore.

The other kids don't think I am so funny and witty when I am feeling down. They just leave me alone, or tease me, "Oh, the clown forgot her nose today?" Nobody wants to hear that you're having a bad day or that you just "feel down." It's funny how that works, but it's true.

I got so depressed. Depression is a terrible thing because there is no end in sight. I felt like I was in a deep, black hole and couldn't get out. Trying to be perfect while knowing I wasn't only made it worse. I tried almost everything. When nothing worked, I attempted suicide. Now I've been diagnosed with bipolar disorder, so I'm on three kinds of medications: Depakote, Paxil and Ziprexia. Before I was on these medications, I thought the problem was me and that I just wasn't as tough as my friends are. I worried that there was something wrong with me mentally, like maybe I was crazy or something. It's a huge relief to find out that what's wrong with me is called bipolar disorder. It's a medical condition, one that can be straightened out. Before I was diagnosed, my parents told me I did stupid things. My friends saw me as the class clown, who had become a drag. But now that I'm getting medical help, I no longer feel like I have two lives. And I feel less frightened of my feelings. Other people feel confused and overwhelmed sometimes, too. I'm not the only one.

Now that I know what's causing me to feel this way, I can give up painting myself to be someone I am not. I am a girl who needs medication to help my body do what it's supposed to do, to feel like it's supposed to feel. These days I'm worrying less about being perfect enough to fit into a bouquet. I'm just working on being an individual bloom. I like to think of myself as a flower. Forget the class clown act.

Alana Ballen, 13

Love, *Me*

I once wrote my girlfriend a letter and signed it "Just me." It surprised me when she told me she didn't like the way I signed it. "I'd rather go out with someone who thought more of himself than 'just me,'" she commented. "I deserve more than a 'just me' boyfriend."

What she said made me realize that when I wrote "just me," I was really saying "I'm no one special." But that's not how she feels about me, and it's not how I feel about myself, either. When I thought about it, I realized that I underestimated the importance of talking (and writing) about myself in a positive way.

So I'm giving myself a whole new "paint job." I've decided to stop (unconsciously) putting myself down. Before, I'd say things like, "School isn't for me, I'm a horrible student." Even saying or thinking those words made me feel like I was a horrible student and so I'd dislike school even more—which was crazy because it wasn't even true. I'm not a bad student. And I don't hate school. I'm a bright guy, and I like most of my classes.

Now I say things in a better way, a way that doesn't make me get down on myself. Now when I talk about school, I say something like, "I like school even though I'm having a tough time with algebra. When I learn the concepts of algebra that I don't understand right now, I'll get better grades. I'm going to keep working on it."

By being more positive and not putting myself down, I actually help myself do better. I like it when other people encourage me. So it only makes sense that I encourage me, too.

I've learned that what people call positive thinking and positive self-talk is like giving yourself a paint job. Why be a "just me" when I can be a "great guy"? Why be a lousy student, when I can be a student who just has a little trouble with algebra?

I'm glad that my girlfriend made the comment she did

because it helped me understand a simple equation: Just as I sign the letters I write to her, "Love, Dan," I can sign thoughts to myself that way, too. When I write "Love, Dan" to her, it's intended to let her know that my feelings for her are positive and loving, so why not make my own thoughts and words to myself as positive and loving as possible, too?

I think the words we use are like a coat of paint. So, be sure you choose the "right" color!

Dan Belana, 17

I Wouldn't Go Out with Belinda Even *If* . . .

Brian had been out of school for three days with the flu. On the morning of his return, he noticed a group of friends clustered around talking about Belinda, the "new girl" at school. All of his friends said how cute and fun she was, and how much they were looking forward to sitting with her at the next day's sports assembly. Even though Brian had no idea who Belinda was, he began his usual habit of being critical of others. "I don't think she's all that cute," he remarked. "She's got skinny legs, and my little sister's got bigger boobs than she does. And she ought to get a new hairstyle!"

Though his friends looked on in disbelief, neither their looks of surprise nor expressions of disgust could deter Brian from making even more disparaging remarks about Belinda—whom he knew nothing about. When Brian announced, "I wouldn't go out on a date with Belinda even if she paid me," one girl in the group, Peggy (a girl Brian secretly liked and hoped to ask out), quipped, "Brian, you are really a geek! And don't worry, no one I know—including Belinda—would go out with you, even if you paid her!" Having said that, she turned and walked away.

Belinda, the one Brian thought needed a bigger bosom, shapelier legs and a more modern hairstyle, the one Brian was too good to date (even if she paid him), was the new school mascot . . . a goat!

Making sure we don't "vandalize" others can be a real "taste berry"—to ourselves and to others!

Jennifer Leigh Youngs

2

You Can . . . If You Think You Can

*If think you can or if you think you can't,
you're right either way.*

—Henry Ford

FERRARI, ANYONE?

A young boy came home crying from school one day. His grandfather was visiting and greeted him.

"Why are you crying?" his grandfather asked.

"Because Paul called me a sissy! Do you think I'm a sissy, Grandpa?"

"Oh no," said his grandfather. "I think you're a Ferrari."

"A *car*?" said the boy, trying to make sense of what his grandfather had said.

"Well, if you believe that just because Paul called you a sissy that you really are one, you might as well believe you're a car, and a terrific one at that," explained the grandfather, asking, "Why be a sissy when you can be a Ferrari?"

"Oh! That's cool, Grandpa!" the boy exclaimed, now realizing that he got to have a say in how he felt about himself.

"Yes, it is," replied his grandfather. "The opinion you have of yourself should not only count as much as anyone's—but even more."

A Word from the Authors

Self-worth—what we think about ourselves—shows up in the things we say and do. We may even misinterpret the words and actions of others because of the view we hold of ourselves. The boy's grandfather knows how important it is that his grandson see himself as having great value—in this case, seeing himself as a "Ferrari" instead of a sissy. It's important to see ourselves in the most positive light that we can. Seeing the good in ourselves helps us to do better, to "be" better. We all have days when almost everything about our lives looks bleak. On those days, it's easy to feel bad about ourselves. Looking on the bright side of things can help us transform tough times: "Just because I'm having a difficult time in one subject doesn't mean that I'm not a good student," or, "Even though the girl I want to date won't go out with me, that doesn't mean I'm not a likable, lovable person."

The good news is, psychologists tell us that we are hurt less by the calamities of life than we are by how we see them. And this is never more true than when applied to how we see ourselves. Not only do we have the choice to paint the events and situations in our lives in the color that we choose, we also have the choice to paint *ourselves* in the color we choose. In other words, you get to choose whether the cup is half-full or half-empty when it comes to how you see yourself!

Like the grandfather in the story above, the many teens we heard from also know how important it is to cast a positive vote when it comes to their own self-worth, saying that self-esteem and actions went hand-in-hand. From becoming a better athlete, to getting better grades; from being a friend, to attracting better friends; from getting along with your parents, to being granted more privileges, self-esteem plays a big role. Jennifer Jones's story of Sergio—her sister's boyfriend—received your first-place vote for being an example of a Ferrari, even if her father wasn't all that happy about Jennifer's sister wanting to marry him. Thirteen-year-old BeShawn Niles explains why his stepfather is a first-class Ferrari—in spite of the name-calling BeShawn's step-dad suffers at the hands of BeShawn's father. He admires that his stepfather is self-confident and doesn't allow anyone else's opinion of him to be more important to him than his own self-image. And Sam Rollins, fifteen, tells us why he thinks being a Ferrari means being *his* best—not necessarily being *the* best. Fourteen-year-old Noreen Nicoles said if she was "so smart," the good grades she gets would come easier for her. When her dad tells her she shouldn't be so tough on herself, Noreen decides at least she's willing to try seeing herself as a Ferrari—and said she'll keep us posted as to whether it works. And your ninety-year-old friend Elmer Adrian pondered what another person with the "same frame, background and foibles would have done with his life—if it had been theirs instead of his!"

If you deserve an A, why settle for a B? When his teacher let him grade his own paper, seventeen-year-old Paul Drexler had a chance to think about that question. He concluded as did the rest of you: Seeing your value means treating yourself accordingly. After all, you wouldn't enter your Ferrari in a demolition derby!

A Ferrari Without an Engine

Last semester, after we had turned in our final class project in our biology class, the teacher told us to assign ourselves a grade based on how well we felt we had done on the project. My buddy, Reese, gave himself an A. He really did do a great job on the project, and probably it was an A project.

I knew my project was even better than his. After completing a unit on mollusks, our class was supposed to do a report of our choosing related to the subject. Reese did his report on the New Zealand Paua, a mollusk with a blue-green iridescent colored shell that's often used in costume jewelry, like in the ring his little sister had. He wrote up his report, and then when he presented it to the class, he showed them his eight-year-old sister's ring.

I decided to do my report on the differences between a natural and cultured pearl. The more I got into reading and researching the pearl, the more interested I became. I really put my heart into the project. I found out that the formation of a pearl is actually the result of an irritant, such as a grain of sand, that has gotten into the shell of the oyster. In order to protect itself from whatever is invading it, whether it's a piece of sand or something that feeds on this sort of mollusk, the oyster secretes a white liquid substance to protect itself. It will encrust anything within its reach. Sometimes when a natural pearl is cut in half, a grain of sand or some small creature is found inside of it.

I was surprised to learn that a pearl's size can vary from between that of a pinhead to that of a pigeon's egg. The Hope Pearl, which is the largest pearl ever found, is nearly two inches long! The Hope Pearl is kept in the South Kensington Museum in London. So, for my report, I wrote the museum and asked for information on the Hope Pearl. They sent me a lot of material, including some really great photographs, which I included in the report. Everyone, especially the teacher, was impressed. This made me feel pretty good because I really put a lot of time and work into my project—and it showed. It was a great report.

I knew that the project I handed in was A quality. Reese's report was good, but mine was much more complex than his. Even so I gave myself a B. And you know what, the teacher gave my friend Reese an A and gave me a B! I think that says a lot about the value we place on ourselves. There was no reason for me to devalue the amount of work and time I had put in on this project to make sure it was excellent. I'm not saying that Reese overvalued his paper, but if his was worth an A, for sure mine was worth one, too! But I didn't stand up for myself and the quality of my work on the project.

It was a good lesson for me. I'm making an effort to be more honest in presenting my own worth. It's obvious that my buddy Reese considers himself a Ferrari. And while I would never want to give myself an A when I don't deserve it, I don't want to give myself a B when I deserve an A, either. I know my report was a Ferrari of a report! But it didn't get the A it deserved because its engine stalled—that engine being the confidence I had in myself. If I had considered myself the Ferrari that I am, rather than a Ferrari without an engine, I would have given myself the grade I deserved.

Paul Drexler, 17

Charmaine . . . and Jerry Springer

Last year I hung out with Charmaine, a girl who had a very colorful vocabulary, especially when she was being critical of someone—which was often. I can't tell you what her favorite phrases were, because they were too X-rated to write here. But sometimes it got pretty bad. My parents taught me not to swear, but hanging out with Charmaine, it was hard not to. It wasn't long before every other word out of my mouth was a swear-word, too.

Charmaine's favorite pastime was watching television, especially some of the "livelier" talk shows. She taped her favorite shows, since they were on while she was in school. As soon as school was out, Charmaine rushed home to watch them. She especially liked Jerry Springer—but only when the people on the show were "dissing" each other. Jerry Springer was Charmaine's high point of the day.

Each day, at the end of the talk show, there was a preview of the next day's show, so Charmaine knew a little of what the show would be about. But from hearing Charmaine talk about the next day's show—before it had even aired—you'd swear she had already seen it. Boy, did she have a good imagination! "Oh, Karen," she'd say, "We can't miss tomorrow's show! It's going to be about sisters who . . . and then they . . . and then they get into this huge fight. . . . It's going to be just great! We can't miss it!"

We usually didn't. If I didn't have anything special to do after school, I'd go to her house and we'd watch the show. On the way home, the *Jerry Springer Show* was all Charmaine talked about—the focus being all the trouble the people might get themselves into. "Oh, I hope they get into a fight!" she'd say, looking forward to it. The instant we got to her house, even before we raided the refrigerator for food—if you can even imagine that—she'd turn on the television and rewind the tape. While the tape was rewinding, we'd dash to the kitchen to get a quick snack, so we didn't waste one minute in watching the show. "Oh, oh, look!" she'd say, pointing at someone on the show who was beginning to get on the nerves of another guest—which usually turned out to be a relative or supposedly good friend—"I think they're going to have it out!" If the people on the show did get into a fight, she'd scream, "Come on! Come on! You know you want to hit her. So hit her!"

I think Charmaine thought the people were faking the way they were behaving because sometimes she'd shout at the people on the TV, "If you're going to hit her, really hit her!" Then, she'd turn to me and demand, "Do you think this is for real? Who really swings like that?" (As if I'd seen my share of "real" fights and knew a real "swing" when I saw one.)

"I hope it's not real," I'd say, cringing at the sight of two people shoving, pushing and ducking each other's swings. The fight scenes didn't bother Charmaine at all—she'd replay them a time or two—as though they were good fun.

I have to admit that some of the shows were very funny. Even though I didn't like the fighting and yelling, sometimes the people on the show made such dumb decisions they were pathetic—like falling in love with someone after talking for only six or seven days on the Internet or something. Then, when the two of them met for the first time, one (or both) of them was genuinely shocked that the person was different than expected—like he weighed two hundred pounds more than he said he did, or was much younger or older than she had said she was. So then, each was disappointed. When the host asked if either had asked these important questions before, they said it wasn't important to them—but all of a sudden, when they met for real, it was important. I mean, duh! When someone makes that big of a mistake, it makes them look like a goofy person, and it's hard not to laugh at them. But that's where I draw the line. When the audience or host eggs them on to begin blaming each other and "resort to physical violence," as my mom says, now that's too much. I think that when you see people behave like that again and again, you can begin to think that kind of reaction is normal. It's not. I've never known anyone like the people I saw on those shows. My mom calls it the "G.I.G.O. (garbage-in, garbage-out) factor."

Even so, I kept going to Charmaine's house each and every day for my daily dose of "humor," as Charmaine called it. I'm not sure what that says about me, because I thought Charmaine's obsession for wanting to watch people who always seemed to be having a hard time in a relationship, always having someone mad at them for something, was a little weird. Even if some of the things that people did or said on the show were funny to watch, it wouldn't be funny if it were going on in your own home. If it was actually someone you knew, it would be scary, not exciting.

Charmaine and her parents moved to another town and I haven't seen her—or Jerry Springer's show—since.

My new best friend is Tina. She's in my grade at school and we both take the same Russian class. Tina's favorite pastime is riding horses. Twice a week after school and on most weekends, Tina and I hang out at the stable where she boards her horse. Because of Tina, I'm now taking riding lessons and renting a horse (Brockton) at the ranch. I absolutely love riding Brockton! His owners are almost always out of town, so the horse is beginning to warm up to me, snorting when he sees me coming up to him.

Tina has been riding since she was seven years old, so she's a good rider. She owns a horse named Silver who she's been boarding at the ranch for almost four years. It's fun being with her because she knows practically everyone at the ranch, and everyone there likes her. But then again, Tina is easy to like. She's friendly, easygoing and even though she's very competitive, Tina loves to have fun, too.

You should see the way she jumps her horse! She's always

going for a higher jump—just like she's always going for a better time on our quarter-mile runs. It's a lot of fun competing with someone who's good, and when they're a friend like Tina, she knows exactly when to back off. She just knows when I'm at my limit. Because of our competing, I'm getting better at riding and jumping my horse, too. She always tells me things like, "Great jump!" or, "Way to go!" or, "Wow, you're really getting good at this!" If I ever doubt myself, she'll pump me up again. She's good for me. When I first started riding, I thought I was such a klutz compared to her. "Don't take it all so seriously," she told me. "We're just *horsin'* around! Just enjoy yourself. You'll get better with time." She was right.

Recently my parents took me to the circus. In one of the acts, a circus performer jumped on a horse's back, slipped underneath, caught hold of its tail and ended up on the horse's neck! I looked at my dad and said, "I did all that the first time I ever rode a horse!" But now, I'm a pretty good rider.

I realize there are other things that make riding fun. The people at the ranch are a different sort of people, and they are very much alike. They're really into riding, grooming and taking care of their horses and genuinely enjoy being out in nature. They're such nice and happy people. Just like Tina. Being around Tina and the people who board their horses at the ranch is such a good feeling, so upbeat and wholesome.

The more time I spend with Tina, the more I'm finding myself becoming like her.

Charmaine and Tina are so different. It's hard to believe they both could be my friends. But I think the "common denominator" (I learned that in math class) is that they're both fun to be around, and both love the thrill of adrenaline. Tina loves the thrill of jumping and will press herself to do better and better— even when it seems to border on being kind of dangerous. Charmaine got her excitement from anticipating who was going to swing first, or say something outrageously shocking that would be sure to rile the other person. I'd leave Charmaine's house thinking how terrible it must feel to be told some unexpected news or to see someone you hadn't thought you would (or didn't want to see) or to have someone tell you something upsetting, especially on national TV. And I'd feel disturbed. With Tina, I leave with good, healthy feelings.

What's even more surprising than how different they are, is how different *I* am now that I'm hanging out with Tina instead of Charmaine. I have to admit, I feel much better about myself when I'm with Tina. When you're around people who look for the best in others, who get their thrills from bringing out the best in themselves—rather than people looking for the meanness in others—it brings out the best in you.

I think you become a lot like the people you hang around. It's a good reason to hang around Ferraris like Tina—and, like me!

Karen Trusdale, 15

Sergio

My sister is dating a really great guy. His name is Sergio, and he's a fireman.

Sergio is definitely a Ferrari.

My sister and Sergio are pretty serious, and I think she'll probably end up marrying him. This really bugs my father, who tells my sister that she can do better than a fireman.

I think my father is being unfair, first of all because it is my sister who has to live with Sergio, not my father. Second, Sergio is one of the nicest people I know. He's polite and considerate to everyone, especially my sister. He takes her to nice restaurants, to concerts and to almost every special event in the community.

I think being a fireman is an honorable profession, even though my father says it's not much of a "lifestyle." And I can understand Sergio's wanting to be a fireman. When he was a small boy, his family's home caught on fire late one night. The family was already asleep. Luckily, the fire department arrived within minutes. The house was quickly engulfed with flames. Though Sergio's mother tried to rescue her two small children from their bedroom, she was overcome by smoke inhalation. Firemen then rescued each member of the family.

Sergio remembers being carried out of the house by a particular fireman, one who kept in touch with Sergio's family over the years. To Sergio, the men who rescued his family and carried him from the terrible fire are heroes. That fireman is the reason they are all alive. Sergio really admires firefighters. And why not? They literally saved his brother and mother's lives. His, too.

How can you say that someone who uses his life in such a purposeful way is not as good or worthy as an executive like my father, who makes a lot of money in his job, but doesn't particularly like the people he works with (he's always complaining about them)? Sergio's work, on the other hand, makes him feel important and needed by others. He loves what he's doing and is happy with his life overall. And he constantly works to improve himself. Though he's already graduated from college, he's taking more courses, especially classes about saving lives.

My father said it must be boring being a fireman because of all the "down time on your hands." I don't see it that way at all. Firemen do a lot more than wait around for a fire to happen. From the things that Sergio and my sister tell me about his work, I think it must be interesting. He meets a lot of people and he gets to travel—even out of state. Just last month when a huge forest fire broke out, Sergio was called in to help. When it was all over, Sergio was credited with saving the lives of nearly three hundred wild mustangs and other wildlife!

Regardless of what my father thinks of my sister's boyfriend, I think when Sergio looks at himself in the mirror, he genuinely likes and respects who he sees. I know I really admire him. And I think my sister would be wise to marry someone who is proud and pleased with who he is. Sergio is the kind of guy I'd like to have for a friend—and as a brother-in-law. I'm very happy my sister is with him.

When a person genuinely is comfortable with who he is, it shows. I think Sergio is the kind of person we should all strive to be like.

Jennifer Jones, 16

Every Time a Cute Girl Walked By . . .

I broke up with my girlfriend, Allison, because every time a cute girl walked by, Allison started ragging on her, saying how dumb she was, or criticizing the way the girl looked or what she was wearing. At first it didn't bother me because I told myself I was with a girl who was "cool"—and better than the other girls. But then I realized that what Allison was saying wasn't always true. Some of the girls she put down as dumb were not at all dumb, and they looked just fine to me.

At first, I thought Allison was just jealous of the other girls. But then I asked myself, "Why should Allison be jealous if she believes she's prettier, smarter and dresses nicer than they do?" I came to the conclusion that Allison's habit of putting others down didn't really have anything to do with the other girls. Allison just didn't feel good about *herself*. She didn't see herself as a Ferrari.

I think Allison thought that if she found something wrong with other people, it made her look better. She made others seem "less" so she could be "more." I really "got it" about Allison at our last Talent Day. Sometimes you don't know how talented your friends are, but at Talent Day students get to share their talents with everyone in the school. Some of the kids sing or play musical instruments, other kids get together and perform a skit. They really get into it, making costumes and props. Talent Day is supposed to be fun, and I think it is. It's a day to display another dimension of yourself. It's great!

At our school's last Talent Day, everyone was laughing, cheering and clapping for a friend who was on stage. Everyone was having a great time—in the audience and on the stage—all except Allison, who for some reason felt it was her place to act as the event's critic. As though she expected a Broadway performance, Allison judged and criticized each person. As usual, she was especially critical of the girls, most especially the really popular or cute ones.

There I was enjoying myself and my friends, having a good time, while my girlfriend—sitting right beside me—seemed grouchy about the whole thing. I wasn't sure what to do. You're supposed to feel loyal to your girlfriend, right? I mean, I'm supposed to like her personality and the things she says and does.

On that particular Talent Day, I realized that I disliked more things about her than I liked. Even though Allison is pretty and smart, it didn't make up for her jealousy and put-downs of others. I began to feel bad about myself for being with Allison. I broke up with Allison that day.

Since then, Allison has had two different boyfriends. (She's not with anyone right now.) Maybe they've discovered what I did. It's not really all that much fun to be with someone who continually puts everyone down.

I think that when you bad-mouth other people, it's a sign that you don't feel all that secure about yourself. I've decided that no matter how cool you are (or think you are), when you tear others down, it takes away from your image of being "cool"—from being a Ferrari.

For people who put others down, think of this: In the end, you're going to find yourself alone, like Allison.

Shawn Hamilton, 16

How Big Is Your Splash?

Now as I look inward,
I find that by comparison,
I haven't jumped as high
or made as large a splash
as others that I know.

I'm told
there is no face or mind
like mine.
I am one of a kind.

This makes me wonder
what another person
with the same frame,
background and foibles
would have done with it.

Elmer Adrian, 90

Something's Always Wrong With . . .

I used to have a friend named Toni, who always found something wrong with other people, even strangers. She'd say things like, "Look at those hideous shoes that woman is wearing. You'd think she'd have enough sense not to leave the house in them!" Or, "Can you believe he's wearing that ugly old shirt with those pants? He must not have any mirrors in his house." Or, "Look at her big butt. I'll bet she weighs three hundred pounds. She ought to get her mouth wired shut."

Another thing Toni always did was gossip, even when someone told her something in strict confidence. It never mattered to her if what she said might hurt someone's feelings. "Tommy told me not to tell anyone, but he says Brad's thinking of breaking up with his girlfriend Kathleen," she said to me as we were standing in the lunch line, with Kathleen in earshot. Kathleen heard her, just as Toni knew she would. Kathleen was very upset and started crying. Toni acted like she'd had no part in hurting Kathleen's feelings. Toni has a really strong personality.

Another bad habit of hers was criticizing other people openly and humiliating them in front of other people. She did that to Mr. Sams, our history teacher. Mr. Sams has a really long nose. Toni drew a picture of him—complete with a cartoon-like exaggeration of his nose—and hung it on the bulletin board. She'd sketched his desk beside him with his nameplate sitting on it, so everyone would know it was Mr. Sams. Beneath it she wrote, "If you filled your nose with nickels, you could afford to get a nose job."

I thought Toni was pretty funny until I was on the other end of her habit of criticizing people. But now I see it was because she didn't feel like a Ferrari.

One day, I asked Toni if she wanted to go with me to watch my little sister's softball game. When the team took their seats on the bleachers in front of us, Toni pointed to a little girl wearing braces and thick glasses and said, "That girl is so ugly, she'd have to play in an open school team, because she couldn't find anyone in her neighborhood to play with her. In fact," Toni added, "she's so ugly, I bet her mother has to tie pork chops around her neck to get the dogs to play with her!"

That little girl with the braces and thick glasses was my sister!

I was very upset, and decided Toni had gone too far. But it did teach me a lesson. Toni's mean comment made me realize that when she was making fun of people I didn't know, I thought it was funny, and it all seemed harmless. But when a demeaning comment was directed at my sister, it sounded especially cruel. When people say things like that about strangers or people you know, they're mean-spirited—period. People who feel really good about themselves don't get satisfaction out of hurting others.

And I learned another lesson, as well. My mother told me that if someone is comfortable with talking about others, then she's probably not going to hesitate to talk about you, too. My mother was right. Even though I thought Toni and I were the best of friends, it got back to me that she had made a comment about me behind my back—one that was not very flattering.

When Toni turned her "put-downs" on me, I got a chance to feel the effects. It was not a good feeling. For sure, it didn't make me feel like a Ferrari.

Rita Sultanyan, 14

Because I'm So Smart

Kids always tell me that I get good grades *because* I'm naturally smart. I don't see it that way at all. I mean, if I am so smart then I wouldn't have to work so hard at getting good grades—which I do.

Good grades don't come easy for me. *If* I were smarter, getting good grades would be so much *easier*.

My dad says I shouldn't be so tough on myself. He says that if I encouraged myself instead of putting myself down, then getting good grades would be easier for me.

I have a history exam coming up and I want to do well on it. My dad says I should see myself doing well and say positive things to myself like, "I'm going to get a good grade on the exam. I've read the chapters; I've studied; I know the material." I think basically what he's telling me is to see myself as a Ferrari.

I'll keep you posted if my dad's theory works.

Noreen Nicoles, 14

One "Hot" Ferrari

My father really dislikes my stepfather, Mike, and is always calling him names, saying what a "good-for-nothing" guy he is.

Mike knows about his name-calling because sometimes when my father comes to pick me up, he'll say inconsiderate things right in front of my stepdad like, "Is *what's-his-name* going to pick you up after the game, or am I supposed to bring you home?"

Even though it's rude that my father doesn't call Mike by his name, my stepdad doesn't hold it against my father. "Sure, I'll pick up BeShawn at 3:30," he'll answer. Nor does Mike make a big deal about my father's inconsiderate attitude towards him. He lets the comments go.

I asked my stepfather if the way my father treats him bothers or upsets him. "Oh, not really," he said. "You don't always have to be right, as long you do what's right." I like it that Mike is secure with himself. My father's taunts don't bother Mike because he likes himself. My dad's opinion of my stepdad doesn't change the way Mike feels about himself.

I really admire Mike. I especially like how he's good to my mother. And I really like what a good father he is to me. I appreciate all the things he does for me, like teaching me to throw a fastball and helping me with my homework—without becoming impatient like my father does. Mike even volunteered at my school's carnival this year. No other stepdads were there.

Though I would never tell my real father that I think my stepfather is one of nicest guys I know, he is. I'm happy to have Mike as my stepfather. Sometimes, I even call Mike "Dad" because he acts like a dad to me. In my eyes, my stepfather is a really great guy—one hot Ferrari.

BeShawn Niles, 13

Part 2

Friendship: Finding, Keeping and— Sometimes—Losing It

*A friend is someone with whom I can reveal
many parts of me, even those I am meeting
for the first time.*

—Jennifer Leigh Youngs

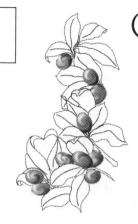

3

Good Friends Are a Necessity of Life

ELEPHANTS AND FRIENDS HAVE A LOT IN COMMON

When an elephant is ill or injured, other elephants in the herd gather around to protect the animal, and to bolster it up. They know how important their support is because if an elephant in such a condition lays down, it won't be able to stand up again on its own. So, the other members of the herd literally surround the weak elephant and help it remain standing. Even when on the move, the other elephants walk next to the ailing elephant, supporting it as they travel.

Just as elephants intuitively know when one of their friends needs assistance, they also know when that friend no longer needs support, and so, they gradually give the elephant a little more room until it walks and functions on its own.

A Word from the Authors

Amazing, isn't it? Animals, like people, intuitively know when one of their friends needs their help. A good friend is someone we can count on, as well as being so much more. A friend is someone with whom we can relax and just hang out, have fun and share our innermost thoughts—deep dark secrets, lofty and noble goals, or our hopes, joys and fears. A good friend allows you a safe space to share your deepest thoughts and needs—without worry of being judged, criticized or made to feel silly for feeling the way you do. Friends cheer each other on, laugh and cry together, and just plain commiserate and listen to each other. That's *why* friends are *friends*.

A good friend helps you become a better, wiser and more compassionate person than you might have been without that friend in your life. Friends help us grow into being who we are or, as Jennifer said, "A friend is someone with whom I can reveal many parts of me, even those I am meeting for the first time." What a wonderful gift, a real taste berry.

As you'll see from the teens you'll meet in this chapter, it's crystal clear that teens sincerely value their friends, and can speak eloquently about the important role their friends play in their lives. From coping with the death of a loved one (which so many teens had experienced), to dealing with the everyday ups and downs of life—like sharing a secret too good to keep, or mourning a breakup with a special someone—teens agree that friends are *very* important.

Making no secret of the fact that they treasure the support they receive from each other, teens shared openly about the sense of connection and strength they gain in knowing their friends will be there to understand and support them. Seventeen-year-old Roma Kipling's friends gathered around when she lost her beloved grandmother, as did a friend of fifteen-year-old Curt Lindholm when Curt lost a brother. For both Roma and Curt, it was a friend—as much as the love and support from their families—who helped them through a painful experience. Experiences as painful as the loss of a loved one stir up a lot of deep feelings—everything from doubt and anger to guilt, grief and depression. Many of these feelings can be difficult to handle. Because they are emotionally painful, these feelings can even lead to physical illness if not dealt with in a healthy manner. While friends are there for us when we walk through the heartache and grief of the death of a loved one, sometimes we need even more support. Should you be going through such a difficult time, we urge you to seek the support of your family, as well as the counseling you need to process your grief. As we discussed in part 1, many schools offer peer crisis counseling, which can provide you with crucial support. If your school doesn't offer these services, you can turn to an adult you trust—whether it's a parent, teacher, school counselor or clergy-man—to help you find the counseling you need.

A friend came to the rescue of fifteen-year-old Susan Hinkle when she found herself the only member of the group unwilling to leave a private party at a pizza parlor to "go look up some guys," while seventeen-year-old Lamont Henry tells of the heartbreak that results when he and his two friends are split up at a party during a police raid—breaking a pact they had between them and leading to tragedy.

Seventeen-year-old Bradley Dawson's best friend is the first person he looks for the moment he leaves the locker room after a game—especially if he's played poorly. Barbara Allen, thirteen, describes how completely different her friends Kayla and Sara are from each other. Though Kayla's support can border on insulting, and Sara won't always give her honest opinion, Barbara explains why both are really good friends.

Yes, friends are important as they help each other along the road of life, especially *real* friends. Sixteen-year-old poet Peggy Nunziata tells us how to know *for sure* if a friendship is "real."

Enjoy their stories!

Our Friendship Is Real

I'm sitting here thinking about the past,
Hoping in the future our friendship will last.
We have been friends for a short period of time,
And been through a lot, even so, we're just fine.

I've seen lots of people come and go,
Saying and doing whatever—careless, you know?
That's why your friendship means so much to me,
When I'm with you, I feel secure, whole, and so free.

Free from those who won't be around,
When times get tough, and I am down.
You'll be there for me and understand how I feel,
Because we both know our friendship is real.

Peggy Nunziata, 16

For You to Cry In

My grandmother was one of my very favorite people in all the world. Her name was Tilly, but I called her "Grams." She liked that.

Grams was so much fun to be around. She lived in a small apartment about forty-five minutes away from my family. She visited us often, and we visited her quite a bit, too. She lived her life to the fullest, and was always very involved in each one of ours. Just this past summer, she took me with her on vacation, a vacation she planned with just the two of us in mind. It was a vacation for, as Grams told everyone, "Just us two girls." We went to Washington, D.C., for eight days. While we were there, we went to the White House and the Lincoln Memorial. We visited museums Grams said I had to know about, and other "places of interest." And we got to eat dinner in a restaurant every single night. It was so much fun!

Grams had a way of making everything exciting. One night we went to a theater to see an opera. Everyone was dressed up, really dressed up, like in tuxedos and long gowns. Grams and I dressed up, too. We even had our hair styled at a salon. In my opinion, the opera itself wasn't all that great, but being with Grams sure was. And she was right when she said it was fun to "appreciate the ambience." Everybody at the opera was so cool!

Besides being fun to be around, Grams was one of the most positive people I've known. She had a way of making me feel like I was truly special. She believed in me and felt I could do anything I wanted, and that I would. She told everyone that I was "destined to grow up and change the world." She'd tell everyone she introduced me to, "My granddaughter is going to become a very important person, you just watch and see. Someday she'll be president of the United States, or maybe she'll just create the cure for all diseases—or the formula to make everyone in the world happy and forever young!"

She was like that. With her, I was an "unlimited" person.

But then, when she was only sixty-one years old, Grams died. I had visited her only two days before. She seemed healthy and was her usual, happy self. Mom said she died from a brain aneurysm.

When it happened, I was heartsick.

Knowing how much I loved and missed my grandmother, my two best friends pretty much did what the herd of elephants did for their sick friend: They rallied around me. Their parents allowed them to stay home from school and go with me to my grandmother's funeral, a gesture I hadn't expected. And the days following my grandmother's death they were so extra kind and sensitive to my feelings. Regularly they asked, "Are you doing okay?" or "Are you feeling better?" I found that so loving, and it showed me that they understood the hurt I was feeling.

The evening after the funeral, both of them came to my house. They brought me a stuffed animal with a note: "For you to cry in." They both stayed over that night, which was really nice. We just hung out, doing things like rearranging my closet, playing CDs and just talking.

My friends' empathy toward my sadness was like a big comforting pillow. They really cared and understood. It was so consoling, and it gave me a sense of friendship that I hadn't really felt from friends before. For sure, my friends helped ease the pain I felt over Grams's death.

Since that time, our friendship has been solid, and we're tighter than ever—inseparable really. We share everything. We help each other through the tough times—like being grounded, failing an important test, not being asked to a big dance and painful breakups with guys we were certain we were going to be in love with forever. And we help each other with the important things—like getting dressed to go out on a big date (a team effort), and planning what to wear to school when something big is going on and we want to look extra-great, like for class pictures or a school assembly. We trade clothes, fashion and makeup tips or model a potential outfit and exchange brutally honest opinions about what looks best and where and why something doesn't work. Because we are such good friends, we can do this without misunderstandings and hurt feelings.

I will always miss Grams. She was such a good friend; it showed in everything she did. I think it's possible to take friends for granted, and to think that friends are friends no matter what—which is not necessarily so. It doesn't just happen. More than anyone else, it was Grams's "style" of friendship that helps me understand that a friendship is special because of the things that people do to make it special. The relationship between my grandmother and me was special because Grams made a point of making it special—like my friends and I do for each other.

We laugh together, cry together, cheer each other on and commiserate and listen to each other. Like the elephants, we gather around to help each other. And because we do, we each know we can count on the other—in good times and in bad.

Roma Kipling, 17

Always Your Friend

Sometimes it's hard to write the words
That you, my dear, should see.
Or say the things you need to hear,
Or be as I should be.

You grow so fast and learn so much
It's hard for me each day,
To say or do just what is best
To help along the way.

Should I be silent or give advice?
Should I answer yes or no?
Should I have control—set many rules,
Or simply let you go?

One thing is certain . . . I'll make mistakes,
And some'll seem hard to mend.
But if nothing else seems clear right now,
Know that you can *always* count on me as your friend.

George E. Young

A Bad Day for the Rest of the Day

Some parents think that their own kids like and need their friends more than they do their parents. It's not true. When I'm in an argument with my mom or dad, I have a bad day for the rest of the day. It's not like I can have an argument with my parents and then go to school and just forget about it. It's very upsetting. If my parents and I have had an argument, I can be sitting in class, but I'm not really paying attention to what's going on because I'm off in my mind, still thinking about the argument.

Rather than concentrating on what the teacher is saying, I'm still involved: *What* were my parents thinking? *Why* did they say what they did (or didn't)? Then I wonder why *I* said what I did—or why I didn't say what I should have! And then I try to decide on a good time and a good way to reopen a conversation with them so I can go where I wanted—or get what I wanted or have what I wanted—in the first place!

So I sit in class, planning a new strategy, and playing through every possible response—several times. Which means, of course, that I'm still not paying attention to what's going on in my class. This upsets me too, so then I get worked up all over again.

I'm sure I'm not the only one this happens to. My friends feel equally upset when it happens to them. So, even though it's really important to me to feel close to my friends, it means even more to me to feel close to my parents. Like me, most of my friends respect their parents, and want to have a good relationship with them. I think a good friendship with your parents is like the elephants' scenario, where they all help each other. When my parents and I are seeing eye-to-eye, a lot of things in my life look okay to me.

Megan Burres, 16

My Stand-In Brother

One day when I was in the eighth grade, my grandfather came to school to get me. This was in the middle of the day, so I knew something was wrong.

We drove to the hospital, and it wasn't until we were getting out of the car that he told me that my brother, Tim, had collapsed on the school playground during recess. They had rushed Tim to the hospital, where he lay in a coma. He was only seven years old.

When I saw my brother hooked up to the wires and tubes, I felt sick to my stomach. It was scary. There were all sorts of monitors on, and he had wires attached to his arms and legs, and tubes in his mouth and nose. I didn't know what all the tubes were supposed to do, but I did know Timmy needed them to stay alive. I wanted to touch Timmy to let him know that I was there, but I didn't because I thought one of the wires or tubes might come unhooked and he'd die because of it. I was worried that Timmy might be in a lot of pain, only we wouldn't know it because he was in a coma and couldn't tell us. I felt so helpless. There was nothing that I or anyone else could do. We just had to wait.

The doctors advised my parents to stay at the hospital with Timmy as much as they could. Sometimes they took turns staying, but mostly both stayed. Because I had to go to school each day, my mother called the parents of my friend, Stephen, and asked if I could stay with their family until Timmy got better and my parents didn't have to stay there every night. Stephen's parents said it was okay and that I could stay as long as was needed.

Stephen's parents were really good to me. They made sure I got my homework done, but they also let me watch television a little later than my normal bedtime. And each day right after school, Stephen's mother took me to the hospital to see my brother. Stephen came along.

Seeing my brother in the hospital bed covered in all those wires and tubes never got easier. And I never got over feeling that the tubes might come unhooked if I touched him, so I wouldn't go into Timmy's room unless someone was with me. Seeing Timmy so lifeless was just a very sad feeling. And even when I just sat there, talking with Timmy, hoping he'd wake up and say something, I felt sad being in the room. Not only was it sad to see my brother that way, but my parents were so upset over Timmy's condition, that it hurt to look at them. They tried to be brave and positive, but I could see how fearful they were. I knew that wasn't a good sign; even though they said Timmy was getting better, I didn't believe them. It got to a point where I didn't want to go to the hospital unless Stephen went with me. Seeing my brother must have been as frightening to Stephen as it was to me, but he always went with me anyway. He never complained about going, either.

One night at Stephen's house, I was sleeping on the floor of his room in a sleeping bag. All the nights while my brother was in the hospital, I didn't sleep very well, but this one night was the worst. I was crying and it woke up Stephen. He asked me if he should get his parents. I thought that showed understanding. He didn't just go and get his parents, he asked if that's what I wanted.

I told him that I didn't need his parents, that it was just that I had a nightmare that Timmy had died. When I told Stephen more about the nightmare, he didn't think I was weird. He just listened. And even though I started crying, he didn't tell me not to. And he didn't pretend that everything was going to be alright, which is what my parents did. He didn't say, "It'll be okay," which is what most people will tell you when something's wrong. Even my parents had said, "We know Timothy will get better." But from the way Timmy looked to me, that wasn't going to happen. In fact, I was pretty sure that he would die. Stephen just said he was sorry that my brother was so sick and that he was scared for him, too.

Stephen said, "It's gotta be really hard to think of losing your own brother." And so we started talking about dying and what that must be like. My parents never talked with me about dying. They didn't want to think that it might really happen. But Stephen was more honest about it. It helped that I could be honest about everything I was feeling.

"The thought of Timmy dying scares me," I told Stephen. "He's just a little kid. And he's the only brother I have." Stephen nodded in perfect understanding, and then he said, "I hope Timmy doesn't die. But if he does, and you ever need a brother, I'll be your stand-in brother."

My parents called very early the next morning for me to come to the hospital. When I got there, they told me that my brother had died.

I miss my brother every day. We shared a room and sometimes we shared things like our video games and jokes and what we thought about school or different people. Timmy was a good-natured and funny guy, and a very good friend.

Now, on those times when I miss Timmy the most, or just need to remember Timmy by talking about him, I know who to call: Stephen, my stand-in brother. He's always there for me to talk to. And many times, just to listen.

Curt Lindholm, 15

Broken Pact

Nick and Peter were my two best buddies. We always had so much fun together. One of the things we did on the weekends was look up a "happening" party.

Six months ago on a Saturday evening, we were on our way to a friend's house when we drove by a houseful of people obviously partying. The front door was open, and you could hear the music blaring. There were so many people there that they spilled over onto the front lawn. We recognized a couple of the kids from school. They waved at us, so we turned around, parked and went in.

Peter, as usual, was already stoned when we picked him up at his house. Then, at the party he drank a whole lot of beer. We could see that he was really getting wasted. But we were having fun and didn't try to stop him.

That wasn't our biggest mistake that evening.

The three of us had a pact between us that we always looked out for each other. If one of us got into a fight or something, or was asked to leave a party for some reason, or if the cops showed up, we always made sure that all three of us left together. If we got separated, the plan was always to meet back at the car.

But on this night, we didn't look out for each other as usual. I think we were just too out of it. We could barely take care of ourselves, let alone be responsible for each other. The police raided the party, so we all hightailed it out of there.

We got separated. But instead of meeting at the car like we planned, Peter didn't show up. We just figured that maybe he had left with a girl he'd met or something. Or, maybe he had gotten arrested.

As it turned out, in trying to get away from the party and not get arrested by the police (as some people did), Peter had gone down to the beach. He was so messed up that he just laid down and went to sleep—right there next to the breaking, rising tide. I guess that he was too drunk and messed up to save himself.

They found Peter the next day, drowned.

I still can't believe that my friend is dead.

His death changed my life. For one, I don't hang out at parties as much as I used to. And his death also ruined the friendship between Nick and me because seeing each other is a painful reminder of Peter's death and how we let him down—and each other.

It's taken us a long time to get over Peter's death. Actually, we still aren't over it, and I doubt we ever will be. I know for sure that we'll never get over letting him down. We let each other down because we didn't stay with our plan to look out for and protect each other. We lost our friend.

We should never have allowed Peter to continue drinking that night. We knew he was messed up, and we didn't watch out for our buddy, our friend.

My friends tell me it wasn't my fault, but because of the pact we had, in many ways it was. I'm sorry that we ever got to a point that we started just losing it at the parties. We should have looked out for each other—been better friends—and not have gotten so screwed up.

I would give anything to see Peter walk through the door, full of life again.

Sometimes, you just don't know the importance of the responsibility you have in being a good friend. But now I've learned how important it is that I always take a buddy's friendship—and life—seriously, because it really can be lost forever.

Lamont Henry, 17

Most Valuable Player

I've discovered that being around someone who believes you're a terrific person makes you feel that you *are* a terrific person. And because of that, you automatically want that person for a friend.

The person who sees and brings out the best in me is Chad Diamant. People say that Chad is a "really together guy," and I can see why: He feels really secure within himself and makes others feel more confident, too. Chad has a special knack for seeing the "up" side of life. To him, the glass is never half-empty. It's always half-full. A good example is when I play in a football game. If I do well, he has no problem congratulating me on a good game and making me feel like a hero. And if I have a really bad game, in which I play really poorly, he doesn't focus on that. Instead, he points out some of the good aspects of my playing, like how I helped another team member to score or make a good play. He turns it around so that once again I end up looking like the most valuable player.

Even if our team lost, he won't dwell on the loss. Instead, he'll talk about some aspect of the game or particular plays that were especially good. "Lousy game," I'll say.

"No way!" he'll counter, and then say something like, "You were great in the third quarter! I saw the way you blocked that pass. The team's very lucky to have you!" With Chad I can't lose: I'm an MVP every game.

Because of Chad's support and positive attitude, he's the first guy I look for when I come out of the locker room. I consider him the most valuable friend I have, a real MVP in the game of life.

Bradley Dawson, 17

I Keep My Earplugs Handy

Sometimes you don't think about your parents as being friends, but they can be. Mine are.

My dream is to be a professional musician. I'd like to be a real star. Sometimes when I tell that to some of my school-friends, especially those who don't know me all that well, they look at me and give a little laugh, like they don't know how to take it. You know . . . am I a serious talent or am I an egotistical jerk? My parents don't laugh or question me. And they didn't doubt that I could learn to play a saxophone. They bought me one last year.

I didn't realize a saxophone was so hard to learn!

I know I must have made a lot of racket as I tried to play it, but my mom and dad never complained. "Sounds great!" Dad tells me. "You're really getting good!" Mom says. Four months ago, I had just about decided it was too much for me to master, but both Mom and Dad assured me that they had no doubts I could do it. So I didn't give up. I can't wait to be a rich and famous sax player. Like my Dad says, "You can do anything you set your mind on." I love how my parents support *me* just like the elephants support one another.

So, when I do make it as a professional, I'll owe a lot of my success to my parents for buying me my saxophone of course, but also for believing in me. So until then, I just picture myself up there on stage with the bright lights. And in the front row I see my two best friends—my mom and dad—with their little black shades on, clapping their hands, smiling.

Oh yeah! I'll make 'em proud! I just need to keep practicing. And my earplugs handy.

Jeremiah White, 17

4

The "Rules" for Being a Friend

DID I PASS YOUR TEST FOR FRIENDS?

I try to read your eyes,
surmise,
just what you think behind that brow.
As you nod,
are you thinking that I am odd?

You seem not to be impressed
at what you see;
I am
a nonentity?
You're in a hurry to forget,
What made me second-class?
I see I didn't pass the standards you have set
for friends.

Our story ends.

Elmer Adrian, 90

A Word from the Authors

As much as friends are friends, they still have to pass the standards you set for friendship—being able to talk openly and honestly is one of them. As your friend, Elmer Adrian, said, if you can't talk openly, the "story ends."

Many of the teens we heard from said that they *expected* their friends to acknowledge them when they did something especially good—like aced an exam, or played well in a tournament or looked extra good. That a friend is able to give you feedback about these things is more than just a matter of praise. It encourages and inspires you to continue to do your best. Being able to express yourself is an important thing between friends—as an entire auditorium of teens found out during a school assembly when Rob Ballen, seventeen, the good-looking, three-time-elected student-council president took the stage. Rob was "a scholar and a gentleman," "every girl's dream date," "every guy's idol." His classmates were in awe of him. You can imagine how dumbfounded they were when they learned he was not as happy as they thought he was—and they were absolutely shocked to find out that he had once considered taking his own life! That Rob reached the point of considering taking his life is a good example of what can happen when teens do not understand their intense feelings or know whom to turn to for help. Again, we urge you to reach out to friends and family. As so many of the stories in this book show, teens can be a good source of help and understanding. Remember, many schools offer peer counseling programs, in addition to programs staffed by professionals trained to help teens and sympathetic to their needs—both can be extremely helpful. Most important, just remember you are never alone—there are people who care and who can help if you reach out to them.

Good communication is not always easy, as Belinda Carr, sixteen, points out, but it has its benefits—as sixteen-year-old Beth

Brown discovered: "being allowed to spend time with my friends means knowing how to communicate with my parents!"

"You know, Mom, expressing yourself, saying what's on your mind and in your heart is so important. Caring enough to show compassion and empathy for what others are going through is what endears us to others and shows our humanness. But, an often overlooked fact of good communication skills is that they are primarily based on good *listening* skills. If you watch closely, you'll notice that the best-liked and most popular kids spend as much time listening to others as they do talking. I think being a good listener is one of the most ignored aspects of making and keeping friends, and of getting along with others in general.

"Good listening means you are really paying attention. Everybody knows someone who pretends to listen, but really only listens with 'half an ear,' continually interrupts, acts bored or shows indifference to what you're saying. It doesn't feel good to have someone do this to you. In fact, it makes you feel unimportant, inferior and generally insignificant. After all, this person has made it pretty clear that you had nothing interesting to say. When I was a senior in high school, a teacher did an experiment that clearly pointed out how unnerving this is. It was a day when we each were to give an oral report in front of the class. Trent—a really popular and well-liked student—was called to the counselor's office in the middle of his presentation. This was a set-up, but Trent didn't know it. When he left the room, the teacher instructed us to be 'an obnoxious audience.' Some of us were to lay our heads down on our desks, others were to gaze out the window and still others were to pretend to scowl or shake their heads in disagreement. When Trent returned to the classroom and continued his presentation, we went into our 'awful listeners' mode. After only a few minutes of speaking, a very frustrated Trent stopped and asked, 'What is going on? Why are you treating me this way?'

"It just goes to show you that listening is an attitude. We must *want* to listen and not just wait for our turn to talk. We need to give our full attention when our friends are talking. Don't comb your hair or fidget with your jewelry when someone is talking to you. Look at that person, show your interest, suspend all judgment and just *listen*. Don't play with the rubber bands on your braces or look around to see if anyone you know is nearby. Let the person who is speaking finish before you say anything. This shows that you care enough to listen and that you respect the person enough to care about what she has to say. It also gives you time to think about what the person is saying and an opportunity to gather your thoughts and decide how to respond. Try it and you'll be amazed at how much it improves your friendships—and all your interactions with people—and even increases your popularity with others."

"It's a good point, Jennifer. Listening is only one of the skills of effective communication, but it is a very important one—especially with your friends.

"Of course another good communication skill in friendship is being kind and treating friends as you would want to be treated. Being kind shows that you are a happy person who likes herself and other people, that you are open to getting to know people better, and that you are considerate and thoughtful."

"Don't forget the boomerang, Mom."

"The boomerang?"

"Yes. My friends and I always say, 'Remember the boomerang!' Basically, it means, 'Don't send out what you don't want to come back.' Like a boomerang, the things we do and say—both good and bad—usually come back to us sooner or later. If you say something inconsiderate about someone, your words will act as an immediate payback—you'll feel ashamed of yourself for being inconsiderate and cruel. Everything you send out boomerangs back to you. If you project an attitude of gratitude, it comes back. If you project happiness and goodwill, cheerfulness and consideration, these, too, return. If you gossip, it'll come back to haunt you, too, as I'm sure Mia in the story 'My Friend, the Thief' will find out! You receive what you give. If you can remember that one phrase, you can help yourself be kinder and nicer to others—a 'taste berry'!"

What I'd Like to Tell You—If I Could

I was testing the microphone in the high school auditorium where I was going to conduct a workshop for teens, when a voice nearby asked, "Do you need anything? Is there anything I can do to help?"

I fully expected to see a custodian, vice-principal, counselor or any other adult who might have been assigned to oversee my needs for the program I was doing for students. Instead, there stood a handsome, muscular, well-dressed young student. "Hi!" he said, "I'm Rob Ballen."

"Nice to meet you, Rob," I said. "I'm Bettie Youngs, and I've heard many good things about you—including that you have been elected student-council president three years in a row. The first thing I noticed as I drove onto the school grounds today was the billboard that read, 'Welcome, Dr. Youngs.' By the way, I heard you were responsible for putting up the billboard and I want you to know it's a nice touch and made me feel welcome!"

"Oh, it was nothing," Rob replied.

"Well, it was meaningful to me, and yes, there is a way for you to help. A good friend of mine, Helice Bridges, has developed a little exercise that's sort of like an award ceremony. A blue ribbon with the words 'Who You Are Makes A Difference' is used to acknowledge a person for something they've said or done that has made a difference to you. In my workshop with your class today, I'll be calling on a number of students, but I need a volunteer to start it off. Would you mind if I called on you to come forward first?"

"Oh, that'd be fun!" he said, without hesitating or asking anything more about exactly what it was he would be expected to do.

"Good," I said. "I'll count on you then!"

The students filed into the auditorium in various states of

anticipation and expectation. "Sometimes we don't express what's really in our hearts," I began. "This is particularly true when it comes to telling others, 'Thanks for being there for me, for making a difference in my life.' But it's important that we do this. First, it lets a person know that what he did was significant to you. Second, it gives the person the courage and motivation to do it again, to you and to others along the way.

"We needn't wait for some major event to happen. We can acknowledge others when they accomplish a worthwhile goal, as well as for their acts of kindness, for acting out of integrity—especially when it's not always popular to do so. I'd like to show you a simple exercise that can help you acknowledge someone for making a difference to you in some way. I'd like to ask you to pay close attention to your feelings as we go through this process. I need a volunteer from the audience. Who would like to . . ." Rob's arm shot in the air. ". . . volunteer? Okay, Rob, would you come up, please?" His classmates hooted and cheered and whistled good-naturedly. He was obviously well-liked.

Rob came up and stood beside me. The top of my head just barely reached his shoulders. His presence with me in front of them caused his classmates to giggle nervously and fidget with their belongings. After all, here was their handsome classmate standing beside a visitor who held a microphone in her hand, and who had the ability to call on them in front of their peers. It was their school, however, and they held the power to pay attention in a noisy manner or pay attention in a respectful manner. Power danced between them and me in perfect balance.

"Rob," I said, "I would like you to know that the wonderful welcome that your classmates gave me when I arrived at school today made me feel warmed, honored and welcomed. Since you were the one responsible for organizing it, I would like to thank you for being so thoughtful." My words were met with claps, whistles and cheers. Even so, I knew they were happy it was Robby up there and not them. Now only quiet chatter could be heard among a few friends. "As you can see, I'm holding a blue ribbon with the words, 'Who You Are Makes A Difference.' Your leadership actions made a difference to me. Thank you. Because you have acknowledged me, in a sense, you have asked that I acknowledge you. Best of all, your actions caused me to want to connect with you and your classmates in a meaningful way. May I pin this ribbon on your shirt?" Little gasps, nervous giggles— and a few good-natured and mild-mannered catcalls—arose from the audience of adolescents.

Rob looked first to me and then glanced over the faces in the audience. "Yeah, sure," he acquiesced. Smiling from ear-to-ear, he leaned down so I could reach the pocket of his shirt and pin the ribbon on it. All eyes were now upon Rob, all motions stilled by my audience's nervousness. This was far too close for comfort in the minds of these young people still learning the social rules of human touch. Classmates poked each other to distract them- selves from getting too close to the experience, no doubt relieved this was happening to Rob and not to them.

I continued the ceremony. "When you take this shirt off, Rob," I said, amplifying my voice a bit because of the hoots and howls these "risqué" words brought, "I would like you to remove the ribbon and place it on the mirror in your bathroom, so that as you get ready for school each morning, you will be reminded that your thoughtfulness was genuinely appreciated. Your car- ing actions were important to me."

I backed up a few steps. Now acting from the emotional energy of a speaker, rather than from the personal one-on-one I had just used, I looked at Rob and asked, "How does it feel to be acknowledged in this way?"

"Oh," he said sincerely. "It feels good. I'm not sure if anyone has ever told me 'thank you,' for anything." He became solemn and reflective. Shaking his head, he quietly repeated, "I don't think anyone has told me 'thank you.'" It didn't seem appropriate for me to examine that further, although I'm sure the audience "got it." Here was a young man who had on occasion done many considerate things for others. Yet, Rob hadn't been told—or he didn't hear—their thanks.

"Rob," I continued, "now that we can all see how this exercise works, I'd like for you to call someone up from the audience and acknowledge that person for making a difference to you."

"Oh," said Rob, macho posturing to impress, "that'll be easy. Chad, get your booty up here." Chad, his best friend, bounded up. Once again, the classmates cheered and clapped. The two guys playfully punched each other a time or two, then stood at attention in front of me. Standing next to Rob to oversee and assist him with the ceremony, I nodded for him to begin.

"Hey, bud!" Rob began in a voice filled with spunk and spirit, "I've got a blue ribbon here, as you can see, with the words 'Who You Are Makes A Difference.'" He turned to me and mouthed the words, "Now what do I say?"

"I would like to tell you how you made a difference to me," I instructed.

"Yeah, I'd like to tell you how important you are to me," he mimicked and then added, "And why."

I observed, but said nothing.

"Why you're important to me," he began, looking first at Chad, then the floor, then at the ceiling, then at me, "is because . . ." He stopped, cleared his throat and tried again. "Why you're important to me is because," and once again he looked first at Chad, then the floor, then at the ceiling, then towards the back of the room and back again at me, "is because . . ." He stopped, cleared his throat, sniffled, and this time Mr. Football used the hand of his "golden arm" to clear away the cloud of tears blurring his vision. The audience watched in disbelief, and perhaps in fear. Oh, no. Was it possible that their hero, the pillar, was going to cry?

"Oh Chad, ol' bud," Rob began again, "I've never told you, I never really wanted you to know . . . but you . . . you . . . saved my life. I don't know if you ever knew it, and if you did, you didn't let on. Remember the time last year when I came to your house at 11:30 at night, and you knew I had been drinking? You took my car keys from me, and though we argued over it, you refused to give them to me. You knew that I couldn't drive, and you called my mother, told her that I had fallen asleep and asked if I could spend the night at your house. I never told you, but my parents had gotten in a huge fight that night, and my dad said he was leaving. He had filed for divorce. I was so mad and hurt, and I thought, 'What will my friends at school think? How can I tell them that my parents are divorcing when my mother is the PTA president and my dad always helps drive us to the football games? Now he's leaving my mother and moving away. My class isn't going to want me to be class president anymore,' and . . ." Rob covered his face with one hand, then letting out a big sigh, continued. "You saved my life, Chad." The silence of the audience blared louder than any words could. Robby, now looking into the eyes of a very shocked Chad, continued, "I was going to drive off of old Highway 164 that night. You saved my life." Chad reached over and pulled him into his arms. The two boys hugged each other for what seemed like a very long time.

The audience sat stunned, aghast that their hero had once entertained such thoughts—or was even capable of them.

Now just another teenager, Rob, with shoulders slumped, took a seat.

Chad, still dealing with all this, stood motionless beside me.

"Chad," I said softly. "Here's a blue ribbon for you. I'd like you to acknowledge someone who has made a difference in your life."

It was a fairly sedate Chad who called upon Mr. Hudson.

"I'd like to call up the shop teacher," he said. A bewildered-looking teacher in the second row of the bleachers got up and came forward, taking his place beside Chad.

"Ah, you know that I gave you a hard time all last semester in shop class," Chad stammered. All the students in the audience were all but holding their breath. Though I didn't know the situation at the time, they knew just who the shop teacher was. "I guess I better begin by saying, I'm sorry," Chad said. "It's just that . . ." he stopped, as though choosing his words carefully. It caught me by surprise, too, when Chad continued with the words, "Dad, it just seemed to me that you'd touch the other guys on the arms or shoulders, or help them with their projects, but you didn't do that for me. It made me so jealous. You stopped touching me when I was in the seventh grade. I thought, 'Why do these kids deserve his touch and I don't?' Anyway, I gave you a rough time and I'm sorry. I admire you because you are such a good teacher and all the kids like you and think you're great. I do, too, Dad. I want to give you this blue ribbon because I think you're the best teacher ever. And you're a great dad, too. And I love you. Can I pin this on you?"

It was a meek and tearful father who received the blue ribbon.

"It's your turn, Mr. Hudson," I said.

"I'll call Suzee Merril," said the best teacher at the school.

"Suzee," he said, "as you can see, I'm holding a blue ribbon with the words 'Who You Are Makes A Difference.' I would like to tell you how you made a difference to me. You were the first girl to take shop class, and that was a courageous thing to do. I'd like to. . . ."

Suzee called up Bob, her brother. And her brother called up Tammy.

"Tammy," Bob said, "as you can see, I'm holding a blue ribbon with the words 'Who You Are Makes A Difference.' I would like to tell you how you made a difference to me. I'm no Einstein, but here I am, finally a senior, and it's because of you. For the last three years, I got up and came to school only because I knew you'd be here. Though we've broken up and aren't dating any-more," he paused to look to Rebecca, his new girlfriend, sitting nearby with his class ring around her neck and his coat draped around her shoulders, "I know that I'd have dropped out of school, maybe worse, if it hadn't been for you. . . ." Though he noticed, he seemed unfazed by his new girlfriend's scowl and look of absolute dejection. He looked again at Tammy and repeated, "If it hadn't been for you."

Tammy stood next to him, her arms tightly hugging her chest. This was difficult enough, loving him still—yet watching as he now dated another classmate was even more painful. Tammy didn't want anyone else. She had hoped to marry her Bob. She was so hurt that she couldn't lift her eyes to his, not even after his kind words. When he said, "You were the most important thing that ever happened to me," her arms unwrapped and followed her hands to her face, where the heavy black mascara and eyeliner she wore now streamed down. She buried her face in her hands and sobbed uncontrollably. The only boy she had ever loved had confessed her importance—humbly and genuinely. It left her visibly shaken emotionally, but more, her entire body was literally shaking. He pinned the blue ribbon on her collar, looked at her tenderly and said through his own tear-filled eyes, "Thank you for being there for me. I will always love you."

It was a good place to stop; what I had wanted to teach, to communicate, had been accomplished.

Bettie B. Youngs,
Excerpted from Gifts of the Heart

The Secret She Kept

For almost the entire school year, I liked a boy named Ben. I was pretty sure he didn't know. I never told him. Besides my mom, the only other person who knew was MaryAnn Drew, and I'd sworn her to secrecy! I didn't tell anyone else because it might get back to Ben. What if he didn't feel the same way? I was too shy to take the chance he might feel differently than I did.

"Asking Ben to the Sadie Hawkins dance?" Mom asked.

"I'd love to; I just don't have the nerve," I told her.

"Hmmm," she said, and then told me a story about "two very close friends" of hers when she was in school.

Katie liked a boy named Sean. But she never told him, forever keeping the secret to herself. When she saw him sitting at the other end of the lunch table, or with friends, she couldn't help but admire the way he listened intently to his friends, and always seemed so considerate and attentive.

Eventually both Sean and Katie began to date—but not each other. On so many occasions, Katie secretly wished her date was Sean, rather than who she was with—but it was her date, and not Sean, who asked her out. The night of her senior prom was especially bittersweet. When a favorite song of hers by Anne Murray was played (a song that always made her think about Sean), she looked to Sean, dancing with his date. Sean was looking in Katie's direction. They smiled at each other, their smiles lingering. For the entire evening, Katie gazed at Sean dancing with his girlfriend, Annie Pauls. Annie was so outgoing, Katie just knew she'd never stand a chance, even if she did get up the nerve to talk to Sean. But that didn't keep her from looking and dreaming—and wishing it was her dancing in Sean's arms.

After graduating from high school, both Katie and Sean went away to college in different states. But Katie never stopped missing him.

Both Katie and Sean attended their five-year high school reunion. When the band began to play, both Katie and Sean found themselves standing alone, each looking for a dance partner. Many of their classmates were married and were there with their spouses—but neither Katie nor Sean had married.

Katie looked at Sean across the room, and though butterflies took flight in her stomach, she walked over to Sean and asked him to dance.

"You're even more beautiful than you were in high school!" Sean whispered to her as they were dancing.

"Oh," she accused, "in high school, you didn't even know I existed."

"On the contrary," Sean corrected, "you were the love of my life. I was just too afraid to tell you. There wasn't an event that went by that I didn't wish you were my girl. You were so beautiful, so bright—and so reserved—I just knew you wouldn't go out with me. I decided I would rather secretly believe that you loved me than to have my Katie turn me down. Our senior prom was the worst. I kept looking at you, wishing you were my date. There was one song, one special song that just broke my heart. It was 'Can I Have This Dance, for the Rest of My Life,' by Anne . . ."

". . . Murray," Katie said, finishing his sentence for him.

"Yes," said Sean. "Do you know it?"

"Yes," was all she said.

My mother knows the story very well—you see, my mother's name is Katie. And Sean is my father. Later that long-ago evening, he asked the band to play "their song," and that's when he asked her to marry him.

It's a great love story. Even though this story ended happily, it's bittersweet, too, because my parents missed out on all those special times in high school when they wanted to share things with the other. They could have been "boyfriend and girlfriend" for all those years.

My mother's story gave me the courage to ask Ben to the Sadie Hawkins dance at school. He said yes! I doubt "our story" is going to end up like my parents' romance did, but I'm having a great time!

Stephanie Cohen, 16

Party On!

Five of my friends and I had gathered at our favorite pizza place for our friend Nicole's birthday party. We were all having a good time, talking and laughing, when all of a sudden, Michelle said, "Hey, I've got a great idea! Let's go to my house, call some guys I know, and party on!"

"I'm not sure that's a good idea," I said. I looked to the others for support, but it looked to me like the other girls were considering going. Either that or they didn't know how to say "no" to Michelle. Michelle always tries to bully the rest of us. Michelle knew that we'd all get in trouble with our parents if we left the pizza place, but that didn't keep her from pressuring us to go. So I reminded her that Nicole's mother had said, "Under no circumstance are you girls to leave before I get here!" I knew she'd heard the words as clearly as I had. "She's bringing Nicole's birthday cake at 8:30," I said. "We can't just not be here when she arrives!"

"So what?" Michelle said, like it was no big deal if Nicole's mother showed up with the cake and we weren't there. I thought it would be pretty rude if Nicole's mother came with the cake and we were gone. Plus, I knew my mother wouldn't give me permission to go to Michelle's house. In fact, she'd be furious if I left without getting permission. So I suggested that we should wait until *after* Nicole's mom had arrived with the cake. Michelle just laughed, and said, "Oh, stop being such a dweeb. Let's go. She'll find us!"

Four of the other girls, including Nicole, started to get up to leave. I couldn't believe my dilemma. "Hey, I'd like to go, too," I said, standing my ground, "but I just can't. My mother is expecting to pick me up here in an hour."

"Call her and tell her to pick you up at my house instead!" Michelle said in a really sarcastic tone of voice.

"She and my father went to dinner someplace, and I don't know where they went!" I lied, not really wanting to tell her that I knew my mother would say "no."

"Suit yourself," Michelle said. "The rest of us are going."

"You guys, it's really not a good idea—think about it," I pleaded. Then Michelle started swearing at me, calling me names worse than "dweeb." I felt tears coming to my eyes, so I ran to the bathroom.

I felt so childish, standing in the bathroom, crying alone, while my friends were getting ready to do something more exciting. But I knew it wasn't right to leave the pizza place. It's really hard to go against your friends, especially when you're hoping to be more popular with them. I was standing in the bathroom wondering how long I was going to stay there, assuming they'd all left, when Amanda came in. "I'm sorry that Michelle is being so mean to you," she said, trying to comfort me. "She's just that way. I agree with you that we shouldn't leave. I mean, Nicole's mother is expecting to find us here, and she's even bringing a cake. And besides, I'll get into trouble with my parents if I leave and go to Michelle's house, so I'd better stay here, too."

"Did the other girls leave?" I asked.

"No," she said, "not yet. But I think they may. But if we get out there right now, maybe we can convince Tammy and Ellie to stay—and Nicole, too."

"Okay," I said, feeling a little bit relieved. I dried my eyes, and we left the bathroom.

"I'm staying here with Susan," Amanda announced as soon as we returned to the table. Then she said something I hadn't expected. "If I leave I'll get in trouble with my parents, too, so I think we should take Susan's advice and just stay here."

Nicole looked relieved as she blurted, "I'll stay with you guys. My mom would ground me until my next birthday if I just took off when she told me not to."

"Okay, I'll stay, too," Tammy said, shrugging her shoulders.

"Me, too," Ellie added.

"Well, I'm not going alone! I'll stay, too. Geez! What wimps!" Michelle griped.

"Better wimps than grounded," Amanda said.

I was so surprised it was that simple. None of the girls left, and I know it was because Amanda sided with me.

Not only did Amanda's siding with me make me feel better, but she was also the deciding factor in the other girls staying, too. Even though the two other girls had seemed willing to go along with Michelle, it only took the two of us to convince them to stay.

I guess it's true what they say: There is strength in numbers. Friends can influence each other. For good and bad. "Alrighty, then," I said, feeling like a victor. "Party on!"

Susan Shrinkle, 15

My Friend, the Thief

When I was in the eighth grade, a girl named Mia spread a rumor that I was a "thief" because I had "stolen" from her. I don't know *why* she got all *dramatic* about it. I mean, all I did was take a cupful of grain from Mia's bag of horse food in the tack shed she and I shared at a stable where we both board our horses.

It's not like I wasn't going to replace the amount I'd taken. And, I would loan her grain if she needed it for her horse. Besides, all of us who boarded our horses there did this—it was a regular thing. And she *knew* that!

But Mia exaggerated the story and made me out to be a thief and spread the rumor throughout the entire school! She made it out like I belonged on the FBI's Most Wanted list. The problem is, I didn't know the rumor was circulating throughout the school until one day when I was putting a note in my good friend's locker and a teacher coming down the hall saw me. She got really funny and began questioning me, then asked to see what I had taken—as if I would steal something from my friend! Next thing I knew, girls in my gym class with lockers next to mine were glancing at me sideways, then shielding their locks from me, so I wouldn't see their combinations when they opened their lockers. Becky, who had been a friend for almost a full two years, suddenly asked me to return a blouse she'd loaned me, as if I was trying to keep it! "You better not think you can keep my blouse, I want it back," she said loud enough for everyone around to hear. She completely overlooked the fact that she had borrowed and still had a blouse of mine, too.

It took me nearly four months to explain myself and for the rumor to die out. Not only did I have to regain the trust of a lot of people—trust I didn't deserve to lose in the first place—but I also had to put up with being treated with suspicion—like some kind of criminal. And even though I knew I hadn't done anything wrong, being treated like I had still made me feel really bad about myself. It was the most terrible semester of school in my whole life. I know how awful it feels to be the butt of a rumor. Because of the experience, I will never do it to someone else. I also know that *I'll* never believe that just because someone *says* something is true that means that it *is* true. I won't believe any rumor without absolute proof that it really happened just the way it's being told. I've learned a really important lesson in friendship.

Sally Thornton, 14

"Cooler" Than You Think

When I was in junior high, Kent wasn't exactly the most popular guy in school. Actually, he was sort of a nerd. Hardly anyone talked to him—not for any particular reason, just nobody said much to him.

One day, after getting my lunch, I looked around for my friends in the cafeteria. They weren't there yet, and it was kind of crowded, so I took the first open seat I saw. I found myself sitting next to Kent. We started talking.

As it turns out, he's not so "different." In fact, Kent is a pretty smart guy. He's just quiet.

I was surprised to learn that he collects sports cards like I do. He even has a Ken Griffey Jr. rookie card—which is worth a couple hundred dollars—that he got from a three-dollar pack of cards! What luck! And, for his birthday this year, his uncle gave him a game-worn jersey card (that's one of the really cool cards that come with a small piece of the athlete's jersey right on the card). We had a really good conversation about where to find some good deals on some of the rare and hard-to-find cards. Kent told me he has both "Tough Stuff" and "Beckett" card books, which are the best ones to tell you what every card is worth. While we were talking, we found out that we each have a couple of cards that the other wants. So now we're going to get together to compare our cards. To tell you the truth, I'm really looking forward to getting together with him. He knows all about which ones are really hot and which ones are supposed to be going up in value. It's totally cool.

It just goes to show that sometimes people who are not popular might be cooler than you think. If I hadn't taken the time to talk to him, I would've missed out not only on knowing all those things about sports cards, but also on knowing a really cool guy.

When my friends saw me with Kent they teased me about it

later. When I told them about what we had talked about and that he was an interesting and pretty neat guy, they didn't say much. But now when my friends see Kent, they talk with him. And they treat him like a regular guy.

All because I sat with him for a few minutes that day in the lunchroom and found out that he definitely passed my test for being a friend.

Carl Galloway, 14

If You *Really* Want to Know

Kayla and Sara are both friends of mine, but they're very different. For instance, the other day the three of us were going to go to the movies. "Do I look okay?" I asked Sara.

Without even so much as looking at me, she replied, "Yeah, sure. You always look great."

"How about my hair?"

"Yeah. Looks great," she responded.

The moment Kayla walked in, she took one look at me and demanded, "You're not going to be seen in that, are you? No way am I going to be seen with you if you wear that!"

"What's wrong with it?" I asked.

"Well, for one thing, you look like a little kid in it, and for another, there's a mustard stain on the left sleeve." She paused, frowned and then added, "Having a bad hair day?"

So you can see how different they are. Sara is a person who doesn't want to upset you, so she always says something nice and would never want to make you feel uneasy, no matter what. Kayla is very blunt and outspoken. She has very definite opinions and isn't afraid to be honest. Kayla is definitely not afraid of what you'll think about what she has to say. So if I really really want to know how I look, while I ask them both, it's Kayla's advice that's worth the most. She has no problem telling me her honest opinion about anything. If the way I look passes her inspection, I can be sure that it will pass with others. Now, if I was worried about a big test at school, I'd go to Sara for help. Kayla puts as little energy as possible into her grades. Sara, on the other hand, is very smart, understands what it's like to want to get good grades, and will help you out when you need it. So both Kayla and Sara are good friends, each in her own way.

Friends. They're so different. That's why you need lots of them.

Barbara Allen, 14

So I Threw His Letter Back at Him

I remember the night my boyfriend and I broke up. We went to a movie, and on the way home I mentioned that I was planning to get a new dress for the big school dance that was coming up. I asked him what he thought he was going to wear. That's when he told me he couldn't take me to the dance. That really upset me. And frustrated me. I really, really liked him, but I often found myself without a date for many of the special things going on. If he was my boyfriend, my *only* boyfriend, why wouldn't he want to take me to all the many things going on?

By the time we reached my house, I was even more upset. Thinking that we wouldn't be going to the big dance upset me so much that I didn't even wait for him to finish what he was saying. I got out of the car, and as I was slamming the door, I hollered, "Well, fine, if you don't take me, then I don't want to go out anymore. We're through!"

Later that night, he called and asked, "Can we talk?"

"No!" I yelled and hung up.

The next day at school he walked over to me while I was at my locker and tried handing me a note. I was still mad, so I grabbed the note and threw it back at him. Looking sad, he just walked away.

I picked up the note so none of the other kids who saw it when it fell to the floor would read it, stubbornly tossed it in my history book—where it stayed on the top shelf of my locker for the next several days. I was just miserable.

Sitting at home—the night after the dance—I took my history book from my backpack, retrieved his letter and read it.

> *Dear Connie,*
>
> *I'm sorry I can't take you to all the things that I'd like to. I'd love to take you everywhere—to every dance, every movie, to the fair when it comes to town, to restaurants. I don't know how to*

tell you this and still be fair to you, but it's just that most of the money I earn from my part-time job goes to help my mother pay our bills. She works hard to take care of me and my brother and sister, but she just doesn't make enough money to do it alone. I love being with you. . . . going places and doing all the little things that make you happy. . . . I just can't afford to right now.

I miss you. . . . you know that we should be together. . . . I know how important it is to you to go to the school dance. If you don't mind that I don't rent a tux, if you don't mind that the corsage I give you isn't made of the orchids I know you deserve, then I'd love to take you to the dance. I miss you so much. Please reconsider.

Love,

Kurt

Now whenever I hear about good communication skills, my heart aches because of the way I treated Kurt. He is such a good guy and I really hurt him—all because I refused to listen. The irony is that because I wouldn't communicate, I ended up hurting myself, too. I'm a better listener now and I don't jump to conclusions so fast. That's been helpful, too! And, I now read love notes the instant I receive them!

Connie Hunt, 16

Sometimes You Just Outgrow Your Friends

My older sister is in her first year of junior college and having a great time. It's all she talks about. So I've decided I want to go to college, too—the same one she's attending.

I haven't always wanted to go to college. My two best friends, Lindy and Rianna, and I had planned to find jobs and share an apartment right after we got out of high school. Now that my plans have changed, I have a bit of a problem. For one thing, my grades haven't been all that great, so I'm going to have to put more time into my school studies to make sure I can get accepted to junior college. This means I'm going to have to spend less time with Lindy and Rianna. I'm no longer as interested in being a high school student as I am in becoming a college student.

Lindy and Rianna and I have always spent nearly all our free time together. We go to the arcade every day after school, and sometimes on the weekends. If we're not there, we're at the movies—or somewhere. Lindy and Rianna are a lot of fun to be with. Even so, being with them takes up a lot of my time. While this was once okay, now it's more time than I'm willing to give up.

So the problem is, now that our lives are starting to go in different directions, the friendship is really strained. I'm beginning to spend more time with my sister—and her friends. At first Lindy and Rianna were okay with this, now they seem annoyed. "Are you going with us to the movies on Friday, or are you going to hang out with your preppie friends?" they ask. "What do you mean, you can't go? It's only homework," or "Don't be such a drag." I can tell by their comments that they resent the plans I've made.

I think that when you change, your friends have a hard time with it. Sometimes you can't prevent hard feelings. The sad truth is, sometimes you just outgrow your friends.

Belinda Carr, 16

Anything . . . for Friends

I worked long and hard at getting accepted by the group of guys I hang out with—Jared, Todd, Dennis and Greg. I'd do anything for them. When they all took karate, I took karate, too. At first, most of them were better at it than I was, but I kept at it and practiced my moves. I wanted to show them I could hold my own with them. And I did. When they all got skateboards, I got one, too. We do some pretty cool stunts with them. I learned how to handle my board better than anyone else. I'm not just saying that, you could ask any of them.

Being their friend means a lot to me. So, like I said, I'd do anything for them. Like when Todd asked me to get the answers to the second-period math test, I said, "No problem." I got the answers for him. That's what friends do. They do things for each other; they especially help one another out when they need it. At least that's what I thought!

Then, last week my skateboard got trashed when I was going over this really huge ramp, and it shot away from me. I wasn't hurt, but my skateboard was totaled. So I asked Todd if I could use his. He said, "No way, I want to keep my board in one piece." I asked Jared and Dennis and Greg, too. They all laughed and said just about the same thing. I couldn't believe it because I'd let them at least have some time using my skateboard if the same thing had happened to theirs. But not one of them would do it for me.

Maybe my sister was right. She said I shouldn't have to keep proving myself with my friends. I'm pretty upset with Jared, Todd and Greg right now because I thought friends did things for their friends, but they didn't return the favor.

Mike Madson, 13

Part 3

Love in Our Lives

Love is the irresistible desire to be irresistibly desired.

—Robert Frost

5

Love Makes the World Go 'Round

We live in a world that needs love.

—Bettie B. Youngs

LOVE IS EVERYWHERE

"It's Friday night! Tell me what other girl, with the best-looking *new* boyfriend in the world, two days before my birthday no less, would want to be sitting at a dinner table—with relatives—discussing her mother's engagement?"

Newly engaged, I was home to share the news with my parents and five brothers and sisters. While happy for me, my daughter Jennifer was in a bad mood because the object of her affection was an hour and a half away. Young, restless and feeling insecure about the depth of what she and he shared (or as she put it, "He's the type that 'when the cat's away, the mouse will play!'"), Jennifer really wanted to be with her boyfriend and not here with us.

Sitting at the dinner table, I looked around the room at my

97

family—my brothers, sisters and their children ranging in ages from newborn to nearly grown. I saw love—many forms of it—everywhere. I glanced first at my parents, husband and wife for nearly fifty-three years now. Even after all these years, they were still in love. Pointing to an amaryllis plant in the middle of the table, Dad was telling my sister of the single stalk he discovered in the backyard, and how he waited for just the right moment to surprise my mother, his love, with the flower. Theirs is a love rooted in passion, honor and commitment—and supreme attachment to their six children, all of whom adore, respect and honor them.

Next, my attention went to my brother as he leaned over to his seventeen-month-old son, sitting in a high chair next to him, and wiped his face with a napkin. He gently rubbed the baby's fine blond curls and kissed him on the head. His gesture, so natural, demonstrated clearly his great paternal love, making it clear that a kiss is the *language* of the heart. His wife, seated beside them, her hand on his knee, smiled at her husband and son, her love for them apparent.

Across the table, another brother and his wife of twenty years joked playfully and laughed intimately with each other, oblivious to the "noise factor" from all of us now involved in individual and separate conversations. Yet another brother and his wife, watching their five-year-old try to force a fork into his mouth that was loaded with more food than could possibly fit, looked at each other, their hands over their mouths, trying to stifle their laughter so their son wouldn't think they approved. My older sister sat next to her husband, smiling and intently listening to his words, nodding her head in agreement to whatever it was he was saying.

And of course, there was my daughter, who by now had slipped away from the dinner table and sat huddled in the corner on the phone, her whispered conversation punctuated with occasional giggles. She was experiencing yet another sort of love, maybe not as stable or as deep, but probably as intense as any other at the moment.

Love, many forms of it, was everywhere.

Looking at my family reminded me that love, with its many stages, all equally as important as the next, "makes the world go 'round." I was warmed at the idea of sharing love as my family knew it, and became even more sure that I wanted to marry David, my fiancé.

Bettie B. Youngs
Excerpted from Taste-Berry Tales

Love—has the power to fill life with joy and meaning.

A Word from the Authors

"Gosh, Mom, I should have stayed at the dinner table! The guy you're referring to in the story above is now history! Funny isn't it, how important some things seem at the time. Whoever said, 'Love makes the world go 'round,' wasn't kidding. I mean, the heart just keeps on believing in love. Even after a tough experience, like losing a special friend or breaking up with a boyfriend, the heart isn't discouraged—it just ventures right out there again. I've been in love a couple of times and each time when love ended, so did the world, or so I thought. But the heart is such an optimist. Time and time again I'd rebound, and my heart would be right back at it, ready to love again. I am getting wiser though! When you think about it, when it comes to love, you can't forget how important it is to look out for your heart— you have to take care of it. I've started referring to mine as 'my little heart' because this endearment reminds me that though I'm a big, strong, independent girl who is learning to handle almost anything, my heart is sensitive, fragile and always seeking love, and so it sometimes calls people and experiences to it that come with a high price.

"But like I said, I'm becoming wiser, each year. I'm setting higher standards for myself in choosing friends and the guys I date. And, I'm learning not to take it so personally when someone I'd like to be with isn't interested in me, and not to get so panic-stricken over breaking up with someone, even though that rates right up there with having your wisdom teeth pulled—all four of them on the same day! Gosh, do you remember being with me when I did that? Was that a dumb idea or what?"

"Well, it wasn't one of your wisest decisions! The dentist had wanted to extract your four wisdom teeth on two office visits, but you insisted on having it done in just one visit."

"That's right. Then, because I did, I had to take painkillers for two days. Talk about being out of it! I actually defeated my purpose; I had wanted to get it over with so I didn't have to miss yet another afternoon of work, but having all four pulled at the same time was so overwhelming that I missed two full days of work! As I recall, you canceled a couple of days of appointments so that you could stay home to take care of me. I love you for all the nice things you do for me, Mom. I know that you love me because it shows in everything you do. We've been through so much together! What's that phrase you use, '*I love you because I know you so well; I love you in spite of knowing you so well!*' Now I better understand the meaning of the first part, and see the humor in the second part! Thank God for parents! They love you no matter what!"

"Yes, they do, don't they! I have no doubt that the strongest bond in love is the one between parents and their children."

"Well, you guys are just so . . . so . . . so cute!"

"What does that mean?"

"Well, I'd wanted to say vulnerable and gullible, but if you combine vulnerable and gullible you get 'cute'!"

"Jennifer! What on earth does that mean?"

"Look, Mom, one of most endearing things from one person to another is when a person is honest in revealing the things that pain them, and things that make them feel frightened or insecure, basically when they are vulnerable enough to reveal their cracks and flaws. A best friend, whether a guy or a girl, becomes the 'best' friend *because* that person makes it safe to be yourself, and to reveal your own cracks and flaws. When I'm missing you, what I bring to mind are the times you cared for me when I was hurting or sick or in trouble with someone, or when something major was going on in my life and I needed a strong and sure anchor. But on those times when I just think about my 'Mom,' it's not the strong and competent and successful 'you' that comes to mind and puts a smile on my face as much as that person who gets flustered for having made a wrong turn, or who, when first learning to ski, came down the slope mostly on her butt. It's the times when you just 'blew it,' the times when you revealed your vulnerability that linger in my mind as reasons why I love you as much as anything else. That you are fragile and human and need me to love you gives me a reason to be needed in your life. And I need you to need me."

"You know I'm going to edit out that part about the learning to ski, but I agree with you that it's these times of seeing another person be vulnerable that create powerful and lasting memories of love. For me, and probably for most parents, we see our children in their young years doing everything for the first time, scared and yet displaying such courage as they venture into new experiences. Everything from standing up—and taking terrible falls as they do; to being up to bat for the first time and sweating bullets that they'll connect with the ball or make it to first base. When you're hoping for a date with a special someone, we're praying you won't get stood up. When you're hoping a special person will want you as a friend, we're hoping she wants your friendship in return. We watch with admiration as you're yearning for 'wheels' of your own; or making plans to go out into the world and test your wings—all that you put to the test. Watching, hoping, helping, rooting for our children—all creates a love that is unparalleled. Our love for our children deepens as we realize that our children must tolerate our shortcomings. As we watch our children unfold, we wish we knew more about how to help our children—these angelic and irritating creatures we've fallen in love with. And, we worry that our own flaws and inexperience will somehow hurt or deprive our kids (and they usually do!). To be a parent is to always wish we'd done some things differently. It's certainly a learning curve. I'm reminded of a statement made by author Betty Eadie in her beautiful book *Embraced by the Light.* She said that of all the prayers that are sent heavenward, God answers those of parents first because they are the most unselfish of all the prayers—they are always about our children's well-being."

Laughing, Jennifer replied, "Yeah, I'll bet they are. Like, please, God, help my kid score high on his SAT test today; please, God, let my kid get to be one of the six girls selected to be cheerleader; please, God, let that boy she's going out with be a nice decent guy; or please, God, don't let my kid make any really dumb decisions today!' Just kidding, Mom, I think you're right. Parents are so hopeful when it comes to their kids. I'm just saying that I'm sure God has heard from you on my behalf."

"As recently as yesterday," I reminded her.

"Love is a wonderful thing, isn't it, Mom. I love the heart-strings between you and me."

"Jen, I do think that we share an extraordinary bond, a real soul mate relationship, but no matter where I am, it doesn't matter what town, city or state I'm in, whether I'm talking to a group of parents or a group of teens, the heart connections between parents and children are undeniable. When the relationship is good, they're 'happy' about it, and when they haven't found a way to respect each other and act accordingly, parents say they are 'disappointed.' Teens, on the other hand, are angry about it, and their anger shows up in a number of ways. For both parents and teens, there is a passionate longing to share a mutual love and respect."

"Mom, enough about parents, let's talk about guys! Did I tell you about Ben? Wow, he's too cool, Mom. He's just out of college, has a place of his own, a job with a production company and . . ."

"Would I want him for a son-in-law?"

"You're hopeless, Mom! Luckily, I love you in spite of knowing you so well!"

Love, what a wonderful and precious thing—what a miraculous gift. We don't have to search far to see the importance we place on love. We even wear a ring a "special someone" has given us (like a friendship ring, an engagement ring and even a wedding ring), on what we refer to as the "ring finger," which became the "romance finger" because it was thought to have a vein that went to the heart—and the heart is the universal symbol for love. The very symbol of a heart brings up feelings of tenderness, affection and caretaking, which is why it represents the most priceless gift of all—love.

Almost everyone agrees on the importance of love, and teens are no exception. You know its value and feel its power. You want to love yourself and others better, and you would like the whole world to be a more loving place. Luckily, there is no shortage of love in the world. Love is everywhere, you said, and it can be expressed in many ways. We agree, and as the stories in this chapter show, this is true even for an umbrella cockatoo named Snowy Bird. Now living in a bird sanctuary because his owner left the state and could no longer care for him, Snowy Bird plucked the feathers from his chest because he is in distress. Snowy Bird is mourning—though he's hopeful that one day he'll find love again! Several weeks ago, he thought he had. When he spotted a visitor to the sanctuary that reminded him of his previous owner, he hopped on the woman's finger, scuttled up her arm, perched himself on her shoulder, buried his head in the collar of her shirt and cooed, "I'm Snowy Bird, I'm Snowy Bird." When the woman looked surprised, the attendant informed her that she looked and sounded like his previous owner. Snowy Bird thought it was his lucky day to "go home."

He may just find a home. The fan mail Snowy Bird gets from teen readers is mounting in our office! And speaking of homes, my mother once said that one of the nicest things about the love of a family for its members is that no matter how the world treats you, a family "always reclaims its own." Love gives us a home, giving us those who will always take us in. In Hanoch McCarty's moving account of the ups and downs of being a stepson, he finds that love is so powerful, so wanting of a home, that sometimes the reclaiming of its own is even outside of bloodlines. And speaking of homes, George Young tells us why our "house" is not our only "home."

Almost without exception, we are told that love is the most potent force in all the world. There's no greater force for good, no greater power for creating changes in our lives. Most all of the teens we heard from agreed and said that love has the power to color all things; it can make a sunset more spectacular, it can ease the bitterness of disappointments, hurts and losses. A kind word or deed by someone makes a victory seem more satisfying, a joy more sweet, a broken heart ache less. This is the power of love in action.

One of the most important things we do in life is learn to love ourselves and others and to do things *with love*. We can rise to the challenge of a world that needs love. Love after all, is the greatest "taste berry" of all.

Robert Frost said, "Love is the irresistible desire to be irresistibly desired," and you agreed, saying there's nothing quite like love to bring out your desire to please—as Tito Montes, sixteen, found out when he fell in love with Camerina. Only after she left him for another guy did he breathe a sigh of relief over the detention he'd been spared. It can be tricky knowing when you're giving too much—or going too far in the name of love. Christopher Gillian, seventeen, learned how far he would go for a girl named "Sheree," as did seventeen-year-old Nick Barry when he ended up in a fight with a guy who had "muscles the size of Arnold Schwarzenegger," and all because his girlfriend wanted "proof" of his "undying love."

When Matt didn't love Sheila Sam forever—as promised—it broke her heart. But in the process of getting over him, she found someone else to love, someone who would never "sign out" on her.

Love is everywhere, even in the kitchen, as Cory Griffin, seventeen, discovers when he comes upon his parents dancing in the kitchen, holding each other close and singing to each other. Probably it wasn't the first time his parents had danced together. Maybe because he had recently fallen in love himself, Cory finally noticed! And your friend Elmer Adrian, ninety, con-tributed quite a bit to the subject—his poems speak of the love of a grandfather, and the love of a lifelong romance! Oh, to be young at heart, forever!

Being loved affirms that we are lovable, worth loving. Giving love gives us a purpose—we are needed. Whether it be a pet, parent, grandparent, teacher, boyfriend, girlfriend or cockatoo, we are reminded that we live in a world where everyone needs to feel wanted, needed and included—in a word, *loved*.

The world needs loving people. And there is no question that teens are rising to the challenge. Love is life's greatest "taste berry." Enjoy these stories of its power and importance.

Unconditional Love

Remember, dear, when you're a success,
I'll be happy as can be.
But remember, too, that when you fail,
You can always come to me.

There's little in life we cannot share.
We'll share the bad times, too.
For my love has no conditions, dear,
That's what I give to you.

George E. Young

Love—is unconditional.

Dancing in the Kitchen

The other day I walked in the house and found my parents dancing in the kitchen. They were holding each other close and singing the words of a song on the radio to each other. They looked so in love.

I never thought about my parents dancing, showing off their romantic dance "moves." But as I watched them for a brief moment, I thought it was pretty cool that they still loved each other enough to dance together in the middle of the kitchen, in the middle of an ordinary day.

Watching them sway together, so wrapped up in each other that they didn't even notice I was there, I decided it wasn't so different from how I would look, or what I could imagine myself doing, if I were dancing with my girlfriend. I could see the two of us, looking exactly as my parents looked, only younger.

They didn't see me, and I didn't stay around. But it's cool to see your parents dancing. It's a nice feeling to know they are in love. Somehow, that feels reassuring.

It was a very beautiful moment, a real expression of their love—my parents, dancing in the kitchen!

Cory Griffin, 17

Love—has happy feet.

Snowy Bird

I was visiting a bird sanctuary, when in the distance, I spotted a young man with a white bird on his fingers. As he moved the bird up and down, the bird got into the spirit of things, lifting his little wings up and down in perfect rhythm with the man's movements. The man gave a little signal, and the bird began to swing around the man's fingers, as if a circus acrobat.

Enchanted, I walked closer to see the beautiful white bird perched on the finger of the attendant. "Marty," his name badge read.

"Hi, Marty," I said. "Great bird. What is it?"

"This is Snowy Bird," Marty replied. "He's an umbrella cockatoo." The cockatoo was snow white in color, a regal-looking bird with a high plume of feathers fanning from the crown of his head. But there was one exception to his majestic appearance—Snowy Bird has no feathers on his chest. Jarred by seeing this beautiful and obviously talented bird with such a raw and featherless chest, I asked Marty, "What happened? Did he have mites?"

Marty shook his head and explained, "No, Snowy Bird plucks out all the feathers on his chest himself. You see, two years ago his owners had to move out of the state and felt they could no longer care for him, so they brought their bird here. Snowy Bird is heartbroken. He still hasn't stopped pining for them. One of the ways he mourns them is to pluck the feathers from his chest."

"And he still hasn't gotten over it?" I asked, feeling for this beautiful little bird with a heartache.

"Apparently not," Marty explained. "Whatever it is that goes on in Snowy Bird's head or heart, he is still missing them." By now I was standing next to Marty observing the bird. My husband, David, was beside me and he held out his finger for Snowy Bird to step on to, but Snowy Bird backed cautiously away. "C'mon over, little guy." David coaxed. "You sure are a pretty bird." The bird turned his head away from David and then, looking at me, began clawing the air, a motion I interpreted as his wanting to perch on my arm. Once again David put his finger up to the bird, hoping the bird might now be ready to perch on his hand. Once again, Snowy Bird turned away from David, and once again he gestured for me to take him. So I put my finger up next to the attendant's hand. Instantly, Snowy Bird leaped from Marty's fingers to my wrist.

Snowy Bird wasted no time making his way up my arm. Scuttling up the length of it, he perched on my shoulder, then nestled there, rubbing his head back and forth against my neck. I reached up and gently stroked Snowy Bird's soft silky feathers, comforting him with baby-talk. Snowy Bird loved this and continued to rub his head against my neck, back and forth, back and forth. Leaning his little body taut against my neck, Snowy Bird then buried his head inside the collar on my shirt and cooed sweetly, "I'm Snowy Bird . . . I'm Snowy Bird."

My heart went out to him. I was also surprised to hear the bird speak, and most especially in the sweet yet forlorn way the little bird said his words. Reading my face, the attendant said, "We hear Snowy Bird say his name every couple of weeks, especially when he's stroked in that manner by someone who looks and sounds like you. It must be a similar look and sound to those of his former owner—at least Snowy Bird thinks so." Turning to look at the bird, whose head was still inside my collar, Marty added, "Too bad Snowy Bird doesn't have someone to give him the same kind of love he once had."

Love, so important—to all of us. Even to umbrella cockatoos, especially one by the name of Snowy Bird who pines to bring back a love and closeness he once knew.

Bettie B. Youngs

Love—makes its presence
known from the inside to the outside.

Oh, Camerina!

I'll never forget Camerina and the way she made me feel. She was my first love! I met Camerina at a soccer game when her school played our school. (Her team won!) I fell in love the instant I saw her. She lived on the other side of town from me and attended a high school there. I asked her if she would like to go to a movie on the following Friday night. She told me her parents didn't allow her to date at night yet, but that she was allowed to get together with friends after school as long as she was home by six o'clock. Then she asked me if I would like to pick her up from school on the following day and give her a ride to the Burger King where she worked three days a week.

The problem was that I didn't get out of school as early as she did, and it took twenty minutes to drive from my school to hers. But did that stop me? No. There was no way I was going to refuse!

For Camerina, I left my last class twenty minutes early—a pretty drastic measure for me, since I never cut a class before. I was worried that I would get caught sneaking out of class and leaving school early—but not enough to stop me from being with my Camerina!

Camerina enjoyed my giving her rides rather than taking the bus to the Burger King. It wasn't long before she needed a ride to other places, too. Sometimes we'd take her friends along with us, and sometimes we'd take them anywhere they wanted to go. Though this was an inconvenience to me, and used up a lot of gas, I would have done almost anything to spend time with her. And I did. I willingly and gladly became her taxi for the next three weeks. Until one day when I had a dental appointment and couldn't give her a ride.

But Scott Schamatenburger could. I guess she prefers his car to mine. Now he's her new taxi driver. Well, I suppose it's a good thing that my love affair with Camerina lasted only three weeks. Who knows how much detention I might've ended up with! Even so, at the time, it would have seemed well worth it!

Tito Montes, 16

Love—goes wherever it wants.

How Far I'll Go

How far will I go? Pretty far, when it comes to Sheree.

I asked Sheree to the school dance. She insisted I wear a tux, even though it was black-tie optional. I rented a tux to please her, even though I prefer clothes that are more casual and comfortable.

How far will I go? Pretty far, when it comes to Sheree.

Sheree insisted on arriving at the dance in a limo! I really couldn't afford it, but nevertheless, I worked the extra hours on my part-time job—even though it was finals and I needed the time to study.

How far will I go? Pretty far, when it comes to Sheree.

It was time to sign up for the next semester's schedule. I'd planned to take a third year of Spanish to complete my college entry requirements for a foreign language. But Sheree wanted me to take French with her. "It's so much more romantic," she said. I took French for the sole reason of being in the same class with Sheree.

How far will I go? Pretty far, when it comes to Sheree.

"Let's double-date with my best friend Tom," I suggested. "Let's not," she said. "He's a geek, and besides, I don't like the girl he dates." Sheree had a different circle of friends, so I went places with Sheree and her friends, and I didn't seem to see much of my friends anymore. When it came to going out with friends, we just always seemed to end up with hers.

How far will I go? Pretty far when it comes to Sheree.

Sheree called and said that if I didn't take her to the library, she'd get an F in tomorrow's assignment. I told Sheree I'd made a promise to my father that I'd never take the car without his permission. Despite the fact that I couldn't reach my father until later that evening—and because Sheree was so insistent—I took Sheree to the library.

How far will I go? Six weeks all totaled—that's how far I

would go with Sheree! Six weeks into the relationship, I started the new semester with a lie between me and my father, not having seen much of my friends, and a class I didn't need—and without one I did.

How far will I go? Well, pretty far now that I'm not with Sheree.

I've learned not to give up the things that are really important to me, the things I value and that make me happy, and move me toward my goals, keeping the promises I make with important people, like friends and my parents. But that doesn't mean I've signed off on love—I just learned not to ever go *that* far again.

Christopher Gillian, 17

Love—values what is important.

The Pickle Fork

When I was eight, I asked my father for money to buy a gift for Mother. He gave me a whole dollar. Off I trudged to find something wonderful.

The elegant shop owner suggested I could find something "maybe at Woolworth's" for my dollar.

Suddenly, a miracle. There it was! It was beautiful in its box, on a bed of cotton like a precious jewel. "How much is this?" I asked the lady.

"It's your lucky day," she said. "That's on sale, marked down to one dollar. Hardly anyone needs a glass pickle fork nowadays."

I did! The next day before lunch I presented it to her. My father leaned over to see. "Isn't it beautiful?" Mother said. "Why it's hand-blown glass. . . ."

"It's a pickle fork," I said proudly.

"I shall treasure it," said my mother and kissed me. After that, we had lots more pickles at meals.

Later she hung it on a ribbon in our sunroom window. "Now it's a suncatcher," she said. "Too bad to hide it all the time when we aren't having pickles."

At Christmas, it hung on the tree, with the lights making it sparkle even more.

Years later when she died, I went to the safe deposit box to take out precious things. There was the glass pickle fork in its old box, with a special note. "You were always so thoughtful, so loving. You always made us so happy. I love you. Mother."

Priscilla Dunn

A pickle fork? Why would a mother place a glass pickle fork in a safety deposit box meant for valuables? Because to her it was valuable. And so it became a treasure, one important enough to be tucked away with other valuables for safekeeping!

Love can make a treasure out of any gift given in its name. Even a simple flower, whether a rose or a dandelion, can become a treasure of love when it brings with it the memory of someone you love. We treasure those memories, like those of a favorite grandmother, a favorite teacher, a favorite aunt, a favorite friend—or anyone who has endeared themselves to us because of something they said or did that was loving, caring or giving.

One of the greatest things about love is its power to live on in memories. And because it is so, it is endless—like that pickle fork, purchased for only a dollar, now a priceless memento.

Love—creates memories that are cherished and priceless.

To My Teenager

It's hard sometimes, when people are changing their lives,
to understand each other, or even to talk.

You are struggling right now for independence
and the right to live your own way . . .
and I sometimes struggle for the strength to let you do it.

I wish now and then for the days when a kiss or a hug
could make your world bright again;
but your world is more difficult now,
and you want to make your own
way in it—which is as it should be.

I want you to know that when you get hurt,
I will hurt for you;
and that deep down, I always have confidence
in your ability to find your place in your world.

When you need a caring heart,
or someone to listen to your deepest dreams or concerns,
I will be there for you because I love and care for you.

Above all else, know that I love and care for you.

                                                    M. Joye

A parent's love—a promise to love us because *they know us
so well; a promise to love us* in spite of *knowing us so well.*

Proof of Undying Love

Whenever my neighbor's playful young dog gets too close to my cat, Max, my cat takes on the posture of a daunting opponent. He draws back, stiffens his legs, arches his back, puffs his fur and hisses with authority, and this makes him look nearly twice his size. My neighbor's dog is a Doberman, so bravado aside, my cat is not foolish enough to believe he can outfight the Doberman. Instead Max counts on the dog being convinced otherwise. It works every time!

It doesn't always work for me.

Last year I went out with Brenda, the best-looking girl in the entire school. For some reason unknown to me, Brenda thought my fighting for her was proof of undying love. I know some girls think it's a romantic gesture when a guy is willing to get into a fight over her, but quite frankly, there's nothing glamorous about having a fist smashed into your face. It hurts. I know some people say that fighting is a real "rush." For me, the rush is more about fear and wanting to run away than giving someone a black eye.

Brenda had the idea that I had to "win" her. At the time, I thought she was beautiful. And you know how that can make a guy as stupid as my neighbor's Doberman who never fails to be intimidated by my cat.

"Todd Jensen keeps flirting with me," Brenda announced one afternoon when I met up with her at her locker after class.

"I'm sure it's just because he thinks you're beautiful," I said, trying to play into her constant need to be told how great she looks.

"Well, I think you should punch him out. That'll show him you're not going to take having another guy try to take me away from you!" Brenda said, as though it was as easy as that.

A fight with Todd Jensen? The guy was huge—he could be our school's football defense all by himself. Wanting to change the subject, I said, "I want to get a couple of new CDs after school this afternoon. Come help me pick them out, and I'll drop you at your house after that."

"Okay!" she said.

But when the school day was over, Brenda had not forgotten about my needing to level the score with Todd.

"So, are you going to knock his head off?" Brenda asked.

"No," I said. "We are going to shop for my CDs." Sulking, Brenda moaned, "I can't believe you aren't going to do anything about it! Last year I dated Tommy Craighton. He would never let somebody get away with flirting with me like that."

My heart sank as I thought of facing Todd Jensen. Then Brenda sealed my fate with her words, "And I don't think you should let him get away with it. Aren't you going to do *anything* about it?"

Now she sounded indignant. Gulping, I agreed, "Okay . . . okay."

I tried to think of how I could get myself psyched up for this, and then remembered my cat and how he takes on the posture of a daunting opponent. So I figured whether I was psyching myself up or psyching Todd Jensen out, it was a wise decision to do some posturing. I drew a deep calming breath, my chest puffing out as I inhaled. I held it that way—looking like my cat. "Where is he?" I snarled.

Brenda looked thrilled. "We can catch him in the parking lot," she assured me. She trotted along beside me as I huffed, chest still out, to the parking lot. Of course I was hoping that Todd would be long gone, and Brenda would be impressed enough with my attempt. But as we walked into the parking lot, we could see Todd Jensen heading for his car. "There he is!" Brenda called, her voice filled with delight. I've often wondered if girls have some secret code they communicate in because from the time we had gone from her locker—just minutes ago—to the parking lot, she'd somehow gathered an audience for this event. "Go on, stop him!" Brenda instructed.

Remembering how my cat tries to fake out the Doberman, I puffed up my chest, flexed and, strutting like a cock, walked in Todd's direction. "Hey you, Todd!" I shouted in my best macho voice. Todd stopped and looked in my direction, his expression puzzled. I thrust my chest out farther, curled my fists and "assumed the position"—feet apart, head up, eyes squinting, a huge scowl on my face. "You better stop insulting my girlfriend," I growled, all the while secretly hoping Todd would refuse.

Unfortunately, Max's tactics didn't have such good results for me. Todd looked from me to Brenda as if we were both nuts. "I don't know what you're talking about," he said, shaking his head in bored disgust.

"Now he's calling me a liar," Brenda jeered and then demanded, "Don't let him get away with that!"

"You calling her a liar?" I snarled. I don't know what came over me, I guess it was all the psyching-myself-up and psyching-Todd-out stuff—and there was Brenda and her friends watching and hoping for a fight. I had this burst of either bravado or insanity and decided to unleash a mighty punch. Todd caught my arm in one of his big paws, and smacked me just once with the other. I now lay on the parking lot's pavement, stunned, with blood running from my nose. Todd Jensen kind of shook his head, climbed in his car and drove away. Brenda, disgusted that I "lost the fight," left with her girlfriends—and the next day, announced that she was now going to be Todd's girlfriend.

I learned a lot in the parking lot that day. I think it could be boiled down to answering the question, "Is fighting over what you're fighting over worth fighting over?"

I have a new girlfriend now. Her name is Jenette. I was sitting with my friends having a conversation over lunch at school one day, when she claimed with conviction, "I deplore all violence.

There's always a wiser solution." At that exact moment I decided I was in love with Jenette.

Nick Barry, 17

Love—knows when to walk away.

Hidden Beneath the Folded Things . . .

Her diary was in the dresser drawer,
hidden beneath the folded things.
It opened where a pressed wildflower lay,
and on that page the words, "He loves me."

I remembered how we had walked from school,
laughed and shared a cupcake from her lunch box.
Impulsively, I had reached to pluck that flower,
and bashfully presented it to her.

Our eyes had met and what I saw was love.
I wondered if she saw the same in mine.
We walked on in silence, lest a word
dispel the moment's mystic magic.

Now seven decades have gone by,
and her diary still within the drawer,
hidden beneath the folded things.
And in it a pressed wildflower lay,
With the words, "He loves me."

I look at her, and it's still love I see.
And when I look at the flattened flower in cellophane
I can see her laugh, and the way she looked at me
when I handed her that flower.

Looking at the flattened flower in cellophane
It comes alive, like on that day I picked it for her.

Elmer Adrian, 90

Love—is captured in symbols that it uses to renew itself.

If You Want a Ride in *My* Car

There was a time when I thought my dad didn't know a thing about being a good father. I couldn't remember him ever saying the words, "I love you." It seemed to me his sole purpose in life was to say "no" to anywhere I wanted to go and anything I wanted to do. Including getting a car. Some parents bought their kids cars when they got their driver's licenses. Not my dad—he said I'd have to get a job and buy my own.

So that's what I did. "I'll show him," I said to myself. "If he won't get it for me, I'll get it for myself." I got a job as a busgirl at a very nice, ocean-view restaurant and saved every penny I could. And when I had enough to buy my own car, I did! The day I brought that car home, my dad was the first one I wanted to show it off to. "Look, Dad, a car of my own—all on my own. If you ever want a ride, I'll only charge you five dollars," I offered with a smug smile.

"I see," was all he said.

One day, my father's truck had to go to the shop and wouldn't be ready to pick up until the next evening. So he needed a ride to work. "If that five-dollar offer is still open," my dad said, "I'll take you up on it."

"Okay, but you have to pay on delivery. I don't accept credit."

"I see," was all he said.

The sun wasn't even up when we left the house, but it was already getting warm out. It was going to be a hot day. As I dropped my dad off, I watched him, dressed in his work clothes and boots, getting his tools from the trunk of my car. Watching his every move, hoping that he'd hurry so that I could get back home and get ready for my own day, I squinted in the rearview mirror at his sun-weathered face, and even from a distance I could tell there were more lines than I ever remembered being there before. I thought about it and then realized how hard my dad works for his family. My father is a cement finisher.

Watching him lift the heavy tools from the car, buckets full of trowels, knee pads and other finishing tools, there was something about him that looked a little more fragile than I recalled. In that instant, it occurred to me that he actually got down on his hands and knees to sweat over hot concrete to make a living for his family. And he did this day in and day out, no matter how hot it got. Never, not once, had I heard him complain about it. Never had he held it up to his children as being some great sacrifice he made for us. I thought about how much he must love us—so much that he's willing to do this hard labor in hot weather, and without so much as ever complaining or asking for anything in return. To him, we were "worth" it. And never once did he "charge" us for it.

When he slammed the trunk, his tools set off to the side, he walked over to my window to hand me my five dollars. I rolled down the window and said, "Good-bye, Dad. Keep your five dollars. It's on me. Don't work too hard. I love you."

At first he looked puzzled, then in a clumsy sort of way—pleased. "I won't," he said, then added, "Thanks for the ride in your beautiful new car." His eyes met mine then glanced away in the direction of his waiting tools, he cleared his throat and said, "Oh, and . . . me, too."

As I drove away, I knew "me, too" was enough because my father showed me his love with his actions, day after day, year after year. In that moment, I decided I'd give him a ride in my car any time he wanted—free of charge.

Marie Parada, 18

Love—worth every cent of it.

I'll Be in the Bleachers

The rules are different now
that you're almost thirteen.
Some budding sign tells me
you're not the little girl I knew,
and that's the way that it should be.

I sense your leap into maturity.
Your innate prudence
will show you the way,
as you adjust to all
the subtle wonders
just ahead.

But as you turn into the rose I know you'll be
don't forget I love you.
And, as always,
I'm still your staunchest fan.
You can be sure, as always,
I'm somewhere in the bleachers.

Grandpa

Elmer Adrian, 90

Love—creates lifelong fans—no matter what your age.

Secretly, I Changed My Name

I was eleven when Mom remarried. When I was four or five, she and my father had divorced. We'd gone from a bright and cheery ground-floor apartment in a safe, middle-class neighborhood to a fourth floor, cramped and darker apartment in a poorer area of New York City. My brother and I often felt lonely and frightened, listening to police and ambulance sirens piercing the night.

In the six years we lived there, I remember envying those friends who had fathers. It was my dream to get a father for myself. My own father had completely left my life—his whereabouts a mystery. I thought that, if I had a father, he would be a powerful guardian who would magically defend me against the many perils I felt that I faced in the streets. Somehow, in that childhood fantasy, my new father would not have to work. He'd just be there for me, whenever I needed him. If other boys menaced me, Super Dad would appear and chase them off. It was pure wish fulfillment, but nonetheless a powerful dream for a frightened little boy.

Suddenly, Frank McCarty appeared in our lives. He was exciting and interesting because he was a New York City police captain of detectives. He had a gold police shield and there was a gun in a holster on his belt, under his suit coat. I don't remember the day he first appeared, but I do remember the general time and its feeling of excitement and drama. Police were the stuff of movies. Police weren't people you actually knew. I told all my friends about him. Their eyes widened as I described his gun and the stories that he told me about capturing some bad guys.

He didn't like to tell these stories, but my mom wanted him to be accepted by her sons and she knew what kids liked to hear. She'd cue him to tell a certain story and he'd acquiesce and patiently tell the story. As he got more deeply into the story, he became animated and the story took on mythic proportions.

One day, Mom asked me how I would feel if she married Frank. By this time, I was really hooked. He had taken me to the Giants game at the Polo Grounds. He had taken me to Coney Island. He talked with me. He gave me advice on how to fight back when confronted with bullies in the street. His gun gleamed darkly from under his coat. I could have a dad, a protector, someone to take me to the game. "Wow!" I said, "I'd love it!"

The date came. We went to a rural resort hotel whose owner was a friend of my mother's. Another friend of Mom's, a judge, presided over the wedding. I had a dad. Everything was going to be all right now.

I didn't know, as a child of eleven, how profoundly my life would change with that one moment.

A bachelor until that point, my new dad had very limited experience with children. He was suddenly thrust into the role of parent, and he retreated to what he knew. His experience with kids had been limited to arresting some. His memories of parenting were of his own father's turn-of-the-century methods. He assumed that he could sit at the head of the table and issue orders that complaisant children would instantly obey.

Unfortunately for him, my mother raised us to be more independent, more participatory in dinner-table discussions. We were encouraged to have opinions. She taught us to speak up as well as to listen. We weren't taught to be impolite or rude, but we were contentious.

Complicating all of this was the onset of puberty. Frank McCarty became a father—with his need to be in control, all-knowing, the leader—at the very moment that I was becoming a teen and was in the throes of the adolescent search for independence and self-authority. I was so attracted to him, I almost instantly loved him. Yet, at the same time, I was angry at him almost constantly. He stood in my way. He wasn't easy to manipulate. My brother and I could masterfully manipulate our mother. Frank McCarty was immune to our tricks.

Thus began eight years of pure hell for me and for my new dad. He announced rules and I tried to flout them. He sent me to my room for rudeness or for my attitude. I complained bitterly to my mother about his dictatorial practices. She tried hard to be the peacemaker, but to no avail.

I must admit that there were many occasions in my life from age thirteen until I was twenty that I was stuck in a state of anger and frustration at some perceived slight by my father. Passionate as these times were, they were punctuated by great moments with him. Going shopping with him, every week, for flowers to "surprise your mother," he'd say. Going to a ball game. Sitting in a car with him, late at night, watching a house. He'd take me on a surveillance, when he became a private detective back in New York City, if the case was an insurance fraud or something similarly nonviolent. We'd sit there in the darkened car, sipping coffee, and he'd talk about "the job," as he called his career in the police department. I felt so special, so loved, so included at these times. This was exactly what my fantasy had been. A dad who loved me, who'd do things with me.

I remember many, many nights, sitting in front of him on an ottoman and he'd rub my back as we watched TV together. He gave great hugs. He wasn't afraid to say, "I love you." I found the tenderness this rough-and-ready guy was able to express remarkable. However, he could go from these intimate moments to red-faced yelling and sputtering anger if I did or said something that he thought was rude. His temper was a natural phenomenon akin to a tornado. It was a fearsome thing to watch, and it was even scarier to be the target of it.

In high school, the angry moments increased and my closeness with him decreased. By the time I was in college, I was mostly alienated from him. I got a lot of mileage in terms of sympathy from my friends, if I put him down in my conversations with them. I'd tell stories of his latest "atrocity," and stuck in adolescence just as I was, they'd murmur sympathetically about how much we all had to put up with from our dads.

It was my last year in college. I don't know if there was any one event that precipitated it other than my getting a year older and going further along on the road to maturity, but I started rethinking my relationship with him.

I thought, *Here's a guy who falls in love with my mother and he's stuck with two teenage boys as the price of being married to her. He didn't fall in love with two kids, just my mother. But we came with the package. And look what he does: He doesn't just relate to her and ignore us. No, he tries his very hardest to be a real father to me. He risks the relationship all the time. He tried to teach me a set of values. He made me do my homework. He took me to the emergency room at two in the morning. He paid for my education without a grumble. He taught me how to tie a tie. He did all the daddy things without thought of payback. That's really something. I guess I'm a lucky kid to have him in my life.*

I knew that my dad had come from an old New England Irish family. They were never famous, powerful or wealthy, but they had been here a long, long time. He felt sad that he was the last to "carry the name." "It'll die with me," he said. His brother had died without children, and his sisters, having married and taken their husbands' names, wouldn't carry on that name either.

My brother and I still carried the name of our biological father: the man who sired me, but didn't stay around for the rest of the job. The thought troubled me that the man who really was my father, as I understood that word, would not be celebrated by having a son with his own name.

Ideas occur to us and gradually coalesce into behavior. The idea got stronger and stronger. My thoughts were increasingly taken over by this idea. Finally, action was inevitable. I went to an attorney and then to a court. Secretly, I had my name changed to McCarty. I told no one. I waited three months until my dad's birthday in October.

He opened the birthday card slowly. Usually when I gave him a card, it was attached to a box with his gift. This time there was no box, just the envelope. He pulled out the card and, with it, a certificate from a court.

I wrote on the card, "No store sells true gifts for father and son. You gave me roots, I give you branches."

It was one of only two or three times I ever saw my dad cry. Tears came unbidden to his eyes. He smiled and shook his head and sighed. Then he got up and enfolded me in one of his famous bear hugs. "Thank you, boy, thank you. I just don't know what to say. Thank you." My mom was stunned, too. And very happy for both of us. The war was over. I'd brought the armistice agreement, wrapped in a birthday card.

Hanoch McCarty
Adapted from A 4th Course of Chicken Soup for the Soul

Love—creates family ties, even out of broken ones.

Your Long-Term Address

It's strange how some will give such great care
To the house their body lives in.
Yet mistreat and abuse that marvelous place:
The body their soul is in.

Some spend their fortunes to buy a house,
It's a symbol of their wealth.
Such comforts mean little to any of them
If they've also spent their health.

So ponder this question: Where do you live?
But think before venturing a guess.
That number and street belong to a house,
Your body's your long-term address.

George E. Young

*Love—cares for the house we live in—
and asks that we care for it, too.*

Time Cannot Erase Our Love Affair

I lean to kiss your cheek
as you lie there.
"For better or for worse," we promised.
Nothing can erase our love affair.

You run your fingers through my hair.

I lean to kiss your cheek
as you lie there.
You stir and look at me
and in that stare,
even your crippled mind
cannot erase our love affair.

You run your fingers through my hair.

Elmer Adrian, 90

Love—keeps a promise to care throughout a lifetime.

The Little Blue Marble

From space, the Earth looks like a tiny blue marble laying in an endless black ocean. The Earth appears so small, so fragile, and yet it is our home, one that supports and sustains many forms of life.

As I gaze at Earth from space, I cannot fathom that there, in communities around the world, people are hurting each other and being careless with a planet that sustains us. Looking at our Earth home from space, the idea that we Earth citizens are not cautiously caring for each other and taking meticulous care of our environment becomes almost a silly notion, an unbelievable one.

When you look at our Earth home from space, you are filled with the belief that life is sacred. We must each care deeply.

Being in space renews a reverence for the very gift of life, and you feel thankful that you are alive and more fully appreciate that we are gifted with a mind that can dream of stupendous possibilities, and a body that can bring these to fruition.

Do your part. Looking out for each other and our Earth home is an act of love. Pay attention to the things going on around you. In the bigger scheme of things, even things that may seem small and insignificant are vital to a healthy Earth and to healthy people. Do your part.

Ironically, it was seeing how small our planet appeared in the very vastness of this universe that filled me with the greatest sense of love for it.

Steve Smith
veteran of two space flights, over three hundred Earth orbits and
three space walks

Love—asks us to protect all life as sacred.

The Heart's Checklist

"Oh Mom," I groaned, "I have a crush on two boys, both equally as *wonderful* as the other. What am I going to do? Neither guy wants me to date *both* of them at the same time! How will I chose between them?"

"Ask your heart to make the decision," my mother advised. "The heart knows who to choose."

Perplexed, I frowned, wondering how a person knew when it was really their heart making a decision. "But how will *I* know?" I asked. I was in my teens at the time, and I was looking for a fast, short answer in trying to understand the romantic workings of the heart.

"Listen to your heart. Your soul contains an image of the man you desire. In the right-hand top corner, there's a checklist of all the things you need in love. When you meet someone akin to the list, your soul nudges your heart, and you just *know*."

"But how does it know?" I asked.

"Your soul has an innate wisdom when it comes to what it needs," she replied, and then using a popular parable, explained, "There once was a little soul who knew itself to be *the light*. In the realm from which this little soul emerged, every soul shone with the awesome brilliance of profound light. And so the little soul was a candle in the sun—but very much wanted to experience something other than light. So it called onto it the experience of darkness. But the darkness didn't feel right and so the little soul felt out of her element and longed to come back to the light, something that felt *right* to her heart." My mother looked at me and smiled. "The moral of the story is that darkness was inappropriate and unsuitable for the little soul—so, her heart knew to be unhappy in the dark. Just like the little soul's heart gave her correct feedback, your heart will too. Your soul intuitively knows *what* and *who* is right for you and intuitively knows when *something* or *someone* isn't." And then she added the most important words of all: "You must *listen* carefully."

I remember when I went out with Grant. I met him in my anthropology class and he seemed like a really nice guy. He was smart, outgoing and had a great sense of humor. But when we went out, I noticed that his humor could be somewhat cruel and was always at someone else's expense. Although he tried his best to charm me, I listened carefully to my heart, which told me he wasn't the right guy for me.

I've had the chance to test my mother's theory about the innate wisdom in knowing who is "right" for me and who isn't! She's right! The soul points us in the right direction of what it needs, of what is right for it. And, just as important, the soul holds the innate wisdom of what we need in life—of the people that are right for us in friendships, even what is right for us in music, foods and the things we do for work and play.

Listen *carefully*.

Jennifer Leigh Youngs

Love—sees through the eyes of the heart.

See You Later!

Respecting and loving someone can change the way you treat them. There was a time when my father and I disagreed on a lot of things, most especially a curfew. We would go around and around the subject. But now my dad and I are able to talk about things. Since I felt like I was a dependable guy, I'd tell my dad that I shouldn't have to be told when to come home. It seemed fair and made perfect sense to me. But he said I had to be in by ten-thirty on weekdays, and midnight on weekends—no questions asked. When I said, "See you later," as I was leaving the house, it almost always ended up meaning "later" than my curfew. I was almost always on restriction because I'd just come in when I wanted. Not good.

Finally, one night when I walked in an hour later than curfew, my dad was sitting there waiting for me. "Sit down," he said, "I think we need to talk." My stomach knotted with both defiance and fear, as I sat down wondering what he was going to do to me this time. I knew I would be on restriction—what more was he going to do to me? "Brent," my dad said, "I know a curfew sounds like a restriction to you, but it's really about a parent's love and concern for their child's safety. You remember running in a relay race? Well, a curfew is about you and I exchanging the 'baton of responsibility,'" he said, "from me to you, and then from you to me.

"Son, I know you're a responsible person and you can be trusted. But because I love you and I care about your safety, I'm afraid of what lurks out there," then he started counting off on his fingers, "unsafe drivers, you becoming too tired to drive so late at night, friends who might talk you into making a bad choice—you fill in the blanks, they're only part of my concerns."

The way he looked me in the eyes, I could tell he wasn't trying to lecture me. He was just trying to let me know how and why he felt the way he did. This approach really made me listen, because I knew he was being sincere—that he really loved and cared, so he worried about me. "A curfew doesn't mean, here are car keys—go and have a good time and then at midnight I want you to stop having a good time and come home. It means, here are the keys to the car. With these keys I'm handing you the responsibility for taking care of yourself. At midnight, I'll take over again. When you aren't back at the time you're supposed to be, what you are really saying is, 'Dad, it doesn't matter to me that you love me enough to care about my safety.'"

Listening to my dad, I could hear the love in his voice. And once again, he was trying to talk to me "man to man." I really got the message. I decided not to waste my time fighting over curfew any more. Instead, I let Dad know that my own safety is important to me, too. Understanding why a curfew is such a big deal to my father makes it important to show him I appreciate his love and concern. I don't come in late just to prove to him that I can do what I want. When I say, "See you later," it no longer means later than my curfew.

Brent Stephenson, 17

Love—respects and shows honor.

Love Me, Forever

I went out with Matt during ninth and tenth grades. I was really in love with him, and I just knew he was in love with me.

During the summer before eleventh grade, Matt went to Colorado to work for his uncle in the construction business. During the first two weeks he was gone, Matt and I talked by phone every night. We wrote letters to each other nearly every day. During the third week we were still speaking to each at least twice a week, and I was writing every other day. But by the end of the first month, I was the only one making the calls and sending letters. After he'd been gone only five weeks, Matt told me he'd met someone else and didn't want to go out with me anymore. I was devastated. Still, I hoped that when school started, we'd get back together again.

But we didn't. Matt said he considered the girl he met there his new girlfriend, even if she was far away.

It was the worst time of my life. I cried almost every day and tried to change his mind. I wrote him ten-page letters and put them in his locker, or shoved them into his pocket when I saw him in the hall. Matt never wrote back, and though I'd try to corner him to talk, he would never say anymore than he had to. He acted like he was totally over me. I couldn't believe it because he had told me again and again that he would love me forever. I believed him. And, I couldn't believe that he could fall out of love so fast with me, and then fall in love so fast with someone new. So, I spent a lot of time trying to get him to change his mind. And besides, what chance did the other girl have? She was four states away! So I kept hoping. And kept writing and trying to talk to Matt.

On Tuesdays and Thursdays we were in the same section of Spanish class, so on those days I'd dress extra nice and make sure I was seen talking or flirting with a boy as I walked into the classroom, thinking Matt would be jealous and want to get back together with me. I'd try to act really cool in class. But nothing worked. Eventually my friends convinced me that I was making a fool of myself, so I stopped.

My friends tried to be helpful. They said things like, "You're so much better than he is anyway," or "Just find someone new." I know my friends meant well, but their words didn't make things better—nor did it make the ache in my heart go away. My life was just miserable. My grades dropped. I gained weight. I didn't want to go anywhere or do anything. Nothing was fun anymore. Without Matt in my life, there was no joy.

Probably it was my mother who offered the most helpful advice. "No matter what anyone says," she told me, "when you're heart is hurting over love, no one can soothe you and be as good to you quite like you can be to yourself." My mother belongs to a women's workout center and works out twice a week. She asked me to come with her on those days. And she started buying me those little energy bars—the one with lots of extra nutrients in them. I'd find them from time to time in my backpack. Twice she took me to get a massage. And though I didn't figure it out until several weeks later, a counselor friend of hers asked me to baby-sit her younger daughter, though she never seemed to be in a rush to get out the door, and seemed to manage a conversation with me.

My mother didn't tell me a story about what happened to her as a child when she was jilted like some parents do. She didn't say, "Oh, you'll get over him in time," or, "There are lots of 'fish in the sea.'" She said simply, "Sheila, I believe with all my heart that you are worth loving. Let's do everything we can right now to show Sheila how much we love and care about her."

Remarkably, I did stop hurting. And I learned a big lesson about love: while not all love is forever, some love is. At my age, I'm probably going to break up with a lot of guys, but I must never break up with me.

Sheila Sam, 17

Love—demands that you save some of it for yourself.

The Greatest Love of All

Margaret's boyfriend Paul proposed. While happy, she was hesitant. She and her boyfriend seemed so different. They decided to take a little walk along the beach to discuss marriage and its importance. When they reached the far end of the beach and were about to begin their return journey, Margaret glanced down and noticed that their footprints had washed out to sea. Turning to Paul she said, "Well, if our married life is to be like this, we don't stand much of a chance."

Paul replied, "When things are tough for me, you will help me—and when things are tough for you, I'll help you."

They continued walking, until Margaret glanced down again and saw that only one set of footprints had washed out to sea. Again, Margaret suggested that their life together didn't appear to have much of a future. This time Paul responded by gently lifting her up in his arms and carrying her along the beach. Finally, he set her down and said, "Margaret, I want to impress upon you that when life is so bad that we can't seem to help each other, God will carry us." Then, pointing to the single set of footprints the two of them had just created, Paul added, "If you just looked at the set of tracks we just made, you couldn't tell that I carried you—but I did."

Margaret found his words and the thoughts behind them very beautiful. That night she couldn't sleep, so she got up and wrote these words: One night a man had a dream. He dreamed he was walking along the beach with the Lord. Across the sky flashed scenes from his life. For each scene, he noticed two sets of footprints in the sand; one belonging to him, and the other to the Lord.

When the last scene of his life flashed before him, he looked back at the footprints in the sand. He noticed that many times along the path of his life there was only one set of footprints. He also noticed that it happened at the very lowest and saddest times in his life.

This really bothered him and he questioned the Lord about it. "Lord, you said that once I decided to follow you, you'd walk with me all the way. But I have noticed that during the most troublesome times in my life, there is only one set of footprints. I don't understand why when I needed you most you would leave me."

The Lord replied, "My precious, precious child, I love you and I would never leave you. During your times of trial and suffering, when you see only one set of footprints, it was then that I carried you."

Margaret Rose Powers

This beautiful piece, printed time and time again, has a love story all its own. She called the piece "Footprints." Today, "Footprints" is one of the most widely distributed inspirational pieces in existence. It can be found on plaques, cards and jewelry. Its power lies in its message—the message of the greatest love of all.

And yes, they did marry.

Love—is an eternal source.

Part 4

The Right Stuff: Attitudes for Life Success—Becoming a Person of . . .

Success in life isn't a given—it costs attitude, ambition and acceptance.

—Jennifer Leigh Youngs

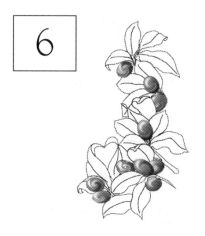

6

A Person of . . . Integrity

*The truth of the matter is that you always know
the right thing to do.
The hard part is doing it.*

—Gen. H. Norman Schwarzkopf

EQUAL PAY FOR EQUAL WORTH

One day my father hired three young men to help him put up the hay crop. At the end of the day he gathered them around to pay them.

"What do I owe you, John?" my dad asked the first young man he had hired.

"Fifty-five dollars, Mr. Burres," John said. Dad wrote him a check for fifty-five dollars. "Thank you for your work, John," my father said respectfully.

"What do I owe you, Michael?" my father asked the second young man who had worked the same number of hours as John.

"You owe me seventy-five dollars," Michael said.

With a look of surprise, my dad asked quietly, "How do you figure that, Michael?"

"Oh," said Michael, "I charge from the time I get into my car to drive to the job site, until the time I get back home, plus gas mileage and meal allowance."

"Meal allowance—even if we provide the meals?"

"Yup," replied Michael.

"I see," said my dad, writing him a check for the seventy-five dollars he requested.

"And what about you, Nathan?" Dad inquired. "What do I owe you?"

"You owe me thirty-eight dollars and fifty cents, Mr. Burres," Nathan said.

Again my father was surprised at the discrepancy in the amount requested. The third young man, like the other two, had been hired for the same job and had put in equal time (and had come from the same small town just a couple of miles away). My father asked for clarification.

"And how did you arrive at that figure, Nathan?"

"Well," said Nathan, "I didn't charge you for the lunch break since your wife prepared and served lunch. I didn't have gas expenses since I came with my buddies. So the actual number of hours worked brings my pay to thirty-eight dollars and fifty cents."

My father wrote him out a check for one hundred dollars.

Dad then looked at the three young men—stricken silent by my father's actions—all of whom were a bit bewildered by the differing amounts on their individual checks.

"I always pay a man his worth, boys. Where I come from we call that equal pay for equal worth." He looked benevolently at the three young men before him and in his typical fatherly style added, "The values in a man create the value of a man."

Bettie B. Youngs
Excerpted from Values from the Heartland

A Word from the Authors

Integrity is being right with yourself—no secrets, no hidden agenda, no dishonesty, just "what you see is what you get." A friend of ours, author and management consultant Dr. Ken Blanchard, put it this way, "There is no pillow as soft as a clear conscience." What's true about integrity is that even if someone else is upset with you, or doesn't agree with you, or doesn't think you did the right thing, if you know in your heart of hearts that you did, their opinion matters less. What they say or think is—in a way—beside the point.

Even though Nathan saw that my father was willing to pay the guys the sum each asked for, his integrity won out, and he treated my father with fairness—and reaped the rewards in return!

"Mom, Nathan's not the only one who has learned a thing or two about the rewards of integrity! When I was in the tenth grade, my friend Sherri always called me while she was doing homework. Then, because she developed a regular pattern of not finishing her homework—and started to bring home low grades—her parents told her she couldn't talk on the phone until she'd finished her homework. They felt it interrupted her concentration. Sherri thought this rule was really unfair and told them that talking on the phone with her friends didn't have anything to do with whether she finished her homework. So her parents made a deal with her: if she earned good grades that semester, she would be allowed to use the phone while doing her homework. Unfortunately, even though Sherri wasn't allowed to call any of her friends that semester, she still received low grades. So, on the day when she knew her report card would appear in the mailbox, Sherri rushed home and took the mail before her parents did so they wouldn't see her report card!"

"Why are you laughing, Jen? That's not funny!"

"Oh, Mom, it is and you know it, but I will admit it's not

honest. Besides, the report card was addressed to her parents, not to her. Her trying to conceal her grades and opening her parents' mail was wrong. But, the good news is she knew it and eventually did the right thing."

"*Eventually?* Something tells me there's more to the story."

"Well, Sherri didn't really know what to do after that. She didn't have any real plan other than 'just don't let the parents see it.' Plus, she has a really good relationship with her parents, and she knew that what she did wasn't right and she felt bad about it. So, she asked a couple of her friends—including me—what she should do. Our friend Carl told her that eventually her parents would start to wonder where her report card was. He suggested that she change the low grades to higher ones and then give her parents the report card. He even showed her how to do it."

"Jennifer, I'm disappointed—"

"Mom, you know Sherri would never have gone as far as changing the grades on her report card. She really wanted to be honest with her parents—it's just that some things are hard to give up, like talking on the phone with your friends whenever you want. Sherri did give her parents the report card and she told them the truth. She did it because she felt bad about having done something dishonest and she didn't want to continue doing one wrong thing after another. She did it because she is a person of integrity."

Jen's eyes sparkled with the affection and appreciation we hold for good friends, as she added, "I'll never forget seeing Sherri at school the next day. I asked her, 'Why didn't you call me last night?' She answered, 'I told my parents everything that happened and I promised to bring my grades up, so I have a lot of work to do in a couple of my classes. But don't worry—next semester I'm going to get great grades. No one can afford to go without talking to her friends on the phone!'"

As Sherri found out, the good feeling of doing the right thing is the greatest reward of integrity. As the stories in this chapter show, teens have a lot of their own experiences in coming to know the value of integrity. Wanting money for a special date, sixteen-year-old Mark Truitt charged for services "not yet rendered," and found he was "no longer needed." Sixteen-year-old Connie Gedding learned a similar lesson when she "snuck" out the back door at work, once, and then twice . . . until she finally got caught. "Integrity," she learned, "is earned."

While integrity may have to do with what other people think of you, it also has to do with what you think of yourself. Many of you realized that integrity is doing what's right even if no one else is looking. No one else was looking when Tomoko Ogata, fifteen, found someone else's money—money no one knew was missing. As teens said, being a "taste berry" means being true to what you know is right—even if you know no one else is looking. Why? Because what you know to be true about yourself is as important as what others think of you. That's being a "taste berry!"

The "Advance"

My savings account is just about zeroed out right now, since I just paid my car insurance. So, I needed to earn some extra money so I could afford to rent a dinner jacket and buy the tickets to a special dinner-dance I wanted to take my girlfriend to.

One of the ways I make money is by doing yard work in my neighborhood. Since I needed the money right away, the next time I worked for one of my neighbors, Jim Thomas, I told him that I had done some extra things—like trimming, hedging, weeding, stuff like that—and charged him for it. Only I fudged on the amount of time I told him I had worked, thinking that I'd make the time up over the next couple of weekends. Mr. Thomas didn't doubt my word, and paid me for the hours I said I worked. I was pretty happy to have the money "in advance."

The next day I got a call from Mr. Thomas. He said it was time his eleven-year-old son "took over the yard duties" and that he didn't need my services any longer. I think Mr. Thomas took the yard job away from me because I had stretched the truth—and he knew it. I felt really terrible I wouldn't be able to give Mr. Thomas the extra work that he'd already paid for "next time." There'd be no "next time" now.

I know that if I had been honest with Mr. Thomas, he would have loaned me the money I needed. Just last summer, when I went to a special two-week soccer camp, he asked me if I needed some extra money to take along. I wish I hadn't taken advantage of him. I think that whenever you take advantage of someone you may think you get away with it, but in the end you usually don't. It's bad enough that I lost a good job, but I also lost Mr. Thomas's trust and respect. And I feel bad about myself for having done it.

From here on out, I'm going to practice honesty in all the things I do.

Mark Truitt, 16

I Have to Live with Myself and So . . .

I have to live with myself and so,
I want to be fit for myself to know.
I want to be able as the days go by,
Always to look myself straight in the eye.
I don't want to stand with the setting sun,
And dislike myself for the things I've done.
I can never hide myself from me,
I see what others may never see.
I know what others may never know,
I can never fool myself and so . . .
Whatever happens I want to be,
Self-respecting and conscience free!

Excerpted from I CAN Ignite the Community Spirit
by Joy J. Golliver and Ruth Hayes-Arista

These Grades Are for You

When I was in seventh grade it was really important to me to earn good grades—to make my father happy. With each report card I took home, I'd sit there eagerly waiting for his smile and praise because I'd gotten good grades. Mostly I got As and Bs. Then one semester I got a D, so I said to my Dad, "I can't believe the teacher gave me a D."

"No," my Dad corrected. "Your teacher didn't give you a D. You earned a D. Nor did your teachers give you these three As and a B. You earned them, just like you earned your D. If you need more help in a course because it's difficult for you, I'll do what I can to help you. But in the end, I want you to do the work and set the standard for the grade you want as something you're earning for you—not for me."

I think my dad made two really good points. First, he was right; my teachers weren't *giving* me a grade, I was *earning* a grade. And second, I should earn that grade for myself, not for my dad. I'm learning to take responsibility for the grades I "earn," and to see them as something I want for myself. I still want to please my father, I can't see that ever changing completely, but I'm the one who sets the standards for what I want for myself. I'm the one I have to please, at least first.

And it's my dad who taught me this. It showed me that he trusted me to set standards for myself. I think that's what integrity is all about: Trusting yourself to be honest—with you. After all, if you can be honest with yourself, you will automatically be honest with others.

Jason Samuels, 16

He Trusted Me, Until . . .

I work at a fast-food restaurant. Like everyone else who works there, my assignments change from week to week. One week I might be working at the front counter serving customers, the next week I might be taking inventory.

Three weeks ago my assignment was stocking shelves in the back room. I was working alone and no one else was around. I was sure that no one would notice if I left a few minutes early. So I did—I left five minutes early. I didn't tell anyone I was leaving, and I didn't deduct the time on my time sheet. The next day I was working in the back again, and once again left a few minutes early. But one of the guys who had been assigned to work at the front counter called in and said he'd be late, so the manager on duty called for me to come up front and fill in for him until the guy arrived. But I had already left.

From that time on, my manager has never trusted me again, and checks up on me for every little detail. I guess I'm lucky I didn't lose my job.

When you take advantage of people, or of a situation, you usually pay for it—or at least that's what I learned. I lost the trust of my manager, and of everyone I work with. The manager has never assigned me to the back room again. When he calls in on his day off to check on things, especially if it's a few minutes before closing, I can hear the assistant manager's end of their conversation, and it always goes like: "Yes, everything's okay. . . . Yes, the deliveries arrived. . . . Yes, Connie is still here." From that time on, everyone treats me as though I am not dependable. The guys I work with give me a hard time, teasing me about it. But I know that I am the one who has made things difficult for myself.

Integrity, I've learned, is earned.

Connie Gedding, 16

I Lost a Fast Twenty Bucks

Several months ago while standing in the check-out line at the grocery store, I saw a twenty dollar bill fall from a lady's purse as she took a check from her wallet. No one even noticed the money float to the floor. I was standing behind her waiting to pay for a bag of M & M's—my regular three o'clock pick-me-up. I leaned over, tucked the cash into my hand and tightened my shoelaces. It was so tempting to pretend the only reason I'd bent down was to tie my shoes. I wanted to go to the fair with my friends on Saturday, and my parents had told me they weren't footing the bill, that I'd have to take care of it myself. I didn't have the money to go to the fair. I looked down at the bill in my hand, thinking that it sure would be handy to have that money! I thought about it—for about three seconds. I knew I had to give her the money back. The woman was very grateful.

If I had taken the money, even though no else might have found out, I would know. Then I'd have to think about how I had stolen it and live with feeling bad about doing it. There are more advantages to being a good person than there are in trying to "put one over" on someone. Even if no one else finds out that you are an honest person, at least *you* know you are.

I know I felt better about myself because I gave the money back to her.

I have integrity—with me.

Tomoko Ogata, 15

I Got Caught Cheating

I thought the worst thing about science class was checking on the growth of mold samples we made from old beans, bread, bananas and other "hairy" food. Whew, what a smell! That was, until my science midterm at the end of the semester. My father knew how important it was that I do well on my science test. So he helped me study, and the day of the test he even fixed me breakfast. Then, he gave me one of his "you can do it!" speeches.

Even with his help, I wasn't all that confident that I'd ace the exam. Since my dad had helped me, I didn't want to let him down by getting a low grade. Then, I made a really bad decision. To tell the truth, at the time it felt less like a decision and more like an impulse.

Anyway, I got caught cheating.

The school called my dad and told him what happened, and they scheduled a parent-teacher conference (with the vice-principal!). Needless to say, my dad and I talked. He explained that failing isn't bad; it's just an outcome, and not a final one. I was really glad that he understood—although he said it would be the last of his "good-guy understanding." He said that he'd tolerate a failed exam now and then, but not cheating. "While failing can mean a lack of preparedness," my dad went on, "cheating can never mean anything other than a lack of integrity." I got the message. And I learned something else: When you cheat, you usually doubt yourself and your ability to master what you've studied. The whole incident, including my father's disappointment in me, taught me something I never would've guessed—I'd rather fail a test honestly, than pass one at the price of cheating. It just isn't worth the way it makes you feel.

Les Williamson, 16

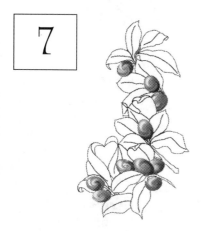

7

A Person of . . . Action

To the proverb which says,
"A journey of a thousand miles begins with a single step,"
I would add the words, "and a road map."

—Cecile M. Springer

YOU HAVE TO BUY A TICKET

Larry was having a really hard time earning a living and paying his bills. "If only I could win the lottery," he thought. "Winning the lottery would end all of my financial problems." So he prayed, "Dear God, winning the lottery is the answer to my problems. Please let me win the lottery."

Each and every day for nearly two months Larry diligently prayed, each time asking God to help him win the lottery. Two months passed, and still Larry had not won the lottery. "Tomorrow," he reassured himself. "Tomorrow."

But tomorrow came and passed, and still he had not won the lottery. Disgruntled, Larry said, "God, I've asked you time and time again to help me win the lottery, but still, I have not. If you have any suggestions on what I'm doing wrong, I'd sure be interested in knowing."

"Dear Larry," God replied, "You have to buy a lottery ticket first!"

A Word from the Authors

As so many of you explained, buying a ticket—taking action—is half the battle. Sixteen-year-old Tom Pierson had been secretly wanting to ask Madison Mason to the prom, but kept waiting for the perfect moment—except that "perfect" moment kept eluding him—while the days until prom night continued to tick away. "What are you waiting for?" asked his father. "I don't want to take the chance that she'll say no," Tom said. "She might say 'yes'!" countered his father. "Why don't you ask Madison and let her decide? But she can't make a decision unless you ask her!" Good advice!

When seventeen-year-old Bob Tyler's plan for the car he was promised was dashed by a family tragedy, he realized he needed a ticket bought with hard work. Fifteen-year-old Marsha Pauls found inspiration for buying an unexpected ticket to win, one she calls "be a better student." Luke Moorehouse, fifteen, bought his ticket because he decided he didn't want to "bum rides" like his twenty-four-year-old brother; and eighteen-year-old Brad Marshall "bought" his because, as he said, "sometimes you have to give up being angry at others for not having the life you want and get involved in making things happen." Brad, we might mention, decided to "buy a string of tickets!" It all begins with action, as Matt Jensen, seventeen—who is "really serious" about going to college—found out. His discovery led him to decide to put a note on his phone to remind him that his homework should be done before he calls his girlfriend!

"Mom, these teens have all learned the really valuable lesson of self-motivation—of just 'getting going.' I'll never forget those Saturday mornings when I wanted to sleep in, but Dad would call, 'Time to get up, buddy!' Five minutes later—because I was still in bed—he'd come into my bedroom, and as he opened the mini-blinds to let in the morning sunshine, he'd repeat, 'Time to get up, buddy!' adding, 'It's a long drive to your softball tournament. We have to leave shortly.'"

"I remember. As I recall, it took a time or two before you 'bought a ticket' to get out of bed!"

Smiling ruefully, Jennifer nodded and said, "Then, as he left my room, Dad would say, 'Gotta ride to the sound of the drums!' I would mimic, 'Gotta ride to the sound of the drums!' a couple of times to myself, not wanting to get out of bed. So one day I asked him, 'Exactly what does that dumb expression mean?'

"He explained, 'It's an old axiom. It originates from wartime, when the troops knew—from the sound of trumpets or drums—that the time was at hand to advance, to march or ride forward into battle.'

"'Oh,' I groaned. 'Another one of those sayings from the Dark Ages!'

"Dad chuckled and said, 'It may be old, but the meaning behind it is still good. It means it's time to get going.' And then he looked at his watch and added, 'In our case that means leaving the house in fifteen minutes.' I may have scoffed then, but I've learned that Dad was right and his words still ring true."

"I have to agree with your father, Jennifer. The gotta-ride-to-the-sound-of-the-drums concept applies to the little things in life—like the minutes on a clock ticking away mean that time is passing and if I procrastinate one minute more, I may be late for wherever I am supposed to be."

"It applies to bigger things, too, Mom, like thinking about the things I want and need in life—from spending time with my family and friends, to going to school, to working. It pays off. I find that the more I 'ride to the sound of the drums,' the more I feel like a capable and competent person. People can count on me—even when at times I might prefer to be doing something else. I've learned to use my time wisely, to prioritize: while some things must be done, others are a matter of choice. I can see that the ride-to-the-sound-of-the-drums approach to life is appreciated by others, too. People don't want to be around those who procrastinate and are always late for things and are stressed out because of it. They prefer being around those who take charge and get things done."

"Good point, Jennifer. Self-discipline leads to accomplishments and productivity—which, in turn, contribute to self-esteem and a positive self-image, leading a person to be successful in whatever she does. It's a positive cycle."

"Mom, if I could sum up in one sentence the importance of being a person of action it would be: 'The more of life I master, the less of life I fear.'"

Waiting for Just the Right Moment

I would give my right arm to go out with Madison Mason! Well, maybe not my arm, but you know what I'm saying. Madison Mason is the best-looking girl that I've ever seen. She goes to my school. She is one year older than I am, so I've been a little shy about asking her out. I've wanted to go out with Madison all year, but she was going with the most popular guy in school. But they broke up.

I really want Madison to be my date for our school prom, which is only four weeks away—I've been waiting for just the right moment to ask her. My dad knows that I like Madison and asked whether I was going to invite her to the prom. "I'd sure like to," I told him.

"What's stopping you?" he asked.

"I'm kind of shy, I guess. And I don't want her to say no."

Dad shrugged and said, "She might say no. But maybe she'll say yes."

"I don't want to take the chance that she'll say no," I replied.

Dad came back with, "Why don't you ask Madison and let her decide? But she can't make a decision unless you ask her."

"I know," I agreed. He had a point. "I just need to wait for the perfect moment."

My dad just looked at me and said, "Son, there's no better time than the present. And like I said, she may say yes, and she may say no, but she can't do either until you ask."

I know he's right. I need to put my fear aside and get up the courage to ask. And I'd better do it soon. If I want Madison as my date to the prom, I'll stand a better chance if I ask her now rather than waiting until it's too late. Someone else may ask her before I do!

"Buying a ticket" means I need to ask her—and soon!

There's a school play this coming Friday, and I know some of

Madison's friends are in it. I'll bet she'd like to see it. I've decided to ask her if she wants to go to it with me. If that works out, I'm going to ask her to the prom. It seems like such an easy thing, but it's a scary step for me. But hey, I can't win the lottery without buying a ticket, right?

Tom Pierson, 16

The Down Payment

I'm finally a senior this year. As a present for graduation, my parents had promised to put a down payment on a car for me. A car of my own is something I've been totally looking forward to.

The problem is, three months ago my father suffered a stroke and he's no longer able to do his job. As a way of cutting back on our family's expenses, we've moved from our large home into a smaller house. And even though my mom has started working more hours on her job, it doesn't make up for the loss of my father's income.

Graduation is only a couple of months away. It's unlikely that my parents are going to be able to help me with the down payment, so if I intend to have a car of my own by the time I graduate, it's going to be up to me.

The change in my father's health and the family finances has changed my thinking from *them* to *me*. Knowing that I'll have to rely less on my parents and more on myself has made me more self-reliant, which is probably a good thing, since I graduate from high school soon. So I got a job waiting tables after school and on the weekends to help pay for some of my school expenses and things like clothes and going out with my friends. I've also started a savings account for my car. Since I want to go to college, I make extra sure to keep my grades up. Now, getting a scholarship is more important than ever.

To me, "buying a ticket" means that my life is up to me. I've decided that I can do it. My goal is to still be able to have a car by graduation day!

Bob Tyler, 17

Lucky If I Get Cs

School has always been difficult for me, and I've always considered myself lucky to get Cs. But recently, as I watched my mother work hard to better her circumstances, I learned something very important. There was a job opening where my mother works. She really wanted the position. It would mean better hours, more pay and a chance to do the kind of work she really wanted to do. There were three other people at her company who wanted the same job.

My mother set her mind on getting the position. She thought about what would make her the most valuable candidate and then made a plan. She did lots of things, from accepting some difficult assignments, to taking two night-school courses to improve her skills. I was so proud of her.

My mother did get the new job. She's been in the position for about four months now. She loves it, and I can see where it's made such a difference in her life. My mother feels better about herself. She can afford to dress nicer. She buys more things for the family. She has time to go to the gym now after work, because she doesn't have to put in so many hours at work—things like that.

Watching my mother has made me realize that you can get what you want if you plan for it, if you set a goal and then work toward it. For me that means to start earning better grades so that I have a chance to get into a college or, at least, a good training program. When I see the way my mom's hard work paid off, how much better her life is because of it, I know that it's all worth it. You just need to buy a ticket. I've decided to purchase one called "be a better student."

Marsha Pauls, 15

Still Bumming Rides

My brother never took high school seriously; he just "hung out." And six years after graduating that's about all he's doing now—hanging out. He doesn't have anything to show for himself: He's still bumming rides, still doing meaningless jobs, still can't afford to go out on nice dates. Don't get me wrong, I love my brother. But I can't say I look up to or admire him. Though he's twenty-four, he's in pretty much the same boat he was in when he was sixteen. I don't know exactly where I want to be when I'm twenty-four, but I know I'll be working hard and achieving my goals.

My friends tell me that I'm ambitious and motivated, and it may be because I don't want to end up like my brother. I'm sorry to say this, but although he calls himself a "free spirit," I'm afraid he's a "freeloader." While my brother says that it's shallow to want material things and "people of real depth" don't need or want them, I think it's a cop-out. Having "real depth" may not always happen to include owning a lot of things, but I doubt if it ever includes just freeloading. Besides, taking action seems to me to be anything but shallow.

I have definite goals: I want a car by the time I get my driver's license; I want to afford nice clothes; I don't have a girlfriend, but when I have one I want to be able to go to nice restaurants, to be able to take her to the prom and do nice things like that. (My brother never asked a girl to the prom. He said it was because he didn't have the money. I think he just didn't make it a priority.) And I love to ski. Last year my parents let me go on a ski weekend with my class. I learned to ski and have been skiing five times since, but it's an expensive sport. I want to be able to go skiing more often.

That's why I've decided to do things differently from the way my brother has. After watching my brother, I don't waste my time arguing with my parents on some of the things that he argued with them about. He was always in an argument, especially over curfew (and then he was always on restriction because he wouldn't follow the curfew my parents set). I've got so much to do—getting good grades, playing football and all the other plans I have—I want my parents to be happy with me. So I talk with them about my goals, and I feel they're on my side. It's not *them against me* like it was with my brother.

And, I don't want to bum rides to get everywhere I have to go. So for over a year now, each week I've set aside a portion of my allowance to put toward buying a car. I've asked my parents if they would agree to adding to my "car fund" for getting good grades. (They said yes!)

For me, "buying a ticket" means being clear on what's important to me and having a plan for getting the things I want.

Luke Moorehouse, 15

I'd Have a Great Life, If Only . . .

In my senior year, I failed my geography course! So, in order to graduate, I had to take a summer school class. Talk about messing up your plans! I wanted to use my summer to work full-time to make a lot of money.

I was telling my woes to my best friend, Roy Ershadi. Roy listened—and then told me he'd just learned he was accepted to a university—the university that was his first choice. I'm facing the possibility of not graduating, while my friend's life is exploding with opportunities! As if all this wasn't enough, my parents informed me that they were separating. Life was looking rotten, and I was really bummed about it all. I thought "I'd have a great life, if only . . ." Then I realized how true that statement was. So I had to get a grip. I had to get it together. Basically, I needed to take charge of my life.

Deciding to get with it has been helpful. I know now that it's up to me. I have to do well in my other classes. I no longer work for good grades for my parents or teachers. Now I need to get them for my own goals—one of which is to get out of high school! Just like I accept that getting passing grades is up to me, so is planning where I go from here. I'm responsible for deciding where I'm going to live after I get out of high school. It's up to me to find a decent-paying job. It's all up to me.

Becoming proactive, buying a ticket, is the first step. I need to pay attention to the things I need and want in life. I need to focus on doing the things that will make me succeed.

I'm feeling better now. I know I'll be okay, that I'll get past the disappointments. I'm going to buy a string of tickets!

Brad Marshall, 18

My Girlfriend Comes First

I have a part-time job, a girlfriend and a lot of friends. I play varsity football and when I'm not playing on the field, I'm playing in the school band. To summarize, my schedule is very full.

I'd like to go on to college—a good college—and get a business degree. I get mostly Bs and a few Cs, so I know there's room for improvement with my grades. But with so many things to do, I just never have enough time to do all the things I need to.

Usually it's my homework that gets done last, since it's my least-favorite thing to do. Then, I usually take a break halfway through it and call my girlfriend—which is my favorite thing to do! And since talking with my girlfriend is a favorite thing to do, usually I don't get all of my homework done, which is a real problem.

Not getting all my homework done affects my grades. And that will affect getting into a good college, so I know I need to get tougher about prioritizing the things that have to get done to reach my goals. But it's tough. I look at my homework, and then to the phone, then at my homework—and then I call my girlfriend. She wins out over homework. Every time!

I think maybe I'll put the words "gotta ride to the sound of the drums" on my phone to remind me that homework should be done before I call my girlfriend. I really am serious about going to college after high school.

Matt Jensen, 17

8

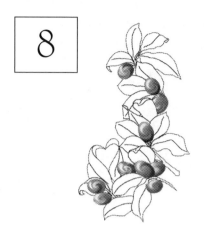

A Person of . . . Determination

Great dancers are not great because of their technique; they are great because of their passion.

—Martha Graham

ARISTOTLE

One day a young man came to Aristotle, the great philosopher, and begged, "Please, Aristotle, I want to learn all the knowledge you possess. Teach me all you know!" to which Aristotle answered, "I'll consider your request. But first let us go for a walk down by the river."

The young man followed Aristotle to the riverbank. Once there, Aristotle picked up a stone and dropped it into the water. "Retrieve the stone," directed Aristotle. As the young man stooped over to pick up the stone, Aristotle dunked the lad's head under the water and held it there until the boy began to swing his arms and squirm for freedom. He needed to breathe and was intent on getting the air he needed.

Discerning the lesson was learned, Aristotle released his hold on the young man. Gasping, the young man heaved in great gulps of air, and once he caught his breath demanded, "What did you do that for?"

Aristotle said simply, "I will give you and teach you all that I know, but it will do you no good unless you want it badly enough—unless you want it as much as you wanted air to breathe."

A Word from the Authors

In his attempts to create an electric light, Thomas Edison tried and tried and tried before he finally succeeded. After many failed attempts, a critic said to him, "Edison, you should give up. You've failed thousands of times."

"No, I haven't failed thousands of times," Edison retorted. "On the contrary, I have successfully eliminated thousands of ideas that do not work!" So remember, don't ever give up!

Just recently, we attended a very special gathering for a group of dynamic and successful people. Gathered together for the purpose of camaraderie and sharing their stories of success were some 350 guests, the likes of physics Nobel laureate, Jim Cronin; Emmy-winning producer of NBC *Nightime News*, Roberta Oster; Charles Bailyn, an astronomy professor who discovered a "black hole"; producer Ralph Winter of Walt Disney Productions; Phil Lader, the U.S. ambassador to England; New York civil court judge, Dorothy Chin Brandt; Bill Broyles, screenwriter for "Apollo 13"; former U.S. diplomat and Harvard physics professor and now president of Queens College, Allen Sessoms; Steve Smith, a veteran of two space flights, over three hundred Earth orbits and three space walks; Bill Perry, U.S. Secretary of Defense—you get the idea.

When you bring together a group of supremely accomplished individuals such as these, you can only imagine the number of stories of success they can tell! We were in awe. But heroes and leaders rarely sugarcoat their successes. If you listen closely while they tell of their route to a gold medal, a peace prize, an invention or discovery, or for an office they were seeking, you learn an interesting truth: Rarely, if ever, did that person succeed on the first try! Most all successful men and women can cite an example or two (or more!) of the times they did not succeed. And each will tell you not to discount or dismiss these failures, but instead to use the failure as an important lesson and feedback to go forward. In other words, the information they glean from what doesn't work becomes as important as information about what does work. Many said that it was a "mistake" or "failure" that led them to an important finding and resulted in new information that led to a new discovery or invention or successful outcome.

What would these accomplished people want you and I to learn from them? First, that almost everything worth doing takes a lot of effort. Second, a failed attempt is as good a reason as any to try again, and this time, incorporate what you have learned in the process!

That's what seventeen-year-old Mark Whitman learned (albeit with a nudge from his father) when an unexpected loss at a state finals wrestling match forced him to rethink "failure." Fifteen-year-old weight lifter Randy Jones said, "I don't think failing is always negative. It pushes me to try harder. It motivates me." It wasn't until his fifth try that Steve Smith qualified to become an astronaut! His advice? "Just as in learning to walk or ride a bike, you keep learning until you don't fall down anymore. Set your goals high and never give in. And never, never, never give up!"

The toughest times call for the fiercest determination, as seventeen-year-old Cory Perea found out. He lost his leg—along with his dream of becoming a pro baseball player—in a car accident. In his case, it wasn't a person but rather a three-legged cheetah named Subira who gave him the determination to build a new dream. Geremy White, twenty, has a message of his own when he says, "As you can see by my address, I'm writing you from prison."

So when a challenge seems insurmountable, or you feel discouraged, think of Edison! What if he had given up because one or more of his attempts did not meet with success? Probably, someone else with more fortitude and stick-to-itiveness would have looked at the progress Edison had made, including reviewing the "failed attempts" to see what had already been tried but didn't work, and then, using all that Edison had already accomplished, gone on to invent the electric light!

To paraphrase Aristotle, "You have to want it bad enough!"

Steve Smith's Dream

As a young boy, Steve Smith was fascinated with the mysteries of space and dreamed of one day becoming an astronaut. When he was in the third grade, he drew a picture of a rocket ship. The picture was so dear to him that he hung it where he could look at it daily. He loved the picture because it coincided with his dream, one in which he saw himself as an astronaut, one who would someday walk on the moon!

Steve held onto his dream over the years. While still a young boy, he read everything he could that was related to space and space travel. He learned everything he could about the National Aeronautics and Space Administration (NASA). By the time he became an adult, only one thing remained: earning a coveted position as an astronaut on NASA's prestigious space team. And so he began the rigorous and arduous training program, a prerequisite in qualifying to become an astronaut.

The day for which Steve had so carefully planned and trained finally arrived. Today was the day when all those who had aspirations to be an astronaut would be put to the test.

Within a few days, NASA announced who had made the team. Steve had failed to make the cut!

As disappointed as Steve was, he was determined to succeed. According to NASA's regulations, a person is eligible to go through NASA's training only once every two years. So, two years later, Steve tried again.

Once again, he failed to make the cut.

So he tried again two years later!

Once again, he failed to make the cut.

So he tried again two years later!

Once again, he failed to make the cut.

So he tried again two years later. On his fifth try, Steve Smith became an astronaut on the United States of America's NASA team!

Today, astronaut Steve Smith is a veteran of two space flights, over three hundred Earth orbits and three space walks! His advice? "Just as in learning to walk or ride a bike, you keep learning until you don't fall down anymore. Set your goals high and never give in. And never, never, never give up!"

Bettie B. Youngs

[**Authors' Note:** *This drawing is the actual picture of the rocket Steve Smith drew as a third-grader! He asked us to please include it for you. Just imagine how this simple picture gave birth to a noble dream. Through hard work and great determination, Steve Smith made that dream reality. He is now a respected astronaut and an American hero.*]

The Three-Legged Cheetah

Seventeen-year-old Cory Perea had dreams of playing major league baseball one day. That was his one and only goal. He lived and breathed baseball and dreamed of the day when he would have a following, fans who knew he was "the man."

No one doubted Cory's ability, certainly not Bob Shepard, the lead university scout for baseball talent in the state. He had recruited Cory, confirming a promising future. But that was before a tragic car accident had claimed Cory's right leg.

Cory lost more than his leg in the car accident: He also lost his hope. And his spirit. Nothing could replace the dreams the accident had dashed.

The accident left him not only physically disabled, but emotionally crippled. Unable to dream of anything other than being a major baseball talent, Cory was bitter, jaded and feeling just plain useless. Hopeless.

Today, he sat in a wheelchair with a chip on his shoulder, angry at the world—and on another "boring field trip" from the rehab program. Unwilling and unable, Cory had become one of the rehab center's few "un" patients: unable to reconstruct a plan for his life, one that compensated for the loss of one leg and didn't allow excuses to impede it; unable to summon the courage to dream new plans for the future. He gave up on not only himself but others. "Get off my back," he had told the rehab director. "You can't help me. No one can." But someone did—a three-year-old cheetah named Subira.

The rehab center had taken its patients to Shambala, a sanctuary for large cats in the Santa Clara Valley, forty miles north of Los Angeles, run by Tippi Hendren. Tippi was talking to the group, telling them about Shambala, how it came about, and a little bit about the animals there. Subira laid atop the large, long, low branch of a massive oak tree, observing quietly. As Tippi continued talking, Subira jumped from the tree and began blazing a trail of speed around the enclosure. Cory looked on, at first bored and then noticed that the animal only had three legs!

No one was more stunned by the sight of this incredible animal running at full speed than Cory. Amazed at the cheetah's effortless, seemingly natural movements, in a whisper, he remarked, "Incredible. Just incredible." Looking bewildered, he commented, "Imagine being able to run that fast with three legs."

Tippi explained, "Subira's umbilical cord was wrapped around her leg in the womb, so it atrophied, causing her to lose the leg soon after she was born. Born in an Oregon zoo, but with only three legs, she was cast off. Her fate seemed hopeless. They were considering euthanasia—putting her to sleep."

Surprised, Cory asked thoughtfully, "Why?"

"Because," Tippi responded, "they thought, 'What good is a three-legged cheetah? What would people say?' They didn't think the public would want to see a deformed cheetah. Since it was felt that she wouldn't be able to adapt, you know, to run and act like a normal cheetah, she served no purpose. She had nothing to do. But we all need to do something, don't we?"

With a kind and wistful look, Tippi looked into Cory's face and said, "That's when we heard about Subira and offered her a sanctuary. It was soon after she came to us that she demonstrated her own worth—a unique gift of love and spirit. Normally cheetahs are solitary animals, but not this cheetah. She decided to love people, and made herself a part of our family immediately.

"And more than that, she's world famous, and has touched the lives of people everywhere because she had to create her own worth by overcoming her handicap." Tippi lovingly looked at the animal and said, "We are so happy to have her. She truly is a most cherished and priceless gift."

Cory grew reflective and, with tears in his eyes, asked softly, "Can I touch her?"

Perhaps in that poignant moment, the boy understood that Subira's courage did not allow a missing leg to hinder her—and that opened the gates of his own heart and mind. Whatever it was, it changed his demeanor and willingness to participate. When the leader of the visiting group was preparing to leave at the end of the tour and asked for a volunteer to push and hold the large rolling gate open so the van could exit the ranch, Cory dared to take his first step in creating his own worth. He volunteered.

As the rest of the group looked on, Cory wheeled himself over to the gate. Struggling to maneuver it open, he gripped the high-wire fence for support and pushed it open. The expression on his face as he continued to hold the gate until the van passed through was one of great determination and satisfaction. And, judging from the smile on his face, it appeared that Cory was determined to find and live a new dream.

Bettie B. Youngs
Adapted from Taste-Berry Tales

My First Cigarette

I had my first cigarette when I was fourteen. I don't know how my father found out, but he did. He didn't ask me if I did, nor did he give me a lecture on not smoking. Instead, one Saturday afternoon he asked me to come to the garage with him. Once there, he handed me a cigar and made me smoke the entire thing! It made me so sick, I almost threw up. I'm sure I turned green. I'll never forget how terrible it made me feel. When Dad was quite sure I had learned to hate the taste of tobacco, he said to me, "Son, I love you. There are lots of reasons why I don't want you to smoke, but the reasons alone won't deter you from smoking. However, because your life and health are so important to me I am determined to do all I can to see to it you don't smoke—at least while you live at home."

I'm seventeen now, and to this day, I haven't put a cigarette (or cigar) to my lips again. (I can hardly stand the smell of smoke!) I respect my dad for doing what he did, for handling it the way he did, because quite frankly I don't think anything else would have had the same effect at the time.

Many of the kids my age at school smoke, even though their parents don't want them to. Most all of their parents lecture them on not smoking, but they still smoke. Some parents bribe their kids, like my buddy Greg's dad promised to help him get a car when he turned sixteen if he didn't smoke. But none of these approaches worked. My friends still smoke. It only makes them work harder at concealing their smoking from their parents. My father was determined to make me dislike smoking. When I'm a parent, if I catch my kids smoking, I'll use the same lesson my father did. His method works!

Everett Stewart, 17

I'm Writing You from Prison

As you can see by my address, I'm writing to you from prison. They busted me for stealing a car and gave me fifteen years. I'd been arrested two times before, both times for stealing cars, but I never thought they would put me away for it. My life is pretty screwed up now, and my mother feels really sad about my being here.

I had a really tough time growing up and pretty much had to make my own way. Maybe if my father hadn't left my mom and us three kids, I wouldn't haven't turned out so bad and then I wouldn't be here. Maybe if teachers would do a better job in schools, so many kids wouldn't feel so bad about their lives and wouldn't get in so much trouble. I would like you to send me some money because then when I get out of here I won't have to rely on stealing cars to make a living. Thanks.

Geremy White, 20

Favored to Win

Success is not measured by your victories,
but by your recovery from your failures.

—Vic Preisser

Last year my wrestling team made it to the state finals. Of all the contenders, I had the best record and was favored to win. Everyone was counting on me to win—and winning was necessary to advance to the nationals.

No one wanted to win more than I did, but I lost my match! It was such a shock and disappointment to me.

I felt defeated in more ways than just on the mat. For several weeks afterwards, I couldn't seem to get back into the stride of things. I lost interest in working as hard as I had to get good grades and do well in school. I even lost interest in the extracurricular activities I was involved in, and that surprised me because I had been enjoying them before, most especially the photography club. I spent time alone instead of hanging out with friends after school. Everything seemed so pointless, so bleak. I felt really depressed.

My father was the one who helped me pull myself from the fog I was in. He helped me turn things around. He told me that, yes, my having an opportunity to attend the national competition would have been a great honor; and, yes, winning there could have opened up other doors (like being selected to work as a junior coach at special wrestling camps, or getting a college scholarship); and, yes, "It's okay to think about what happened, to understand what kept you from the outcome you had hoped for, but after a review, it's time to focus on your achievements and move on, to recover, to rebuild." Then he said something I'll always remember: "Son, a loss is just a loss, and not your finest achievement. Don't give it so much power. Save your time and energy for the next endeavor. Focus on that. Your finest achievement always lies ahead."

My father helped me realize that failing at some things is going to be a given, and that losing at some things is the flip side of winning at some things. I found his perspective and advice helpful.

I love my dad for believing in me and for trusting in my ability—win or lose. He gave me the push to keep on being determined to succeed—not to give up, but to continue moving towards success. I just hope that one day I can become as inspirational to others and to my own kids, when I have them, as my father is to me.

Mark Whitman, 17

Don't Ever Call Me a Wimp!

"Hey, wimp!" Hank Holton would call. "Seen any good movies lately, wimp?"

"Don't you ever call me a wimp again!" I'd yell.

"Oh, yeah? And what are you going to do about it?" he'd ask. Then he'd punch me on the arm or in the back. It hurt. "So?" he'd repeat, "What'd ya say you were going to do about it?" Then Hank would put my head in a head-lock and flick me on my head with his fingers. That *really* hurt. Then, with my head in a head-lock, Hank repeated once again, "I didn't hear you, what did you say?"

If I answered, "Don't you ever call me a wimp again!" Hank would thump me again. And, if I answered, "Nothing!" he thumped me again anyway. He thought it was very funny.

Hank picked on me and gave me a hard time because I was so much smaller than he was. And my muscles weren't as large.

All that changed! I started lifting weights.

I probably never would have started "pumping iron" if it hadn't been for Hank Holton.

That was a year ago. Now I have well-developed muscles, better than most guys my age and bigger than some of the older guys. And Hank Holton doesn't call me a wimp any more!

Randy Jones, 15

Part 5

Deciding What to Do in Life: Discovering Your Interests, Talents and Direction

The goal is to make your joys your job,
your toys your tools.

—Jennifer Leigh Youngs

9

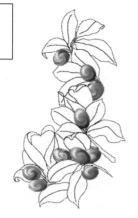

Finding Your Acres of Diamonds

The world makes way for the person
who knows where they are going.

—Ralph W. Emerson

ACRE OF DIAMONDS

An Arkansas farmer, tired of not being able to make a good living on his farm, sold it to a man who had very little money, and went off to seek his fortune elsewhere. Several years passed and still he had not found the fortune he sought. Tired, and now broke, he returned to the community of the farmstead he sold. One day, he drove by the farm he once owned—the one on which he could not make a living. To his surprise and amazement, the farmhouse had been torn down and a mansion now stood in its place. Several new buildings including a large barn, a huge machine shed and a grain dryer and storage unit had been erected. Rows of trees and shrubs had been planted. Beautiful lawns adorned the meticulously groomed grounds. The place had changed so much that he could hardly believe it

183

was the same farm. He decided to stop and have a talk with the new owner. "Look at all you've done," he remarked, clearly bewildered by what he saw. "How on earth did you accomplish all this? You barely had enough money to buy the farm from me. How did you get so rich?"

The new owner smiled and said, "I owe it all to you. There were diamonds on this property, acres and acres of diamonds!"

"Diamonds!" scoffed the previous owner. "I knew every inch of this land, and there were no diamonds here."

"On the contrary," responded the new owner as he pulled a lump of what looked like an oily piece of quartz from his pocket. "I carry around this small nugget as a good luck charm."

The farmer was amazed. "That's a diamond? I remember seeing a lot of those all over this land, so many that I was frustrated thinking what rotten luck it was to have owned a land filled with hard rock formations—so many that it made plowing and planting difficult!"

"Well, it's obvious you don't recognize a diamond when you see one," commented the farmer. "Diamonds in their unpolished form look like lumps of coal."

A Word from the Authors

Finding your acre of diamonds—discovering what interests you—is an important first step in deciding what you'll do for work. The big questions are how do you discover it and how do you know when you have found it? The farmer sold his acre of land, certain there was nothing of value on it. Some of the teens we heard from felt the same way, certain that they didn't have any special talents that they could turn into a job or career. Upon closer examination, they discovered they did.

"Mom, seventeen-year-old Trent Dayton told us, 'I have a passion for the ocean,' and then explained *why* he loves to go surfing. Trent said that some people called him a 'surf bum' and didn't see him as having big goals or plans for his future. 'You can't make a living being a surfer!' a classmate in Trent's careers class jeered. In careers class, the students discussed the issue of turning their passions into a living. Trent and his jeering class-mate, Bruce, had very different opinions and very different pas-sions. Bruce planned to be an attorney. This was his dream and he had his college plans and the goal of owning his own law firm set before him. Right after Bruce made his statement about Trent, the teacher held up his hands and said, 'Wait, I wouldn't be so sure of that.' Another classmate volunteered, 'Trent could surf professionally.' 'I'd like that,' Trent conceded, 'but it's not my dream.' Then, with the teacher's prodding, the class learned that Trent did have very real goals and dreams for the future. They are based on his love for the ocean and it's very possible for him to make a living doing what he loves.

"Trent's dream is to own his own surf shop and to manufac-ture his own surfboards. Trent has already developed great skill at shaping surfboards and he knows all there is to know about what a surfboard shop needs to carry—quite impressive accom-plishments for someone his age. Add his knowledge and skills to his passion for the ocean and for surfing, and you have a large arrow pointing to the entrance of a diamond mine. With just a little unearthing, Trent and his classmates discovered that his goals and dreams were as clear and as possible to achieve as Bruce's were. Learning that Bruce planned to go into business law, Trent was a good enough sport about Bruce's earlier razzing to joke with him, saying, 'Maybe someday I'll hire you to draw up some contracts for me.'"

"Jennifer, that's a great example of discovering that your interests and talents have everything to do with pointing you in the direction of 'making your joys your job,' as you say. Now that Trent has identified his passions and thought about what he'd like to do, he'll be better able to decide what further education and training he needs to give wings to his goals."

"I think that's why so many teens we heard from said, 'Teenagers often have very good ideas about what they want out of life. Some people may think teens are clueless or mindless about these things but they aren't. They just get frustrated when others aren't listening to their ideas, dreams, goals and plans.'"

As you'll see in the stories in this chapter, when teens looked closely at the things going on in their lives, they found diamonds. As a struggling, teenage mother determined to finish high school, Julie Newman, seventeen, found the diamond of her future career. And Julie's not playing around—she's determined to give Mattel Toys some serious competition! An encounter with orphans in Bogotá, Colombia, helped sixteen-year-old Lisa Cartwright refuse to be seen as a "loser" anymore. Finding an injured cat and taking it to the vet crystallized seventeen-year-old Kevin Tulane's love for animals. Having found his "lucky" acre of diamonds, Kevin now knows he wants to be a vet. As a result, he's become a better student, developed better relationships with his parents and brothers, and even with his classmates. In Kevin's own words, "Knowing what I want to do has made all the difference. For the first time in my life, I feel on track. Dreams fill my mind. My heart suddenly has goals that are worth doing. Now I'm energized."

Many teens felt as if they stumbled upon their diamonds by chance. Seventeen-year-old Richard Lewis described his newly found passion for film production as a "gift in disguise"—and tells Steven Spielberg to move over! And fifteen-year-old Mark Knolls tells us why his brother's not being able to afford to take his car to the auto repair shop may help that same brother own his own auto repair shop someday.

It can take time and honest introspection to come to know yourself well enough to be certain of what you want to do. Until you reach that point, it's important not to become discouraged—and to keep looking for those answers.

Luckily there are definite places to look. Just as Brent Lasorda took a class, so can you. Brent's class was a summer course at a junior college, but often high schools offer classes that help teens discover potential career skills by identifying strengths and aptitudes. Your own high school may offer just such a class. If you follow the community calendar section in your local newspaper, you can find out about career-day events in your area. During these types of events professionals in a variety of careers set up booths to offer you information on the kind of work they do. It can be helpful to learn more about what tasks different professionals perform and what different positions and career options are available. You can also meet with your school guidance counselor or school career counselor. These counselors are trained specifically to help you find ways to discover where your talents lie. We live in a world of computers, so take advantage of this resource, too. Ask your counselor about Web sites and software programs that can help you in your search. In addition, there is a wealth of books (including workbooks) that can walk you through nearly every possible phase of figuring out what to do in life. Your school and community libraries should carry these books. Ask your librarian to help you locate them.

A part-time job can help you clarify your interests and talents, too. Look carefully at those things you like and dislike about your job. If you dislike stocking shelves but love waiting on customers, that's a good indication that you'd like a career working with people. On the other hand, if you just love spending your work hours entering data and dislike having to answer phones, you'd probably be happier in a job where you don't directly deal with people. One teen worked in a clothing store, and while she didn't like working the cash register or assisting customers, she discovered she loved window design. This led her to pursue a career as an interior designer. The goal is to find what you love to do—whether it's because you're great at it, or it gives you a sense of purpose or you just think it's fun. Usually, when you find it, it will involve all of these.

In the following stories, teens search for their "diamonds." Let's join them on their search!

A Pain in the Butt

In his acceptance speech for winning an Academy Award for his performance in a motion picture, Oscar-winner Robin Williams thanked a number of people, including some high school teachers. "Some of my teachers thought I was 'a pain in the butt,'" he laughed, referring to himself as jokester, a funnybone who could always see the humor in things as a teenager. And then, clutching his Oscar and growing serious, one of America's most beloved comics remarked for all the world to hear (perhaps attributing some of his success to her), "but one special teacher said to me, 'I hope you'll channel that talent. You'd make a good public speaker!'"

Obviously the teacher saw great possibility in Robin's sense of humor. How forturnate we are that the teacher encouraged him to do something with it: It was to be the start of something very special. As his Academy Award confirms, the "pain in the butt" turned a very spectacular piece of coal into a brilliant diamond!

And of course, that Mr. Williams acknowledged the teacher is the mark of a winner, a real "taste berry!" [1997 Academy Awards telecast interview.]

Bettie B. Youngs

Clueless

I don't have any idea what I want to do after I graduate. Sometimes I get really bummed out about it, because it seems like everyone else knows exactly what they want to do, like what college they want to attend—or at least where they want to apply.

Some of my friends even know what they want to do for work—Sandy wants to be a lawyer, Zach wants to work in the field of computers and Jesse wants to be a rock star. Another friend wants to be a landscaper because he wants to work outdoors. Jordan wants to work for himself, but Devrin wants to work for a big corporation. I even have friends who know exactly what they don't want to do. Like Ricky knows for certain that he doesn't want to travel—he's scared to death of airplanes. He also said he doesn't want to be a teacher because he thinks kids give teachers a hard time.

The only thing that I know is that I would like to do something that I enjoy. Right now, the only thing that comes to mind is that I like surfing the Internet—but no one is going to pay me to do that. Then again . . .

The more I think about it, maybe there *is* something there that could lead to a career. It's worth thinking about. Hey, maybe I could even find a Web site that would help me figure out a career goal!

Matt Jeffries, 16

"Two-Hundred and Fifty-Six!"

Education is not the filling of a pail,
but the lighting of a fire.

—William Butler Yeats

When I was in the tenth grade I had a teacher by the name of Mr. Swede. Of all the teachers I had, he impressed me the most because I could tell he loved teaching and really liked his students. To me, he seemed to be living his dreams, doing exactly what he wanted to do.

He taught American history, of all things. I expected to be bored to tears in that class. Boy, was I wrong. Mr. Swede was brilliant—he knew his subject so well. Facts just poured from him, and he knew how to make them interesting to his students. There was something about his passion for the subject, or maybe he just had a great gift for storytelling; whatever it was, he made history come alive for me, too.

Mr. Swede seemed to intuitively know my interest was piqued, and he took a special interest in encouraging me to learn all I could. It really worked with me. During our timed midterm essay, we had to write all the facts we could remember about the civil rights movement. I wrote eighteen pages, 256 facts—more than anyone else in the class.

After that, as Mr. Swede walked around the room while we were doing our written assignments in class, he would pass my desk and pause to whisper, "Two-hundred and fifty-six, imagine!" as if to remind me of how well I had done—and what I could do. On occasion, he'd say, "Be sure to talk with the counselors about universities!" Other times, he'd say, "You know, you could teach history." I found that so inspiring.

Last year, at the end of my junior year in high school, I asked him to sign my yearbook. In it he wrote: "You have great promise. I hope you'll work hard, go to a fine university, and help change the world. If ever you doubt yourself, just remember, 'Two-hundred and fifty-six!'"

I admire Mr. Swede and value his opinion. If he thinks I'd be a good history teacher, maybe I would be. Now that he mentioned it, I do like finding out all I can about how people used to live and how they struggled to grow and change throughout the years. I also like sharing what I learn with others, so I've been seriously considering teaching. I think I could be a good teacher.

I don't know if I'll get accepted to a college, but I am trying. My grades throughout my ninth- and tenth-grade years weren't all that good, but since I've had Mr. Swede, I'm working very hard to improve them. Every few months, especially when things get tough, I get out my annual and read what he wrote. Mr. Swede's words and his belief in me and my talent reminds me that I really do have promise. I've not lost sight of the goal he helped give me—to work hard, go to a fine college and change the world.

Whenever I doubt myself, I recall the affirming tone of his voice and his words, "Two-hundred and fifty-six!"

Lana Bowman, 17

The Incredible Six

Last summer, I took an eight-week course at a local junior college. The course was all about discovering what's called our aptitudes—our "acres of diamonds." The instructor told the class that we can tell a lot about our aptitudes—the things that we're naturally interested in—if we pay attention to the times when we're doing something and it really captures our attention. He said we'd know when that was because the time would just fly by.

One of our assignments was to keep a journal for eight weeks. The teacher told us to keep track of the books and magazine articles we read, and the movies or television programs we watched. Using a six-point checklist, we had to write about each one, telling what it was about the book, article or show that we either liked or didn't like. He also gave us other assignments to help us discover the kind of things we were interested in.

I learned a lot more about my interests—my deeper interests—because of it. The moment you've finished reading a book, or if you've just come out of a movie, right away you know if you liked it or not. And you intuitively know that there are some you prefer over some others. The bigger question is, "Do you know why?" Before I took the course, my criteria for whether or not I liked a book was whether it bored me or if I fell asleep reading it. And if you asked me to review the book—whether I liked it or didn't like it—before I took this class, I probably would have said, "It was just boring." That would have been my response.

Now, I would answer you with a little more insight and be more specific. Now I might say something like (as I did recently in a book report), "I didn't enjoy it because the setting for the story took place nearly five decades ago and in a foreign country, and I couldn't relate." Or, I might say that it was precisely because of those things that I loved the book.

Another point in the checklist asked us to watch for specific detail. If I were applying this to the book I'd read, I might ask, "What is the nature of the story?" For example, does a human-interest story grab my attention more than a story about animals? If my answer is "yes," then according to the teacher's checklist, the next thing I might explore is to see if I'm caught up in the adventure of how the person's dilemma is going to be resolved, or am I most interested in how the person himself is going to change as a result of the ordeal? Things like that. The checklist we were given helped us examine a lot of different things, all aimed at finding out what we were *really* interested in.

One of the last items on the checklist was to see if we could spot the interests of others, and if we could, to describe what we saw. So I used my friend Kirk as a "guinea pig." One weekend, he and I went to the Wild Animal Park—a place I love no matter how many times I go. I watched Kirk glance from one animal to the next, only occasionally amused or interested by what he saw. I couldn't help but compare it to the way I felt when he showed me all the "great" stuff that he could do on the computer. There'd be moments where I thought it was really cool, but for the most part it bored me. Kirk obviously felt this way about animals.

Though I still don't know exactly what career I want for sure, I think the method I learned in the summer-school class will be very valuable in helping me determine my "acre of diamonds."

Brent Lasorda, 17

Kevin Got "Lucky"

My mother was driving me to soccer practice. I was in the eighth grade at the time. We came to a stop sign, and I looked out the window and saw a cat lying near a park bench licking what appeared to be a wound. I begged Mom to let me go over to get a closer look. She did! The cat was badly injured, so I coaxed my mother into letting us take it to a local animal hospital.

When we arrived there, the vet took care of the cat, then released it to our care. My mother was left with the bill for an animal we didn't own, much less know whom it belonged to. But she paid the bill anyway!

We took the sedated cat home, and I carried her into my room and laid her on my bed. By now I could tell that her medication was wearing off. Still, her breathing was labored. From time to time, she picked her head up to see what was going on around her, then after just a few seconds her head dropped back down. And her eyes had this glassy look of misery, like she thought she should be afraid of me but didn't have the energy to express it. I knew she was in a whole lot of pain. I stroked her soft silky fur and I talked gently to her, trying as best I could to soothe her. She hardly noticed. Inside, I just felt this pain for her—almost like I felt it with her. I wanted to make it go away.

For some reason, tears came to my eyes. Here I was sitting on my bed, stroking this cat that belonged to someone else and crying. I had never seen the cat before. I didn't understand these feelings. At first, I thought maybe the tears were for the cat who was hurt and lying here without her owner's soothing voice. I know that at those times when I've gotten sick at school and found myself lying on the couch in the nurse's office, the one place I'd always rather be is home in my own bed. Just knowing that my mother is somewhere in the house is comforting.

Then, I thought that maybe my feelings were about gratitude

to my mother because she consented to helping this injured cat. Paying the vet bill was more than she could afford—it was a really expensive thing for her to do. She didn't know who the cat belonged to either. It wasn't like she'd get reimbursed. I felt bad that this had cost her, and since I didn't have a job, I couldn't help her with the bill. But then it dawned on me that maybe my feelings were about me. Most of the time I felt bored with everything and everyone around me. I often had this lost, kind of out-of-place feeling inside . . . like I never fit in or had a place where I felt comfortable. I was always getting in trouble for this or that, and never cared much about anything or felt like what I did mattered, except when I felt these strong feelings that pulled at me every time I found myself helping an animal. It was all a combination of reverence, humility and appreciation for wanting to help.

This made me think about the cat's owner, and I realized that whoever it was would be getting worried about the cat. I went to the garage, got a cardboard box, cut it apart so that I had a large flat surface, and wrote, "Lost your cat? Call 827-4534." I took it down to the stop sign and tacked it to the post.

As I was walking home, the most weird—actually not so weird as interesting—feelings came over me. I looked down at the sidewalk as I crossed the street and saw this tall mustard plant in full bloom there. For some reason, the sight of it instantly triggered the idea that I wanted to be a veterinarian. Then, almost instantly, an assortment of feelings rushed into my mind. Immediately, I realized—I knew for sure—that I was most happy when I was with animals. But not just in their presence, like when I was horseback riding or at the zoo, but rather, when I was helping them, like all the times I had rescued a wounded or sick dog or cat or bird. Whether they were lost, hurt or simply hungry, I always took them in and helped them on their way. There was this recognition of a lot of feelings, and these feelings took on meaning. I realized that what I was doing was important and that what I did made a difference. I felt honorable and like I had a greater purpose when I was caring for animals.

This incident helped me understand, in a big way, what it was that captured my attention most, where I fit and what made me feel most satisfied. I can still visualize the crack in the sidewalk at that moment when I decided that I was going to be a vet. It was very freeing, I wanted to run the rest of the way home! Suddenly, I had the urge to get busy. I wanted to find a newspaper to see if there were any part-time jobs in an animal clinic, or maybe even in a pet store. I began wondering if I was smart enough to be a veterinarian, and if it was too late to get better grades in school in order to get into a college. I found myself wondering how long it would take me to become a vet, even where I would go to school, where I would practice.

It was such an energizing feeling. All of a sudden, I was on track. Life mattered, I had things to do. I was important after all. Dreams flooded my mind and filled my head with visions. I saw myself in college, I saw myself in a small practice with other vets, then in a practice of my own and then in an animal hospital that I had built.

Well, someone did come for the cat—a guy who lived not more than seven blocks away. It was funny because I had never seen the cat before and I usually walked down that very street on my way to school.

The man was so grateful. He couldn't afford to repay my mother, though he did promise to trim the trees and hedges in exchange for her paying the vet's bill. I felt good knowing that we'd helped. We'd done the right thing by helping to save an animal's life.

I still have a soft spot in my heart for that cat—I guess I always will. You know, she comes around to visit now and then. I'll occasionally see her on my way to school. Her name is Lucky. Kind of fits, doesn't it? I think she's grateful. She knows. I think animals know when we help them. I took a psychology course just to get some insight into my idea. I think being a vet will be a very important way to spend my life. I'm a senior now, and I still have my heart set on it!

People always ask me how I was able to come to such a clear sense of what I wanted to do for work in life. I usually don't tell them the whole story. I smile and say, "Just 'Lucky,' I guess!"

Kevin Tulane, 17
Adapted from Gifts of the Heart

Now That I'm a Mother

I'm seventeen and have a ten-month-old baby daughter. Now that I am a mother, I'm more motivated than ever to take my education seriously and get a good job. Before my baby was born, I never even thought about what I was going to do once I finished high school. I mean, I knew I planned on getting a job, but it's not like I had any idea just what that would be. I equated a job with earning money to get an apartment, and have the things I wanted.

Now I know exactly what I want to do.

Our school has an infant care center where babies can be dropped off while their parents attend school. One of the requirements is that each parent gives two hours of volunteer time to the center each day. While there, I noticed all the many different kinds of baby toys and mobiles that are used. One of the infant care center's aides explained that these toys are important for developing the baby's brain and alertness and intelligence.

I realized that I loved the work the center is doing with infant children, and that it was my favorite way to spend my time. My time there helped me discover that I would like to design toys for infants, most especially for a baby's crib. I want to design toys that keep them stimulated, alert and learning. Think how interesting it would be to develop a toy that would not only be colorful and captivating but also help the baby develop his brain. Think how many babies there are—and all parents buy toys to keep their children entertained. I can see myself designing and marketing toys for infants.

Now I'm taking a marketing course. It's a class that I would never have considered taking before I got interested in children's toys. I've also decided to get all the education I can to help me achieve my goals. Just in case you ever hear of a company that's rivaling Mattel Toys, such as Newman Toys, think of me!

Julie Newman, 17

READER/CUSTOMER CARE SURVEY

If you are enjoying this book, please help us serve you better and meet your changing needs by taking a few minutes to complete this survey. Please fold it and drop it in the mail.

PLEASE PRINT

BKB

NAME: _____

ADDRESS: _____

_____

TELEPHONE NUMBER: _____

E-MAIL: _____

(1) Gender: 1) ___ Girl 2) ___ Boy

(2) Age:
1) ___ 8 or under
2) ___ 9-12
3) ___ 13-16
4) ___ 17-20
5) ___ 21-30
6) ___ 31-40
7) ___ 41-50
8) ___ 51+

(3) Who purchased this book?
1) ___ You
2) ___ Parent
3) ___ Grandparent
4) ___ Friend
5) ___ Relative
6) ___ Adult Friend
7) ___ Counselor or Teacher

(4) Was this book bought as a gift?
1) ___ Yes 2) ___ No

(5) How did you find out about this book?
1) ___ Friend
2) ___ School
3) ___ Parent
4) ___ Radio
5) ___ Counselor
6) ___ Store display
7) ___ Newspaper or magazine review

(8) What do you like to read?

Teen magazines:
8) ___ Teen
9) ___ Seventeen
10) ___ Teen People
11) ___ YM
12) ___ Jump
13) ___ Teen Beat
14) ___ All About You
15) ___ Twist
16) ___ Christian Youth Magazines
17) ___ Comics

Books:
18) ___ Young Adult Fiction
19) ___ Romance
20) ___ Self-help
21) ___ Sci-fi

(22) Where do you usually buy books?
1) ___ Bookstore
2) ___ Discount Store
3) ___ Grocery Store
4) ___ School Book Sale
5) ___ Web Sites
6) ___ Price Club

(23) How many books do you buy or read a month (not school books)?
1) ___ 1
2) ___ 2
3) ___ 3
4) ___ 4+

As a special "Thank You" we'll send you news about new books and a valuable Gift Certificate!

(24) What are your TWO favorite TV Shows?
1) ___ Dawson's Creek
2) ___ Beverly Hills 90210
3) ___ Boy Meets World
4) ___ 7th Heaven
5) ___ The Simpsons
6) ___ Sabrina the Teenage Witch
7) ___ Buffy the Vampire Slayer
8) ___ Party of Five
9) ___ Other

Describe a book that you would like to buy especially for teens that isn't currently available

_____

_____

_____

_____

_____

_____

BUSINESS REPLY MAIL
FIRST-CLASS MAIL PERMIT NO 45 DEERFIELD BEACH, FL

POSTAGE WILL BE PAID BY ADDRESSEE

TASTE BERRIES™ FOR TEENS
HEALTH COMMUNICATIONS, INC.
3201 SW 15TH STREET
DEERFIELD BEACH FL 33442-9875

FOLD HERE

Thank You!!

Additional Comments:

Because He Couldn't Afford a Car

My seventeen-year-old brother really wanted a car, but my dad said a car was something my brother and I had to get on our own ("so we'd appreciate it")—so there would be no help from my parents with buying one. Although my brother found a part-time job, he was also playing sports, and it didn't leave many hours for his job. I remember my brother telling me that he felt like he'd be out of high school by the time he saved up enough to buy his own car. But then, knowing my brother couldn't afford a car, when my uncle bought a new car, he offered my brother his old one—but it needed a lot of repairs.

Since my brother didn't have the money to spend for someone else to fix it, and because he didn't know how to do it himself, he took a shop class to learn how. Not only did he get good grades in shop, he thought the class was fun. The few hours he was working in his part-time job were enough to pay for the parts he needed, and before long his car was up and running.

One thing led to another, and soon other kids were asking my brother for help with their cars. He even did a few repairs on my dad's car. Then, the shop teacher convinced my brother that he should take other classes that would teach him how to run a successful business, like an auto repair shop. Right now my brother works at the school's auto repair shop.

I have no doubt that one day he'll have his own auto shop—and all because he didn't have enough money to take his car to one!

Mark Knolls, 15

A Loser No More

I'm sixteen and someone many people call "a loser." Surprising, isn't it, that someone so young can still be considered a loser. I've heard people refer to me, and kids like me, as losers—some have even called me that to my face. I am only sixteen and would like to believe that only the first few chapters of my life have been recorded, and that like all books, there are chapters to come.

I dropped out of school at thirteen, because I was pregnant. I had my baby at fourteen. I went back to school after my baby was born, but dropped out again after only six weeks. At fifteen, I got pregnant again, and this time, I had an abortion. I don't think I've ever had a steady job for more than two months. I'd like to say that I lost my jobs because I was laid off, or because I couldn't find a sitter for my baby, or because I had to stay home with my child when she was sick. But that wouldn't be true. I lost these jobs because I was late day after day, because I didn't call my employer when I wasn't going to go in, and because my attitude was so bad that other employees and my employer couldn't deal with me. Those are the reasons I was fired. My irresponsibility didn't end there.

My parents had jobs of their own, but that didn't stop me from leaving my baby with them almost all of the time. Most of the time, I just left finding someone to take care of the baby when they had to go work up to them—like it was their problem. Finally, my baby was taken from me and put in a foster home. By this time, I'd been arrested twice for disturbing the peace, once for having an open container of liquor in my car and twice for possession of marijuana. I was told that if I wanted to see my child again, and not have her put up for adoption, I had to attend the dropout program I'm in now. With all of my other choices looking pretty bad, plus the fact that I get paid for attending the school program, I decided to give it a try.

At first I went to the program mainly because I was paid to go, and I needed the money. I got paid at the end of each week, but only if I attended regularly, so I did. But no one said I was getting paid to be nice to anyone, so in the beginning, for the most part I wasn't. For the first two weeks of the program, I thought, "I hate this school. I hate these people—both the teachers and the students. This is boring!" Those are my usual feelings about everything. But in the third week of the program, something happened that changed everything.

One of the younger, more hip teachers began teaching us how to use the computer. To keep us interested, she linked us to a group of other young people—who were pretty much the same as we were (losers), except they lived in another country, in Bogotá, Colombia. For nearly three weeks, our class and the group of students in Bogotá talked back and forth using the computer. It was really pretty interesting because these other kids considered themselves, like us, losers and so we had a lot in common. But one day our class learned they were very different from us: They were orphaned and living in an orphanage! That was a totally new idea to me.

The more these kids learned about me and my class, the more they thought we were just whiners. They even thought we were privileged because we had what they had never experienced—parents, public schools, shopping malls, arcades, freedom to come and go in our lives—while they lived in an orphanage, were not free to come and go as they liked, had no parents, not even relatives who came to visit. Not one single kid had ever, ever received a gift from anyone. Not ever. Our class couldn't imagine such a life. And of course, they couldn't even relate to a life like ours; our lives seemed very magical to them. As we got to know more and more about them, and understand more about their lives, all of a sudden we did begin to feel privileged.

So, my class decided to send them some things, like T-shirts, fad jewelry, CDs, things they never had. All the students seemed to come alive—everyday the class buzzed with talk about what we could give the kids in Bogotá. We went door to door in neighborhoods to collect things for them, and solicited businesses for things they wanted to donate. This project consumed us. Every day became an exciting adventure of pursuing our goal and of puzzling out ways we could accomplish it. I couldn't wait to return to school the next day to share in the latest development. And I truly believe that each member of our class felt this way, too. And of course, we couldn't wait to get to our computers to tell our new friends what we had found for them and intended to send them. And we couldn't wait to learn of their enthusiasm and awe in what we were doing for them. Their words back to us made us feel so needed, so purposeful, like such good human beings. And the more our friends in Bogotá expressed their joy and disbelief in their good fortune, the more my class wanted to do for them. It was an incredible high!

Our efforts resulted in nearly fifty boxes of things to send! And then came the realization of our new dilemma—we had no money to send these things all the way to Bogotá! As it turned out, our teacher and a friend of hers came to the rescue. She had a friend who worked for Airline Ambassadors, a goodwill volunteer group that provides humanitarian assistance to families and communities. Together they made plans to fly the things we had collected to our Bogotá friends over the Christmas holiday. Our teacher videotaped the whole thing, and when she returned she showed us the video. It was so amazing and touching! The kids in Bogotá were overcome that anyone would want to be so generous with them, most especially other kids, kids who lived so very far away from them—kids who were "losers," too!

Our class watched the video our teacher made of them as they opened the boxes of items we'd gathered for them. And this time, it was our class that was overcome with tears as we watched the looks of surprise and tears of joy on their faces as they saw the things we had collected. And then we talked with them by computer. It was a moving experience.

To say that not one member in my class has been the same since would be an understatement! It has made us want to do even more. We are now in the process of putting together several projects to help raise money. We haven't decided if we're going to use the money to give to these children, or if we will use it to visit them in person. Maybe we'll send it to them so that they can come and visit us. And we're talking about ways to get other teens around the world interested in doing things for other children in other places in the world. And, we've decided that doing things for others is a good way to use our lives. We are searching for ways—each of us in our own way—to make a living out of our newfound interests. For me, I'm now certain that I want to get my high school diploma. I'd like to go to college to study to become a teacher or a counselor, preferably working with kids that others consider "losers."

Perhaps more than anything else, the experience has motivated me to put my life back together. One of my first priorities is to get my baby back. Because of the way I've been leading my life, my baby was taken away from me and put in a foster home. Though I've always missed my little girl, I wasn't responsible enough to do something positive to change my life so that I could change her life. I no longer feel so worthless—or powerless. I've decided to stop blaming others for my problems. I've decided to go beyond merely feeling sad and angry about my not taking care of my little daughter. Instead, I am going to do something about it. I don't want my baby to live without me. I don't want her to wonder if she is loved. I don't want her to be deprived like the children in the orphanage. And more than anything else, I don't want her to grow up ashamed of me. I don't want her to ever think that she is a loser. And I don't want anyone to ever call her a loser. And I want her to know the exhilaration that comes from helping others in the world.

I know these are words on paper, and actions speak louder than words. But I also know that a fire deep within me has been ignited. I intend never to allow it to burn out. I will not allow me—or you—to snuff it out. Ever.

So the next time you see someone you think is a loser, reserve criticism and save your harsh words. Instead, offer up some encouragement. You never know, you may just turn someone's life around, like my teacher did when she believed in a bunch of "losers." Trust me when I say that I know what it's like to have lost your way, and I know how important it is to find someone who will show you a new way—a positive way.

I am not a loser. At least not any longer. For me, there are many chapters yet to write in my book. And who knows, maybe the stories written by those of us who have been losers will be the most important of all!

Lisa Cartwright, 16

A Gift in Disguise

I really wanted a certain part in the spring play our high school drama club was putting on. I knew I'd be great in the part because I'd been in plays for the last three years and really like acting. Plus, it's such an honor to get selected for a good role and all. I've even thought about being an actor.

Well, I didn't get the part. The teacher asked each of us to help with the lighting and sound, as well as with other behind-the-scenes roles. Two of my buddies were so upset at not being chosen for the lead role that they said no to the behind-the-scenes work. I have to admit, it was my first thought, too, because I was disappointed I wasn't getting chosen for the part. At first I figured, well, I'll just wait and try out for the next play—which was only three months away. But then I decided, why not learn all you can about the theater? It might come in handy to know this stuff.

Boy, did I find out how true that was! Not only did I learn that I was really good at production and behind-the-scenes work, I also found out I enjoyed it. What I didn't know was that I would enjoy it even more than acting! Now I'm certain that I want to be a film producer. Move over, Steven Spielberg!

As it turned out, it was really good that I didn't get chosen for the part. I'm happy that I agreed to work backstage. It was a gift in disguise—because I've discovered my acre of diamonds.

Richard Lewis, 17

College Is My Next Destination

When my cousin Alex, who is already a college graduate, asked me what college I planned to go to, I said, "To tell the truth, I'm not sure what kind of career I want, so how can I know what college I want to go to? Why should I even go to college?"

"Go to college," Alex said firmly. "Believe me, it gives you four more years to think about what you want to do and that can be helpful because sometimes it's hard to know what you want to be when you're still in your teens. It'll give you time to get it all figured out—and besides, except for studying, college is *great* fun!"

Alex gave me some great suggestions. First, he told me to go talk to my guidance counselor at school. It turned out she had all sorts of information for me. Once I started looking into colleges, I began to get a lot of different literature with information on all sorts of different schools. I received brochures, applications and other information from colleges all over the country.

Next, Alex told me that I should go visit all the schools I was most interested in attending. Through my guidance counselor, I found out that my high school even offers a tour of four of the major universities in my home state, so I signed up for it. Alex said if my school didn't offer the tour, I could have called the admissions office at each of the universities and asked to arrange tours that way. Most universities offer tours and orientations for potential applicants during spring break, but Alex said it's even better to see the schools during their regular day-to-day operations—that way you can walk around, check things out, sit in on classes and ask yourself whether you'd be happy going to school there.

I also learned about books that rank colleges. You can find them in any library reference section. They rank each school academically, financially and by certain majors—some books even describe campus life. When I went to check out these books, I found another book that shows which colleges to attend and which subjects to study if you want to make a difference in the world. That book really gave me a lot to think about. Now, I'm looking into becoming an environmentalist.

For my birthday, Alex gave me a great gift: a software program that helps you choose the right college! There are lots of different software programs designed specifically for that purpose. Mine gives me information—good, brief overviews—on sixteen hundred four-year colleges and universities. It prompts me with questions and my answers create my own personal profile. Then, I can rank and categorize my own college preferences. All this will help later when I have to answer questions on the college applications. After using the program, I realize that college is the best choice for me. I'm also learning tips for coping with dorm life, writing application essays, getting letters of recommendation and qualifying for financial assistance.

I'm glad I'm lucky enough to have Alex for a cousin. He really pushed me in the right direction. Every time he sees me, he asks how I'm doing and what progress I'm making. "Going to college is one of life's most important road trips," he always tells me, "so it takes a lot of thought and research. But don't let the stress of all those major decisions take the fun out of planning for it! In the end, it's the adventure of a lifetime—make sure you have fun as you mark your destination."

I still don't know my exact career destination, but I do know I'm going to go to college. Now I see college as an important step toward choosing a career. And, as Alex helped me see, a good education, even if just for its own sake, is a worthy goal.

Danny Benjamin, 17

My U-Turn in Life

Drugs consumed me. My life went from bad to worse, and then worse still.

I was selling everything I owned, borrowing from everyone I could think of, stealing and lying all the time. My whole world crashed in on me. Drug abuse made a complete disaster of my life.

Luckily, I got pulled over for an illegal U-turn one day and the police officer suspected (rightly so) I was high on something. I spent five days in juvenile hall before I was finally released to my parents. The juvenile authorities only released me with the condition that I promise to get help.

I did. By that time, I knew what a hell my life had become. I also knew that I needed help and change. It was the only way I could save my life. This time, I had to discover myself, the real me; I had to get out of my denial, get honest, become a real person. It was either that or death. I had to practice rigorous honesty in everything I said and did. Before, when I didn't, I'd relapse and return to the hell of addiction, a place I never wish to be again.

I've been drug-free for two years now, and I'm working full-time. Now I'm interested in using what I've learned and experienced to help others. I'd like to be a drug counselor and work with troubled teens. I feel I have something to offer since I've been there. I have had experiences that were vital to making me the person I am now. I have grown to appreciate that I can help others. So, I've enrolled in junior college to get my GED, and I'm taking courses toward a career doing just that. More than anything else, I'm doing more than surviving day by day. Now, I'm thriving on my goals day by day.

Josh Henderson, 19

10

A Mine of Diamonds

I AM, I CAN, I WILL

I AM—two small words, and yet,
It's a powerful "place" in which to be.
It's my life, and I'm living it,
I am everything you see.

I am responsible for my actions,
And all the things I say and do.
I am responsible for my behavior,
And how I interact with you.

I am responsible for the level of my work,
And the choices that I make.
I am responsible for the values I profess,
And for the ways that I communicate.

I CAN—two small words, and yet,
It's a powerful "place" in which to be.

It's my life and I'm living it,
Traveling the land, sky and sea.

I can earn the respect of others,
And gain their friendship true.
I can honor all things living, and
Take care of my mind, health and body, too.

I can do my best each day,
And I can know my best is great.
I can continue to progress,
And move closer to my fate.

I WILL—two small words, and yet,
It's a powerful "place" in which to be.
It's my life and I'm living it,
I will be everything, just wait and see.

I will use my talents wisely,
Learn to manage the moods of life.
I will respect my ups and downs,
Ask for help in overcoming strife.

I will is a promise to see clearly,
It reveals my strength to win.
As I arrive at mutual resolutions,
And look for my answers from within.

I'm young, still learning, growing, changing,
Yet I have ideals, noble goals and plans,
For things like a healthy environment,
World peace and a crime-free land.

No longer a child, yet not an adult,
I am a teenager still.
But don't underestimate my value,
Because I am, I can and I will.

Jennifer Leigh Youngs

A Word from the Authors

Everywhere you look, teenagers are making awesome contributions to the world; their achievements are nothing less than spectacular! Last year, of the twenty teens named to *USA Today's* All-USA High School Academic First Team, fifteen had perfect 4.0 grade point averages and eight had perfect SAT scores. Over nine hundred teens have been honored by the Youth Hall of Fame for their contributions to their communities. Some 120 teenagers made it into the sports hall of fame. Just think about the number of teens who participate in the Olympics and other major sporting events. Teenagers around the world are among those who are winning awards for intellectual achievement, social contributions and athletic excellence. The number of teens achieving great things is phenomenal; their inspiration is precious beyond measure.

"You know, Mom, after reading about teens who are achieving such spectacular things, it's only natural to compare your accomplishments with theirs. To this day, my favorite poster is still the one I hung on my door in high school, the one with the baby chick just outside of the eggshell, saying, 'Now what?' At that time, the big saying was 'Fly with the eagles!' and I just kept thinking, *Fly with the eagles?—I'm still standing outside the shell going, 'What next?'"*

"I thought it was a pretty cute poster, too, Jennifer. I guess we need to remind teens that whether or not their own accomplishments compare to those of the teens in this chapter, they shouldn't become discouraged—even eagles need a push!"

In his beautiful book, *Even Eagles Need a Push*, David McNally reminds us of an important truth about the great soaring eagles. The mother eagle builds her nest high on the shelf of a sheer rock face. Around and below her nest there seems to be nothing but endless miles of open space. Those few moments when a baby eagle peers out of its nest and into the vast emptiness for the first time must be terrifying because it is only upon being coaxed to the edge of its nest by its mother—and nudged out of it—that the baby eagle ventures to fly.

Why are baby eagles so reluctant? Perhaps they wonder if their wings will support them in the air—if they will prevent them from tumbling to the earth below. Perhaps they wonder why the thrill of soaring has to begin with the fear of falling. But the mother eagle knows that in spite of her "children's" resistance to her persistent nudging, until her young discover their wings and learn to soar, they won't make it in life—nor will they understand the privilege it is to be an eagle. Knowing what she must do is a part of her innate wisdom. And so, one by one, she pushes them.

And they fly.

Like the baby eagle, sometimes people prefer to stay in a place of comfort and have someone bring them their "food." But the goal of life is learning "to fly"—or, in other words, learning to do the things in life that help us stand on our own two feet, to accomplish goals that are important to us. We must become capable, willing and able to find satisfaction and happiness in life.

Life isn't easy—nor should we expect it to be. Just as flying is a skill the eagle must learn, for people, finding meaning, purpose and direction presents its challenges, too. Sometimes we need to unlearn a bad habit or correct a bad decision we've made. If we've hurt someone we must ask their forgiveness and make restitution to make things right. Sometimes it seems as if we've lost our diamond and need to mine for another by learning a better way to live.

The search for your acre and the diamond, as well as the route to learning to fly, may be a bit different for each of us. Even so, it's usually our own work to do. While others love us and are there to support us, we soon discover that each of us has to take responsibility for our own flight. We are each responsible for our own life. But that doesn't mean that we can't ask others for advice, direction or support as we set our goals and work toward achieving them. Once again, we urge you to turn to those friends and adults who can help you put wings to your dreams and direction to your goals. The school counselor is usually a good place to start, but teachers, parents and others almost always find it heartening to help teens find their way in life. We've all been there and know how difficult it is and most of us can remember a time when someone helped us.

Just as the baby eagle gains more and more confidence with each flight it takes, people also gain more and more confidence and grow more and more resilient each time we work through and overcome a hardship. This isn't to say that we won't ever doubt ourselves in the process. Just as the baby eagle quivers as it stands for the first time on the brink of the nest, knowing that he must eventually fly into that vast space of "nothingness," people are sometimes doubtful and fearful, too. But, in the end, we find that learning is liberating—plus, it just feels great. It gives us courage. And, if the challenge sometimes seems too great, we can take heart—even an eagle needs a push. For people—and perhaps eagles, too—it's the price of flying!

Diamonds, Diamonds Everywhere

Everywhere you look, teens are doing great things! Kory Johnson, a teenager from Arizona, waged a student campaign against hazardous waste. Recently, in recognition of her efforts, she received the Goldman Environmental Prize to a North American, an award that carried with it a one-hundred-thousand-dollar prize. Kory's commitment to her cause was inspired neither by the desire for recognition nor prizes. Because her sixteen-year-old sister died of congenital heart problems due to the tainted well-water her mother drank while pregnant, Kory founded Children for a Safe Environment. Through her efforts, Kory has impacted a number of projects on a massive scale. For example, she halted a project that would have placed a hazardous waste incinerator and dump in a poor Arizona community.

Kory is nineteen, a freshman at Arizona State University, and continues to travel all over the country carrying her message of environmental justice and responsibility.

Twelve-year-old Hunter Scott is a diamond, too. After seeing the movie *Jaws*, in which Robert Shaw's character recounts his ordeal as a member of the *Indianapolis* crew who watched sharks maul his shipmates, Hunter became interested in the ship's plight—and then focused his interest on its captain, a naval officer found guilty of negligence.

On July 30, 1945, more than eight hundred sailors, Navy officers and Marines were forced overboard after two torpedoes from a Japanese submarine sank the *U.S.S. Indianapolis*. Spending five days and nights floating in the Pacific, the head count each morning dwindled as the wounded, fatigued or those fallen victim to sharks slipped away overnight. In all, 880 men died. It was the largest wartime loss of life at sea in U.S. Navy history. Discovered only by chance, Navy ships rescued 316 men.

Four months later, the *Indianapolis's* Captain was found guilty of negligence for failing to order his ship to "zigzag" in hostile waters—a charge that many believe made him a scapegoat for Navy brass who didn't want to admit that mistakes were made as the war against the Japanese drew to a close. Hunter, a seventh-grader from Pensacola, Florida, agreed. After contacting 80 of the 150 *Indianapolis* survivors, Hunter learned that most of them believed Captain McVay was wrongly convicted. This set Hunter in motion. He set out to right an old wrong.

Remarkably, Hunter Scott (who in the meantime had also tied this into a history project) then resurrected efforts to clear Captain Charles McVay. Hunter went to Capitol Hill with *Indianapolis* survivors, and rallied support for legislation that will erase all mention of court-martial and conviction from Captain McVay's records, as well as to get a Presidential Unit Citation for the *U.S.S. Indianapolis* and her crew. Just imagine! How's that for righting a wrong?

What does a diamond look like? Here's just a glimpse of some of them sparkling from their hometowns:

In Alexandria, Virginia, Thomas Jefferson High School student Paul Bracher won an award for his research of chemical agents that may lead to better antibiotic delivery and lubrication. His classmate, Jordan Feil, helped create a Holocaust Web site that won an international Internet education competition.

In Naperville, Illinois, Sanjay Basu researched why non-steroidal anti-inflammatory drugs appear to delay the onset and slow the progression of Alzheimer's disease. He discovered that the drugs neutralize radicals and prevent brain plaque from forming—which is a remarkable addition to the work being done to find how to treat Alzheimer's.

In Tempe, Arizona, Ravi Shah conducted brain cancer research to find mechanisms of resistance in the cancer cells that remain after chemotherapy and radiation. This has led to progress in finding a way to combat those resistant cells.

In St. Petersburg, Florida, freshman Andrew Nelson developed a way to predict the long-term stability of the emulsion of any sunscreen. This led to his sophomore-year discovery that some natural chemicals strengthen the photoprotection of existing sunscreens. His compound could cut skin cancer rates by providing 150 percent more photoprotection. (Andrew's already applying for a patent!)

In Pasadena, California, Richard Kim—who scored 1600 on his SAT—got donations of computers for kids in a home for abused children and set up a Web site for them. Richard also coordinated a project to connect nonprofit organizations with student volunteers.

In Moorestown, New Jersey, Adam Hornstine, who is co-captain of his high school debate team and captain of its mock trial team, got other kids involved in community service. He organized M.A.G.I.C. (Moorestown Alliance for Goodwill and Interest in the Community). M.A.G.I.C. has raised funds to organize a food drive, reclaim a vacant lot as a playground and renovate the home of a single parent.

In Great Neck, New York, Michael McNabb is what might be called a "saxophone activist." An accomplished saxophonist, he is actively advancing the use of the saxophone in classical music—introducing and advocating its beauty to both the public and to professionals. Michael also became the first saxophonist to win the Lincoln Center Young Artists Chamber Music Competition.

In Hattiesburg, Mississippi, Christine Vanardo wrote a prize-winning letter to Harper Lee, the notoriously reclusive author of *To Kill a Mockingbird*. Harper was so impressed with Christine's words that, though for decades she has not responded to any public contact (not interviews, calls or mail), she sent Christine a handwritten reply!

In Laguna Hills, California, Farzad Alemi secured corporate

sponsorship for the Helpline's funding to found Homework Helpline (which is student-run) to help other students achieve their own academic excellence.

Talk about "taste berries!"

Bettie B. Youngs and Jennifer Leigh Youngs

Part 6

Giving, Sharing, Making a Difference

Whatsoever things are right, just, pure, lovely or good . . . if there be virtue, if there be praise, report on these things.

—Philippians 4:8

The meaning of life is finding your gift; the purpose of life is giving it away.

—Joy J. Golliver

The spirit of charity exists in all of us. Sometimes the brightest sparks come from the smallest fires. There is power in every act of kindness, however small or grand.

—Deborah Spaide, founder, Kids Care Clubs

Why It Feels Good to Give

11

Do ordinary things with extraordinary love.

—Mother Teresa

FORTY-FOUR GLADIOLAS

One spring, while I was planting fifty gladiola bulbs, my six-year-old asked, "What are you planting, Mommy?"

"Gladiolas, honey," I answered. "My favorite flower."

"More than anything else?" she asked in wide-eyed innocence.

"More than anything else, honey," I replied.

"I wish I had given them to you," she lamented.

"Well, then," I remarked, playing into her need to show me her love, "Whichever ones you hand me, I will believe with all my heart they are from you!" There remained only six bulbs to plant.

The next week it was Mother's Day. To my surprise, my little daughter presented me with a gift, a white shoe box on which

she had drawn blooming flowers. Unable to contain her anticipation of my response to her gift, she put her small hands to her
glee-filled face and squealed in delight, "Now you can say ALL
of them are from me!" The box was filled with gladiola bulbs—
forty-four of them! My daughter had dug up the bulbs I had
planted the week prior—so that when I [re]planted them, they
would be from her.

Bettie B. Youngs

A Word from the Authors

"Mom, I can't believe you're telling that story about the forty-
four gladiolas in a book for teens. Besides, it makes me sound
like a little geek!"

"On the contrary, Jennifer, I think it's a darling story. And I
don't think it makes you look like a geek at all, but rather, points
out how natural it is to want to give. You were only a child, and
needed to show your love. Intuitively you knew that 'giving'
was a way to do that. Your gesture was innocent of all hidden
agenda, which makes it even that much more sweet."

"Giving *is* a sweet gesture, but besides that, it feels so good to
do things for others."

Luckily, the need to give never goes away. This past week, my
daughter, now twenty-four, handed me a bouquet of flowers,
watching intently for my reaction. When I swooned at the beauty
of the flowers—and her gesture of giving them to me—her eyes
lit up and a beautiful ear-to-ear smile appeared. Buying the flowers for me had elicited her joy, but seeing my happiness in receiving them had made her joy complete.

In the stories in this chapter, you'll meet teens whose experiences, while sometimes vastly different from each other, all lead
to validating the phrase "It's more fun to give than receive."
Sixteen-year-old Steve Hand volunteered to spend "time" with a
group of young boys in a shelter, and discovered that it wasn't

his time that was valued as much as the bracelet he was wearing! And Mr. Paul, the school custodian, found out what students thought of his "time." After being voted Citizen-of-the-Year by the kids in his school, seventeen-year-old Kevin Lloyd thanked them, and then surprised everyone when he told them he wanted to share the award with someone special—Mr. Paul, the custodian. Shaking as he spoke, Mr. Paul humbly thanked the students and told them that in his entire life, it was the only award he'd ever received. With tears in his eyes, he walked off stage holding the plastic award as though it were a precious piece of crystal.

Robyn also received a gift—every couple of days as a matter of fact! Robyn thought they were left by "angels," but fourteen-year-old Paige Williams tells us who really left them! Thirteen-year-old Rhonda Klemmer made a difference to Cindy Lindburg when she told her she'd have more friends if she didn't "smell so bad." Fifteen-year-old Becky Coldwell did some explaining as well: "What goes around, comes around," her father had told her. When testing this principle, Becky detects something even *more* important.

All in all, teens discovered a simple truth about giving, sharing and doing things for others: While it made a difference in the lives of those they served, it also made a difference in their own. Sixteen-year-old Kevin Pauls said that helping others is a way to "earn a merit badge in life."

Teens say that kind words and actions are among the things we "give." They help make the world a "better place." Being kind and considerate can remind us that while we live in a world where someone may walk through a door and not hold it open for you, or someone may even take someone's life without any regard for it, many teens go out of their way to be courteous, kind and to assist each other. And to make the world a loving place in which to be.

And that's what being a "taste berry" is all about!

Citizen of the Year

My school held an annual end-of-the year awards assembly to recognize those students who, in one way or another, stood out because of their exceptional performance in sports, academics, extracurricular activities or who brought honor to the school in some way. As each award was handed out, the audience clapped, hooted, whistled and cheered wildly. Finally came the award for best citizenship, to be given to the person who had most contributed in a positive and significant way to our school.

The award went to Kevin Lloyd. He was not only on the football team, but was also student body vice-president and president of Youth for a Better Tomorrow. Kevin leaped up on stage, his customary enthusiasm and charisma present in his bright eyes and sincere smile. "Thanks," he said in the midst of our applause. "This is an honor, thank you. I appreciate this honor everyone—*but*," his voice rose to quiet the applause, "there's someone who deserves this more than I do."

The crowd grew silent at his unexpected words. "Someone who spends more hours at this school than any of us. Someone who gets here before we do, and he's here long after we're gone. Someone who can be found picking up a candy wrapper or a soda can carelessly discarded. Someone who has attended just about every special event, every football, baseball, basketball, softball and soccer game this school has held. You name it, he's there, cheering the team on, cleaning up before and after, taking pride in everything about this school. And he never lets that get in the way of offering a helping hand or giving a word of encouragement to any of us, either. I've seen him out in the parking lot helping a student change a tire. I've seen him walking students to the nurse's office when they didn't feel too well. I've seen him listen when someone just needed to talk. I've seen him offering encouragement to us kids to help us turn a 'bummer-of-a-day' attitude into a positive outlook. I've seem him joke with students, and I've seen him just listen and be there for a student with a broken heart, his own eyes looking as sad as the kid's. I've seen him search through garbage cans looking for an assignment that a student thought had been inadvertently thrown away. I could go on and on, but I don't need to. I'm sure you all know who I'm talking about—Mr. Paul—and I'd like to give this award to him."

Rising to their feet, the audience went wild, chanting, "Mr. Paul! Mr. Paul! Mr. Paul!" Mr. Paul looked a little embarrassed and overwhelmed, still he beamed as he was coaxed by students to get up on stage and take his award.

That day, Mr. Paul, our school's tireless and dedicated custodian, was named our *Citizen of the Year* to enthusiastic whoops of applause and approval.

Mr. Paul, with tears in his eyes, walked up and accepted the award, his words simple. "Thank you so much. I don't know what to say other than I've only done two important things in my whole entire life. The first was serving this fine school in a job I've loved. And the second was having you share this award with me, because it makes me realize that you know I love you all as much as I do."

With that, Mr. Paul, who in just three months would retire from the school district, stepped down. With his eyes still teary—and a smile that stretched from ear to ear—he held the plastic award as though it were a precious crystal. It was the only time he'd ever been publicly recognized for his dedication, his consistently thorough work, his endless acts of giving, and for a lifetime of service to others.

Remember, though, it took someone thoughtful and kind and secure in himself, like Kevin Lloyd, to make it happen.

Jennifer Leigh Youngs

"His" Bracelet

I had gone with a group of seven teens from our church to spend a day with children in a shelter for abused and abandoned kids. We all met at the church and then took a van to the shelter, about an hour away from our town.

The kids at the shelter had heard that a group of "big kids" was coming to spend the day with them, and they were really excited about it. When we drove in their gated yard, the children stood anxiously waiting for us. Some were jumping up and down in anticipation, others had big smiles, and some just stood looking, as though they were suspicious. One little boy in particular caught my attention. His hands were jammed in his pockets, his shoulders were drawn up, and his head was lowered. The little guy just glared at us, his eyes filled with a look of incredible mistrust. It was disquieting.

We got out of the van and were playfully "attacked" by children wanting to give us high-fives and wanting us to put them on our backs for piggyback rides, which we did. We'd come to play with the children, to be their "big brothers" for the day. That was the purpose of our coming, to have fun with them, to play, read and sing songs with these boys.

Right after lunch, we did a sing-along. Three of the guys from our group brought guitars and tambourines and we began a session of songs. I sat in the back to see how things were going and to encourage the boys in the back to sing along. As I looked over at the group, Charlie, the boy I'd noticed glaring at us when we arrived, was looking in my direction, staring at the bracelet I wore. I didn't think too much about it. It was a thick silver bracelet, with fancy black hieroglyphic engravings. When I had first seen it in a store window several weeks before, it attracted my attention, too. I loved it the instant I saw it and knew I had to have it, so I bought it. I wore it all the time.

I watched Charlie for a moment, and when he glanced at me, I smiled at him. He didn't return the smile, and quickly turned his eyes from mine. I continued observing the kids in the group. Several minutes later, I noticed Charlie once again just staring at my bracelet. So I just watched him, wondering what he was thinking, and wondering what I could do to let him know that it was okay for him to trust me—at the least, to smile at me.

When Charlie realized I was looking at him, this time, rather than turning away, he pointed at the bracelet—and smiled! Obviously, he liked it. I smiled back, and got up and went over and sat down beside him. Though he seemed a little nervous, Charlie continued to smile, and then, ever so slowly, he reached over—all the while watching my eyes—and gently touched my bracelet.

Thinking it would be a nice gesture to let him try it on, I took the bracelet off and placed it on his wrist. You should have seen how large his eyes became. A smile lit up his whole face. I could see how much it meant to him, so I decided I'd let him wear the bracelet for a while. It was a good move, with good results! Charlie sat beside me for the remainder of the songs, holding my hand and leaning his head against my arm!

As soon as the songs were over, Charlie jumped up and ran over to show the other children the bracelet he was now wearing. His wearing the bracelet attracted the attention of most all the other boys, and within moments, the entire group of boys had circled around him. Charlie, his words serious and insistent, pointed in my direction and said to the other boys, "*He* gave it to *me*!" All heads turned to look in my direction, and then back at the bracelet Charlie was wearing. As though it were a precious object, each of the boys took turns touching the bracelet, murmuring their approval. With a look of pride, Charlie spoke slowly, carefully and with a great deal of respect as he said yet again, "He gave it to me!"

When I saw how special the bracelet was to him, and saw how

much it meant to have someone give it to him—even though it was mine and I loved the bracelet and wanted it for myself—I said, "It's for you. It's *your* bracelet."

Charlie smiled and tears welled up in his eyes. "For me," he confirmed. "It's for me."

"Yes it is," I assured him. Charlie just stood there grinning. It was easy to see how he was moved by the gesture of having been given the bracelet.

I thought about Charlie all the way home. In the morning, he had been scared and mistrusting, by the afternoon he was holding my hand as we did a sing-along. It was such a big change. And the bracelet—it meant so much to him to have someone give him something that he obviously liked so much. Though I had initially expected to take my bracelet back, Charlie's excitement over the bracelet made it necessary that he have it. In turn, I was truly happy that I let him have it.

I went there to volunteer my time, to sing and read and play with the boys. That was to be the gift I was giving. But it was giving Charlie my prized bracelet that was the best gift of all. To him. And to me.

Steve Hand, 16

Left by the Angels

It's amazing how much even little things, like basic kindness and gestures of caring, can help someone—most especially if they are going through a tough time in life. Like Robyn.

Robyn is my father's secretary. She is one of the nicest people I've ever met. She makes me feel special. Probably she makes everyone feel that way.

She likes everyone. Especially her husband; she's always talking about him. And, she's just crazy about her dog, Bandit. She keeps tons of pictures of both of them on her desk at work.

Besides being a very good secretary to my father, Robyn is a good friend to me. My father is often away on business and sometimes my mother travels with him. When they're away together, Robyn takes care of me.

Because she is such a nice, caring and thoughtful person, I just could never imagine that anything bad would ever happen to her.

But it did.

First, her mom died suddenly of a stroke. Less than two weeks later, her husband, a Navy SEAL, had a fatal heart attack while swimming in their pool. But her terrible luck didn't end there. After her husband died, she had to sell her home and move into a small apartment building that didn't allow dogs in the building, so she had to give Bandit away. Robyn gave Bandit to her brother who lived in another city with his wife and kids. While Bandit has a good home with them, she misses her dog a lot. I can't imagine giving a pet away. That's got to be hard.

And it's got to be hard to have so many changes going on in your life—like Robyn has in hers. It's amazing how much Robyn's life changed in just one year. It's been really hard on her, too. My mom says Robyn is suffering from depression. So my father gave Robyn a month off work so she could get to feeling better. I don't think it helped. Whenever we called her, she sounded really in the dumps.

Our family knew that she was going through a terrible time. She didn't have her husband. She didn't have Bandit. And she really didn't see many of her friends now that she'd moved from her neighborhood and into an apartment on the other side of town. I think it was even worse on her that she didn't have her work. At least in my father's office she had things to do. And she had us.

Because I go to my father's office every day after school until my mother arrives to pick me up, I missed Robyn as much as my father did. Which is a lot. We all missed her.

We thought about what we could do to cheer her up. So every other day or so, when my mom or dad was taking me to school, we drove by her place. We'd stop just short of her building and I would sneak up to her door and place a little something on her doormat—without her knowing it. Sometimes it would be a bouquet of hand-picked flowers; a little basket of bubble bath and bath salts; a book. Once we gave her a little music box that played her favorite song. Sometimes we mailed her a card from a post office on her side of town.

A month later, Robyn returned to work. One day when I was in my father's office, she said to me, "It sure is nice to be back, but I'm sure going to miss that little angel."

"Angel?" I asked, wondering what she was talking about.

"Oh, yes," Robyn explained. "Every few days, a little gift appeared on my doorstep. The gifts were from a little angel reminding me that I wasn't alone. Receiving those little gifts was a spark of kindness when my life seemed so sad."

Of course, I pretended that I had no idea what she was talking about, but hearing how happy these things had made her, I was really glad we did them for her.

We never did tell her that it was our family who left the gifts. But, from that day on, our family became even more important to her. And Robyn goes out of her way even more to be nice to me—if that's possible. Just three days ago she took me to see *Titanic*—for the third time. (She said three times would be her limit on any one movie. My parents took me once, and said seeing any movie once is enough.)

I'm so happy our family gave Robyn the little gifts because I think having someone care about her at a time when so many terrible things had happened to her made her less depressed. Though Robyn thinks the angels left the gifts for her, I think it is the angels who gave Robyn to us—to be in my family's life, both as my dad's secretary and as our friend—my friend.

So, if you ever have a chance to do something to help ease the pain of someone, do it. It helps them, and it's a good feeling, too. Every time I was taking a gift to leave on her doorstep and for days afterwards, the feeling inside of me was wonderful. And now that I see how much it helped her stay "together" and get through a rough time, I can see how important it is that we do things for other people.

Doing something kind for someone is a great feeling.

Paige Williams, 14

The Girl No One Talked To

Last year there was a girl at our school who hardly anyone talked to. I think it was because she seldom showered, and she kind of smelled bad. Her name was Cindy Lindburg. I didn't know exactly where she lived, but it must have been somewhere in the neighborhood because we always got on the school bus at the same bus stop.

Cindy Lindburg didn't have many friends. She always came to the lunch room alone and she left alone. On the bus, no one offered her a seat, and she never asked if she could share a seat with others. I thought that maybe it was because she was sort of a shy person. She seemed like a nice girl—who had an odor problem.

One day, I was walking up to the bus stop and I saw Carl Littleton making fun of her. I couldn't hear what he was saying, but I saw the way he was laughing and rolling his eyes in his typical poking-fun-at-you way. I also saw how sad it made Cindy. Clutching her notebook to her chest like a shield, she stared at the ground and moved as far away from him as possible without leaving the bus stop entirely. As soon as I got close enough, I glared at Carl to make him stop laughing—even though I knew he probably wouldn't. He didn't, so I walked over and stood closer to Cindy so she wouldn't feel quite so bad. It was just one of those times when you just know someone needs someone to be a friend.

I didn't think she'd say anything, but she did. Her eyes peeked up from staring at the ground and as though she thought I'd be embarrassed if anyone heard her speak to me, she whispered "Hi."

"Hi," I said. Then as loudly as I could, I said, "Don't pay any attention to Carl. His parents have been unsuccessful in teaching him some manners."

Some of the kids standing there laughed. The comment didn't even rouse a smile out of Cindy. By now everyone there was talking with a friend. Quietly, and with a serious look on her face, Cindy said, "I don't know why everyone hates me."

I was surprised at her words. "No one hates you," I told her.

"Then why don't I have any friends?" she asked.

Her question took me by surprise. I thought for a moment. "Well," I began, wondering if I could tell her that maybe it was because she smelled so awful, "I think you're really nice and I think that the kids at school think you're smart and all, and you dress okay, and . . ."

"So then, what is it?" she blurted.

"Well," I hedged and then figured it's now or never. "Maybe it's because you. . . ." I paused because I almost said "stink" but said instead, "don't smell so good."

She looked up, studying my face as if checking to see if I was making fun of her or being mean. I guess she decided I wasn't. She nodded, like she believed what I said was true. Since she seemed to take this well, I added, "I think you'd probably make more friends if you took more baths." She looked away and, worried that I might have gone too far, I shrugged and added, "It's just a thought." (My mom says that sometimes when she gives me advice.)

Turning back to face me, Cindy took a deep breath and said, "Thank you."

I was so relieved, and the next moment the bus arrived, and all the kids started piling on.

"If I save a seat for you on the bus tomorrow," she asked, "will you sit with me?"

"Sure," I said.

I'm happy to report that Cindy did take more baths from that day on. And it wasn't too long before she started to make friends at school. I was one of them.

I made a difference for the better in Cindy's life. And got a new friend to boot!

Rhonda Klemmer, 14

Merit Badges for Life

When I was younger, I was a Boy Scout. I'm not now, but I miss being involved with Boy Scouts from the standpoint that we did a lot of good deeds for people. The Boy Scouts had a list of things you could do to earn your various merit badges.

One merit badge was in community service. One year, I chose to help out two Saturdays a month in a group home for developmentally disabled adults. I especially enjoyed helping the residents decorate for Christmas. The adults looked up to me, and they appreciated my help. Being able to help the disabled adults do the things that they couldn't do and teaching them how to do things they didn't know to do made me feel needed. Helping them made me realize how we often take things we know how to do for granted, and might not even think about having to be taught to do them—like how to make popcorn in the microwave, or how to plant a packet of seeds.

As I got to know the people more on an individual basis, I began to know more about each of their personalities and the things that just gave them so much joy. I especially got a kick out of Bobby Henry because he loved motorcycles. He really had a thing for them! As soon as I arrived each Saturday morning, Bobby greeted me with the news of every motorcycle he had seen in the past two weeks. He was nonstop chatter, describing each bike in exact detail. When I told him I wanted to get a bike when I could afford one, he got so excited, carefully explaining what model (and why) I should buy! Because he was so into motorcycles, every now and then I'd bring him a motorcycle magazine with pictures of fancy motorcycles in it. He loved that! Then he'd add it to his treasured collection—one he had shown me many times. I knew that when he saw me, there was an instant connection between me and his love of motorcycles. It showed in his face, in his smile and in his eyes. My listening to his detailed accounts of the motorcycles and taking the time as he pointed out and described the various features of the motorcycles made him so happy. Thinking of Bobby always brings a smile to my face. Whether I was helping Bobby or any of the other disabled adults in the home, I always felt needed. Being needed and helping is a great feeling. I stopped working in the group home soon after I left the Boy Scouts, and to tell you the truth, I really haven't done much volunteering since then.

And I've noticed something. When I was in Boy Scouts and helping others, it felt like a "routine" thing to do. And, I saw myself as a helpful sort of person, one who could be counted on when someone needed me. Now it seems like every year I do less and less for others, and sometimes I feel put out, even irritated, when someone asks me to take time out of my day to do something for him or her.

There's an older man that lives in our neighborhood, and his son called from another state and asked if our family would stop in to check on him from time to time (which my mom does). Last week, my mom asked me to stop by a pharmacy to pick up some Epsom salts he needed, and I remember thinking, "I don't want to stop by the pharmacy, park, go in and search around for Epsom salts." It wasn't until I was on my way home that I realized how selfish I'd become, thinking that running a little errand for an elderly man was somehow an imposition for me.

I guess I'm lucky to have thought about how much I've changed, and to realize I missed the more generous, giving me that I was when I belonged to Boy Scouts. Boy Scouts taught me the importance of earning merit badges—most especially the kind you wear in your heart.

I miss the kind of giving I was able to do at the group home. I need to think about how to get involved in helping others again, because I miss that part of my life.

Kevin Pauls, 16

"No Big Deal!"

Last year our class went to the roller rink as a reward for having perfect attendance for a full semester. It was the first time I had ever been to a roller rink. I loved it, but I had a hard time standing up on the skates. I kept falling down, and some of the other kids laughed at me.

A lady who works at the snack bar called me over and gave me a free soda. All she said was, "Looks like you need this." As she talked, she counted out coins from the apron she was wearing. It probably was her tip money. She rang up the soda, paying for it with her money.

I guess she'd seen me falling—and the kids laughing. I thanked her.

"No big deal," she said. "You looked like you could use cheering up!"

It worked. As the other kids watched me get my free soda, I didn't feel like such a clumsy jerk. And I think they must have thought I was someone special to have someone just hand me a soda—one I didn't have to pay for.

That soda made a big difference to me. For the rest of the time I was there, no one said a word when I fell down—some kids even boosted me up as they skated by and saw that I was about to fall. Some even reached out to pull me along with them!

Just one person, even someone I didn't know, taking the trouble to notice that I felt embarrassed and then doing something to cheer me up, made me feel better. It made a real difference to me.

She may have said "no big deal," but a soda on that day was a big deal to me!

Mark Howard, 12

Not Always to the Sender

My father uses the expression, "What goes around comes around." He says that when we're good to others or do good things for them, they're usually good to us back. But my mother says a payback for a good deed doesn't always come back to the sender, but sometimes, to someone else. I think they both may be right.

Three weeks ago, as I was going to class, I saw Gia Hayes making a mad dash to class when suddenly her books and papers slipped from her arms and went flying every which way down the hallway. Gia became so frustrated that all she could do was stand there and cry. So I stopped to help Gia gather her things.

Helping Gia made me late to Mrs. Wentworth's class. I was scared, too, because Mrs. Wentworth is a very strict teacher. You can't be even one minute late to her class without getting a detention, which means you have to stay after school ten minutes for every minute you're late to class. But on that day, for some reason, Mrs. Wentworth didn't say a thing. She wasn't upset and she didn't keep me after school. You can imagine how relieved I was! I'd like to think that was my payback for helping Gia; like my dad says, "what goes around comes around"—and mine came from Mrs. Wentworth.

That very same afternoon, I saw something that made me think about what my mother says, about how payback for a good deed doesn't always come back to the sender, but can come back to someone else.

I was sitting on the bus after school when I saw Lindsey Deutch, running as fast as she could so she'd reach the bus before it took off. She lost her footing and slipped and fell down, practically landing on her face. I mean, her whole body was flat against the ground. It must have hurt, too. As she scrambled to her feet, straightening her backpack over her shoulder, I could see a big rip all the way down the back of her skirt. I could also see her horror as she discovered it herself. Right then, along came Gia Hayes. Gia took one look at Lindsey's problem, whipped off her sweater and gave it to Lindsey to wrap around her hips.

You never know just how, where or when a good deed will come back to you. But I do know we could all make the world a better place to live in just by all of us doing our share of good things. That doesn't seem all that difficult to do.

Becky Coldwell, 15

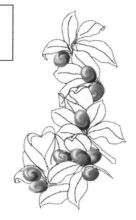

12

One by One by One . . . Makes a Difference Collectively

Do all the good you can, by all the means you can,
in all the ways you can, in all the places you can,
at all the times you can, to all the people you can,
as long as you ever can.

—John Wesley

THE STARFISH

A man was jogging on the beach one day when he came across a boy picking up starfish and frantically slinging them into the ocean. "I'm afraid your efforts are in vain, young man!" the jogger said as he approached the boy. "Hundreds of starfish have been washed ashore here, and they're withering fast in the hot sun. Your well-intentioned efforts simply aren't going to make a difference. You might as well run along and play."

The boy surveyed the many starfish stranded on the beach, then looked at the beautiful starfish he was holding. Flinging it into the ocean, he replied optimistically, "Well, I made a difference to that one!"

A Word from the Authors

"I love this little story, Mom, because it illuminates an ideal we must each take to heart: There is great significance and importance in all our day-to-day actions in both words and deeds."

"That's right, Jennifer. Just as the boy's singular actions made a difference to each individual starfish he touched, we each make a difference one person at a time, one by one by one."

A reporter once asked Mother Teresa, one of the greatest "taste berries" of our times, what she considered to be the single most important thing we can do to make the world a better place. Her answer was simply, "Begin with one single act of kindness—in your family, in your community and everywhere you go. Just begin . . . one, one, one."

As you'll see by the stories in this chapter, teens are making a difference all over the world, one by one by one. Seventeen-year-old Cara Robinson gave up her place in line at the post office and unknowingly saved a mother and her two young children from having the heat turned off in their apartment. Fifteen-year-old Carrie Hague provided "Fred in the Green Shirt" the much-needed exercise he needed to "stay alive"; twelve-year-old Brian Lumke explains the global importance of his rescuing a lizard from the paws of his cat. A "hungry" fourteen-year-old Mike Siciliano tells how thirty hours of hunger helped an elderly woman receive the home cleaning and repairs she needed, and Sadie Murray, fifteen, tells you what she did in exchange for a share in a "stash" of Bazooka bubble gum.

"You know, Mom, I especially enjoyed working on this section of the book because there is something about helping others that just brings out the best in each of us. I'm so happy to include this chapter because I once heard that 95 percent of the news coverage focused on youth is about those involved in drugs, violence and negative gangs, yet only 5 percent of teens ever commit those kind of acts. It seems like teens easily attract attention if they do something wrong, but, in fact, 95 percent of the teens are doing good things. I'm reminded of a story I heard Rabbi Wayne Dosick tell about when his home recently burned to the ground in a wildfire. He said it wasn't just family, friends and the Red Cross who came to his family's aid, but also a group of kids in his neighborhood. They took up a collection of their own money and raised three hundred dollars, then went to the local hardware store to buy tools their neighbors would need to dig through the ashes. When the manager of the store heard what they were doing, he matched their three hundred dollars! As news of what they were doing spread through the store, other customers began donating money, and another five hundred dollars was raised. The next day, all of the kids piled into one of the store's trucks and drove through the neighborhood handing out all the tools to their neighbors—over eleven hundred dollars in shovels, rakes, work gloves, wastebaskets and garbage bags. Teens are thoughtful, helpful and loving."

"Yes, they are, Jennifer, and I think that story makes the point that so many young people are doing such good things."

One act, one word, one person and one day at a time, the stories in this chapter prove that teens are up to the challenge of making a positive difference in the world. Eighteen-year-old Toby Long, an amazing young man, is a powerful example of how teens are making a collective difference in the world. Feeling bad that he refused to give his T-shirt to a little boy who wanted it to protect himself from the scorching sun, Toby organized a T-shirt drive, collecting ten thousand T-shirts for children who need them. Teens involved with Habitat for Humanity travel to places they've never been, with others they've never met, to do something they've never done—namely, build houses from start to finish in two weeks. Like so many other teens, they learn that when joining together for a common purpose, people can accomplish great things.

Everywhere you turn, "taste-berry" teens are helping others. And the effects are far-reaching. There is no absence of "taste berries" in today's teens! Want to get involved? Teens had some great suggestions about the many ways to get involved in doing, giving and making a difference! Authors Joy J. Golliver and Ruth Hayes-Arista have written a book on 301 ways teens can turn caring into action. [See the end of chapter 12.] Check it out!

"Fred in the Green Shirt"

I had only three hours of community service work left for a school project. I was happy to be completing the hours, but bummed that the time it was scheduled for was a bright, sunny Saturday afternoon. I would have preferred to be doing other things.

As my mother dropped me off at the home for elderly Alzheimer's patients where I was to complete my hours, I secretly wished I could leave. "There are so many other places I would rather be," I thought.

Luckily, I willed myself to stay. It turned out to be a very special day.

I was handed a beach ball and told that my first job was to find "Fred in the green shirt" and play "catch the ball" with him. Having been given these instructions, the nurse pointed in the direction of the patio.

I walked onto the patio to find "Fred in the green shirt." He was sitting in a chair, staring into the garden. I asked him if he wanted to play ball. He just looked at me blankly. So I gently tossed the ball at him. A big smile came across his face and as he reached to grab the ball, he almost fell out of his chair. He needed help to stand up, so I helped him up. He stood there grinning at me and then suddenly threw the ball back to me. This went on for about ten minutes, each minute seeming to take forever. It was really a chore for him to concentrate so hard and then to think about each action in tossing the ball back to me.

It was such a monotonous game, and I wondered if he was getting bored with it. My doubts didn't last long. With a serious look on his face he broke the silence with the words, "Good exercise!" And then, with tears in his eyes, he added, "Helps stay alive." The other seniors who had gathered to watch murmured their agreement. Then, all heads turning in my direction, they smiled at me.

In that moment, I knew my afternoon was being well spent. I completed my service hours with a better, happier attitude. I was being helpful after all. Fred needed exercise and was happy that I was patiently providing it.

When it was time for Fred to take a break, he thanked me wholeheartedly—not with words, but with the gratitude and appreciation in his eyes. And it was really important to him that he and I shake hands. "Again, soon," he said, shaking his head with enthusiasm. "Again, soon."

I know that what I did was a simple thing, but I also know that it meant something to someone else. I could see it in his eyes, and in his smile. And it was evident in the seniors who watched with interest as I played ball with him. I believe that what I did was much more than playing ball; by my presence, I had shown an interest in another. I could see that they were thankful and grateful. For Fred getting the exercise—and for me for giving it.

"Fred in the green shirt" was a lesson I won't soon forget. It taught me that all of us—no matter how old or how young, no matter what health condition we are in—need others to show an interest, and to be patient and tolerant. I learned that a simple act of caring can make a difference. I want to believe that I made a difference to Fred that day. And I maybe even made a difference to his children or grandchildren, who would feel good that their father or grandfather had some attention and exercise that day.

Now I stop in at the center every now and then, even without needing hours for a project as motivation for volunteering. And always I check up on "Fred in the green shirt"—who claps his hands in joy the moment he sees me, then searches my hands to see if they're holding a ball.

Which they usually are!

Carrie Hague, 15

Rescue a Lizard

I think that every little thing we do in life makes a difference. This morning before I left for school I rescued a lizard from the paws of my cat. I know it made a difference. That lizard may eat an insect that would have eaten a bud on a flower waiting to bloom, one that a bee would have depended upon for honey, a flower that in turn depends upon the bee to spread its pollen. All species of animals and plants and humans on earth are linked together. As a matter of fact, every living thing is connected to each other in one way or another.

And everything we do, good or bad, makes a difference to living things, including the universe and all its planets. Rescuing a lizard was one way for me to do my part to make a difference. Just like the boy with the starfish, at the very least, I know it made it a difference to the lizard. And I also know how that lizard is connected in the chain of things, so I made a difference on a bigger level as well.

We each have a special role in keeping the world of nature going. Every time a species disappears, the natural world does not work as well as it used to. If too many become extinct, we may find the world doesn't work at all. Think about it.

Brian Lumke, 12

Thirty-Hour Famine

Hard work is usually something I can't stand. In fact, most of the time I avoid it altogether. But recently I found some that I enjoyed. Last year I participated in the Thirty-Hour Famine with my church. This is an event sponsored by World Vision to raise money for starving kids around the world. Teens get together and do not eat for thirty hours straight, and are only allowed to drink juice and water. This was hard enough; usually I eat every hour or two. (Hey, I'm growing!)

The part that was even harder was having to work. The first night was not bad. I arrived at my church and spent the night there. In the morning, however, I woke up starving. But the worst was still not over: A full day of work lay ahead. Our project for the day was to clean up the house of the oldest woman in the church, Alice, who is eighty-five years old. Her house was a real mess. She had piles of boxes and old, dusty knick-knacks lying around. Her windows were so dirty it was nearly impossible to see through them. One of the sliding doors was off its track. Bags of molding garbage lay outside her doorway. The condition of her house made my room look just great.

So we all got to work. With a splitting headache and my stomach rumbling like Mt. St. Helen, I picked up the pail of soap and water and began my assigned task—washing the windows. It seemed like we were cleaning the Empire State Building.

During the time we were all working, all wondering just exactly what we'd gotten ourselves into, and wishing we could punch the friend who talked us into this volunteer stint, Alice hobbled around and marveled at the work being done, remarking what a great a job we were doing and how much she really appreciated our helping her. It was very easy to see that she was not only grateful, but so happy that her house was getting back in order. Perhaps it was just fate, or perhaps it was just because the windows were clean and we could see through them, but as she stood marveling at the windows, the most beautiful little hummingbird fluttered around, hovering to see what was going on inside. The sight of the gracious little bird so delighted Alice. I thought she was going to cry. Her response to the bird quieted the grumbling in my stomach a little, and I tackled the remaining windows with more enthusiasm than the first few I had cleaned.

After all the windows were washed, we stacked the piles of old papers into boxes and hauled them to a recycling bin down at her corner. Several hours later, the place was beginning to look like a real home. Alice kept walking around with her walker, smiling at us, never ceasing to thank us.

My initial bad attitude gave way to my feeling rather good about myself. We had done something really nice for someone, who, because of her age and health, could no longer manage these tasks herself. And, we had turned a cluttered house into a neat and orderly home.

As we were preparing to leave, Alice came out and, grasping our hands, thanked us all. She had tears in her eyes, and she couldn't say thank you enough.

She really truly appreciated what we had done. I thought about her and the work we had done for her all the way home. All the while, the smile on my face was just huge. And it wasn't until walking into my house and being hit by the wonderful smells of dinner cooking that I was reminded that I was hungrier than I'd ever been. I mean, you can only imagine how nearly impossible it is to not to eat for thirty hours!

Months have passed now, but the joy of doing something nice for someone still remains. And I still get a smile on my face when I think of Alice. I had worked hard all day, and it had benefited someone else. I had made an elderly lady very happy, and in the process it made me happy.

Before participating in the thirty-hour hunger drive, I never realized how good it felt to do something for someone else.

Something else also came out of that day. Before it, I never really realized what it feels like to be starving. I've always been sympathetic to those who lack daily food or adequate nutrition, but the thirty-hour famine drive changed my perspective.

Now when I see hungry people, I don't just feel sorry for them, I empathize with them. Helping the hungry is something I now want to make a part of my life. When I pass by a person who is obviously hungry—like those holding those signs that say, "Hungry, will work for food"—I no longer look away or make a funny remark.

Now, when I have some money in my pocket and I can give, I do. And when I don't have anything to give, I become all the more committed to doing what I can whenever I am able. Now, I've also decided to take it upon myself to visit Alice two Saturdays every month, to help her with at least a few of her chores. I won't be starving, so it should be easier than the first time. Besides, making her happy really did make me happy, too.

Mike Siciliano, 14

Bazooka's the Best

It was a beautiful Saturday morning, and I didn't have anything to do, so I went outside to see if I could stir up a game of basketball. The only person around was a twelve-year-old neighbor boy, Matt Henry. "Wanna play?" I yelled to him from across the street, pointing to the basketball hoop that sits in my drive.

"Yeah, sure!" he said, and came running over. He was chomping on a really big wad of bubble gum. I love the smell of bubble gum. When he blew an awesome-sized bubble, I knew I had to have bubble gum, too. "Got any more of that?" I asked.

"I don't know," he said. "Let's go look. I found this in the kitchen drawer just before I was leaving the house. It's Bazooka. I think Bazooka's the best."

We ran across the street to his house, where we searched the kitchen drawers for remaining Bazooka bubble gum. We couldn't find any there, so we searched the drawers in his bedroom, and then the bathroom. There was none in those places, either. So then we searched behind the sofa cushions of his couch and then a big armchair. And that's where we found it! It was old and probably stale but at least it still was in its wrapper—and it was *Bazooka*! "Sorry," he said, handing me the stale piece. "This will have to do. At least it's Bazooka. I'll get a new stash tomorrow when I'm at the store."

We played ball for the next hour or so, and talked about a lot of things, like the schools we each went to. We talked a little about some of our friends and a couple of teachers—especially the tough ones. We discovered we liked some of the same sport teams—and that we had both picked the same guy for the Most Valuable Player. When we got to discussing the new skateboard park in town, Matt said he went there every Sunday morning as soon as it opened, which is at ten o'clock in the morning. Then he invited me to come with him. I told him skateboarding is my most favorite thing in all the world, but that I couldn't go on Sundays because I go to church on Sundays. I told Matt it wouldn't be right missing church.

So then we started discussing church. Matt had a lot of questions. He wanted to know *what* I believed, and *why*. Then he told me what he believed and what "scared" him about religion—and why he admired people who had made a commitment. Then he asked me if he could come with me to church the following Sunday.

He did. He didn't sing the songs or pray the prayers, but I could see that it all seemed important to him. As we were standing outside the church right afterwards, he said, "Thank you for sharing God with me." That's all he said.

We don't always think of telling others about our faith as sharing, but it is. I can't think of any gift that is greater to share with another. As Henry Thoreau said, *"Live your beliefs and you can turn the world around."*

"I owe you a favor," he said as we were getting ready to leave. "Okay," I said, "you can start by sharing your new stash of Bazooka!"

Sadie Murray, 15

Keeping the Heat On

Three weeks ago, I was in the post office buying stamps for a couple of letters I wanted to send. A woman with two very young children was standing in line behind me. Her little kids were cranky and wanted no part of standing in a line. The mother looked as tired and harried as her kids. So, I told the woman she could go before me. She thanked me and got in line in front of me.

There's a cutoff point for serving people at the window of the post office, and it was just a few minutes to closing time. Unfortunately, the line wasn't moving very fast and a postal clerk closed the line off right behind her and before me. His decision meant that I wasn't going to get my letters mailed out that day—and all because I let her get in line in front of me!

At first, I was upset that I had given up my place in line, especially because it meant I'd have to come back another day. But when the woman turned to me and said, "I feel bad that you've been inconvenienced because you gave up your place in line. But I want to thank you for being so courteous. If the payment for my heating bill wasn't postmarked by today, the gas and electric company was going to turn the heat off in my apartment."

By letting her go first, I had made a difference to her and her two small children.

Probably we don't always know when the little things we do make a difference to others, but after learning what it meant to that woman, and how it saved her from having her heat turned off, I've decided to be more thoughtful to others, and to just assume that in some way, it probably mattered to them.

I believe that if we all practice being courteous, if goodwill is our motto, then we can make a really big difference in the world.

When I left the post office, I was not at all upset for the inconvenience of driving there, parking and waiting in line. Instead, I left feeling really good. My having to go back the next day was definitely worth it. Since that day, I've definitely continued to look for ways to help others whenever possible, in whatever small ways I can.

Cara Robinson, 17

The Shirt Off His Back

Feeling a tap on his shoulder while in the middle of distributing food and supplies to people with a group of other workers, eighteen-year-old Toby Long turned around to find an Ethiopian boy standing behind him. Gaunt and looking very tired, the young boy looked first at his own tattered shirt then at Toby's clothes. Next, he asked if he could have Toby's shirt. Toby had traveled to Africa to work for two-and-a-half weeks with World Vision, an organization dedicated to alleviating hunger and suffering around the world. He had a long day of work in the hot sun before him, and wouldn't get back to his camp until night. Toby didn't know what to say to the little boy other than, "I need it, too."

When Toby returned to camp that evening he couldn't stop thinking about the little boy with the big sad eyes, a small child who also spent his days in the scorching hot sun. A boy so desperately in need of a shirt—Toby's shirt. Hunger wasn't the only problem in this area where poverty loomed everywhere. Most people had only one or two ragged pieces of clothing to their name. Haunted by the memory of the boy—and his own refusal to give him his shirt—Toby cried about the decision he'd made. But not for long. Toby vowed not to forget the boy he had denied his shirt.

With the memory of the boy burning in his heart, when Toby returned home to Michigan, he made good on his promise to make a difference in the lives of the people he had seen: He organized a T-shirt drive in his community! Called "Give the Shirt Off Your Back," Toby's campaign soon collected over ten thousand T-shirts.

His next challenge was as great or even greater than the T-shirt drive itself—finding an organization to pay the shipping costs for getting all those shirts to Ethiopia. But Toby was up to this challenge too. He found SOS (Supporters of Sub-Saharan Africa), a group that agreed to transport the T-shirts on their next trip to Africa.

"I think we can all make a difference," said Toby. "One of the things that I've struggled with is wondering if that little boy I met will get one of the ten thousand shirts, and I don't know the answer. But I can pray that he does—or that someone who receives one will give it to him should he ask."

Well aware of the gift of giving, Toby not only spent part of last summer in Africa and much of the fall conducting this T-shirt drive, but he's been involved in many other things, too. He'll spend this coming year in Bolivia as a foreign exchange student. After that he'd like to go to college and ultimately become a doctor. "I'd like to use my life by helping my fellow human beings," Toby said. "I'm most happy when I'm helping others."

Toby's giving isn't just limited to those he directly helps, his example of how one teen with a sincere desire and determination can make a difference in the world serves as a gift of inspiration to many others.

Jennifer Leigh Youngs

Habitat's Twenty-Seven

Picture this: A group of twenty-seven teens from all different backgrounds travel to a place they've never been, with kids they've never met, to do something they've never done: build a house from start to finish—in two weeks.

Sound improbable? It isn't. It happens every summer as part of the Pritzker-Cousins Summer Program coordinated by the Campus Chapters and Youth Programs, a division of Habitat for Humanity. Habitat for Humanity is a nonprofit housing ministry organized around the purpose of building homes for families who need housing. (Two of Habitat's most famous volunteers are former President Jimmy Carter and his wife Rosalynn.)

Each summer, teen volunteers come together to "blitz" a house for a family in need of housing. "Blitzing," the building of a house from start to finish in a short period of time, is an amazing process. Even without time constraints, building a house is a time-consuming project that involves the massive-scale and precision coordination of both the people working and the numerous, labor-intensive tasks to be done. It's a project where the order and sequence of things to be done depends upon successfully completing others. For example, the concrete slab must dry before you can begin installing surface beams. The structure of the house must be complete and in place before the roofing is put on; installing the ducts for heating and air-conditioning precedes putting up drywall; sanding the drywall must be done before the walls can be painted, and so on.

For the teens, the Habitat timeline is condensed into two weeks! It goes something like this: exterior wall panels and roof trusses go up the first day. On days two and three, electrical and interior framing begins. On days four and five, drywall is started, the roof is sheeted with plywood and windows and doors go on, then the insulation and stucco. Around days six and seven, it's plumbing fixtures, cabinets, interior doors, garage doors, tile on the roof, air conditioning unit, carpets, floor covering and hardware. During the next few days, all interior and exterior painting is completed. Then the drapes are installed, and, finally, the lawn is planted. At the end of two weeks, an empty lot turns into a house. On the final day, the teens present the new homeowners with the keys to their new house—then, a family moves in and makes it a home.

It's a daunting task—and perhaps each member of the new group each summer feels this way, too. Like the groups before them, when each new group of volunteers looks at the rendering (the picture of what is to be after the two weeks), many wonder if it's possible to build a house in such a short period of time. Looking from the barren piece of dirt—and then comparing its appearance to the beautiful house in the photo, one that is complete with grass and shrubs—stretches the imagination, most especially for those who have never done it before. Nonetheless, with a six-thirty wake-up call the next morning, the new group of volunteers begins. And on the final day, even those who, in the beginning, found it almost unbelievable to think that a house can be built in such a short period of time have learned that it can be done.

Like the groups before and after them, many will leave with a few new carpentry skills and with a few aches and sore muscles (and an all-important tan). But more than the physical completion of the day-to-day work will be accomplished. As sixteen-year-old Brent Rogers of Ontario, California, said, "The initial demeanor of sizing up each other gave way to many new friendships. Because we share such a camaraderie and sense of cooperation our 'team' could be sent anywhere to do any task and we'd get it done." This is probably true.

In the end, the teens from different backgrounds who travel to a place they've never been, with others they've never met, to do something they've never done, namely, build a house—from

start to finish in two weeks—will leave with a number of amazing discoveries, among them: When joining together for a common purpose, people can accomplish great things. To date, some
seventy-five thousand homes have been built by Habitat around
the world.

[**Authors' Note:** *If you want to get involved, write to The Pritzker-
Cousins Summer Youth Program, Habitat for Humanity, 121 Habitat
Street, Americus, Georgia 31709.*]

Serving Up Something Simple

I needed to do something in my community in order to complete community service hours for my Key Club. Some of my friends had signed up to spend time at the St. Vincent De Paul's soup kitchen, so I did, too. It seemed like it would be a neat thing to do.

I thought that we would just be passing out dinners to the needy, but I found out we would be doing everything from preparing to serving the dinner. We began preparing the food, from mixing salad dressing to separating frozen meat. Much still needed to be done before dinner was served, but already outside the building many homeless people were gathering. Within the next two hours the line grew, until it went down the street and around the block. Glancing out the window, I could see the clouds of steam as the people standing in the line breathed out there in the cold night air, rubbing their hands together, and talking or just milling around waiting for the dining hall to open. It wasn't until a couple of hours later that we opened the doors and began serving dinner.

As the line of people came toward me, I got a little scared. I'd come face to face with the homeless: How should I act? How would they treat me? Would they resent me for having more than they did? I even found myself beginning to wonder, "What am I doing here?" While some of the people looked very friendly, some of them looked so dangerous. I didn't have too much time to worry about it. I was assigned to serve the salad dressing with the lady next to me. She smiled at me and said if I needed help, she'd be right there, which I found reassuring.

I had never seen so many people wanting food. They were all different ages and nationalities; some had lived a rough life all of their lives and others were just entering poverty. A lot of them were holding bags that contained all they owned, others wore layers of clothes. Some of them wore clothes that were ragged and almost all of them wore clothes that were rumpled. Most of them looked a little rumpled themselves—unshaven men, women and children whose hair wasn't shiny, clean and well-brushed. Some looked like they had totally given up on life, while others seemed to be making the best of the situation, smiling and joking. Some were better off than others, but they all needed a good meal and a warm place to eat. It saddened me to think of how many people there were who didn't have a place to call home and the only food they got came from a soup kitchen. For some it might be their one and only meal of the day.

As they came in my direction I put on my brightest and happiest smile and said, "Hello, would you like ranch or thousand island?" Some responses were cold, they just wanted to sit down and eat, but others were friendly. All were grateful. Some smiled and commented on how they appreciated my doing what I was doing. A couple commented that I was beautiful. A little girl of ten wanted to touch my long hair. All made me feel like I was doing something good.

To see the smiles on their faces was so heartening. I realized that homeless people aren't that different from me in spirit. They all want to be treated with kindness. After working at the soup kitchen, I started looking into the problem of the homeless. There's a lot you may not know about the homeless. I know many things surprised me. Did you know that one out of four homeless people works full- or part-time, but they have minimum wage jobs, so they're caught in a struggle to afford to get into a home? One-quarter of the homeless are war veterans. And it's really sad to realize that one out of four homeless people is a child. I learned in school that one child in five lives below the poverty line. I was shocked to find out that over *three million* people are homeless for at least one night during the year. That's a lot of people. It must be very frightening to them. It would be terrifying to me.

I'm really happy I helped out—even if it was just a smile as I helped served them a meal. It's surprising what a little smile and a little service can do for others. My smile and my being helpful was important to them. My presence as a volunteer showed those who came to the shelter that day that other people were aware that they were in need and were willing to lend a hand. At a time when they needed to believe that other people would help them, our being there showed them we would. At the very least, they had a meal and were served that meal by people who did it with kindness, and expected nothing in return. I'd like to think that our caring brought them the strength and courage to get through another day. And if a mere smile and a kind heart could change a life, maybe it would give some the desire and motivation to work on a better tomorrow.

I was so happy that I had earned my service hours in this way. But in the end, it was so much more than service hours. Among other things, I learned gratitude. I live in a luxurious house and have so many comforts. Still, I'm always saying I don't have anything to wear, or that I need this, or can't live without that. My experience showed me that I shouldn't take things for granted.

I hope I was able to make their lives a little happier. At the very least, they might see the world as a kinder place. So whenever you feel that something as simple as a smile or a kind act will go unnoticed, do it anyway. You never know how much it might change someone else's life—maybe even your own. And you never know how much that change might go on to change yet another life, or even the world. Through my experience, I also learned that I want to continue to help others, so I've joined a youth group that's involved in volunteering at local shelters on a regular basis. Knowing that I'm doing something that can make a positive difference in someone else's life has really changed *my* life—for the better.

Erin Bishop, 17

The Heart of Christmas

The man read the church bulletin announcing that the congregation was aware that one of their families was experiencing hardship and could afford neither Christmas gifts for their children nor food for a traditional holiday celebration. Members of the congregation were encouraged to donate food, gifts and whatever else they could. The bulletin asked that members of the congregation bring all donations to the church by six that afternoon. Everyone would then form a caravan and deliver the goods to the family. Nudging his wife who sat in the pew beside him, he pointed to the pamphlet and whispered, "We must help."

Scanning the announcement, she nodded in agreement and returned a whispered, "Yes."

On the way home, the couple told their children what the bulletin had announced and discussed what their family could do to help. It was agreed: The family would spend the afternoon canvassing the neighborhood, going door-to-door asking for donations of toys, canned goods and other items for the needy family. Warmed by the idea of helping someone in need—especially during a season of "giving"—the family enjoyed themselves, and found that most everyone was in the Christmas spirit. "It's just as well that someone enjoy this," said one woman as she handed the younger boy a twenty-five pound frozen turkey from her refrigerator. "I was going to cook it for Christmas, but now that my son and his daughter have invited me to their home, someone else might just as well have a delicious meal, too."

Just before six, the couple and their two sons hurried to the church to deliver everything they had gathered. Once there, they were both surprised and pleased to find so many other families participating in what the father had called "the heart of Christmas." Headed by the pastor and his family, cars and minivans loaded with an assortment of items—food, clothing, even a Christmas tree—lined up to begin the trip to the family who needed the congregation's outpouring of love, donations and sense of community. Like the others, this family took their place in the procession and set out to deliver "Christmas."

Several minutes into the trip, they were surprised to find themselves on their street. Within minutes, the cars in front of them drove into the driveway of their home.

They were the family in need and the recipients of the congregation's outpouring of love and support—and its Christmas heart.

Bettie B. Youngs
Excerpted from Gifts of the Heart

There Are Lots of Ways to Help Others

My little sister, Carrie, is only nine. Once a month she takes her dog, Pal, to a children's home where the little kids take turns holding and petting her dog. One time I had to drive her there because our mother couldn't. A little boy put Pal on his lap and petted him—while he was taking chemotherapy. I heard chemotherapy burns really bad. Petting Carrie's dog helped distract the little boy from the pain of the chemotherapy. To that little boy that day, Pal was a welcome sight.

A lot of my friends "think globally," they just don't know what do to "act locally." What my little sister does with her dog proves there are lots of ways to help others. All you have to do is look around you and see how other people are serving others. Like my family, for example.

My mother gives the clothes our family doesn't need to our local church. Every few months or so, we do the clean-your-closet routine. I always find something that I don't need, don't like or I've outgrown, things someone else should be using. Just this last time, I dug out my shoes. I had two pairs of cleats. One pair I may use again this next season (if I don't outgrow them) and the other pair is already too small. It's not like I need this second pair. I don't have a brother, and my little sister isn't going to ever wear cleats. I'll just bet there's some kid out there who would love to own a pair but can't afford them. So, I "donated" the second pair of cleats.

Another thing our family does is sponsor an animal (a giraffe named Shorty) at the zoo. Each month we write out a check for forty-five dollars and send it in. The money goes toward Shorty's food bill. Even my older sister, Sheree, who's twenty-two and who is really busy, still finds time to volunteer. She works for the airlines and is active in a group called the Airline Ambassadors; they donate their time and flight miles to help families of sick or injured children get the medical attention they need.

So I've learned to keep my eyes open when it comes to look-ing for what I can do to help others. Right now I'm involved with a group in my school, headed by one of the counselors. We're organizing a neighborhood drive where each family donates one nonperishable item or canned good on the last day of every month. There are less than twenty homes in my neighborhood, so I can cover these in probably three or four hours on a Saturday or Sunday afternoon. The food is picked up by a group called Meals on Wheels, an organization that donates food to seniors in need of food. I've discovered I like going around to collect the food—it gives me a chance to talk to everyone in the neighbor-hood. I'm good at it and it's good for the cause. I like it so much that I'm making a commitment to stay involved in the group for at least a year.

Helping is an attitude, more than anything else. If a person is open to helping others, usually you'll find the opportunity right at the tip of your nose.

Randy Bobrow, 16

Help Abused or Abandoned Animals

When it comes to making a difference in the world, I'm most interested in doing it by helping animals. Every community has a shelter for abandoned or abused animals. Just ask around or look in the yellow pages, and you'll find one. You can check out *www.planetpets.simplenet.com* for a list of *101 Things You Can Do to Save Animals*. There are many groups that work to help and protect all different kinds of animals. I know in my community alone, we have six animal shelters and a bird sanctuary. You can donate time to help comfort and care for the animals, or you can donate supplies or pet food.

Every month I send five dollars to one of the animal shelters in my town; and then I help walk Mrs. Hemmeter's dog, Buster. Mrs. Hemmeter is getting really old and she can't walk Buster for herself anymore—but other than that she can take care of Buster just fine. So my stopping by and taking Buster for a walk keeps them together and makes them both happy.

If you're really into animals, like I am, there are also temporary pets available. For example, in my community there is a group called Canine Companions for Independence. This group is always looking for help training puppies and, sometimes, grown dogs. Golden retrievers, Labrador retrievers and sheltie puppies are placed with volunteer puppy raisers at eight weeks of age and are returned to the training center for advanced training at six to eight months. I think it would be so much fun to volunteer as a puppy raiser. My parents aren't going for it right now, but I still think it would be such an awesome thing to be able to do.

When it comes to volunteering, let's not forget the other creatures on our planet who depend on our help, too!

Danny Joseph, 15

You! Yes, You!

If you want to know more ways you can take action to help others, as its title promises, *I Can Ignite the Community Spirit: 301 Ways to Turn Caring into Action*, by Joy J. Golliver and Ruth Hayes-Arista, is a marvelous resource—and will give you 301 ways. You can order it by calling 800-254-ICAN, or writing I CAN Ignite the Community Spirit, 500 West Roy Street, #W107, Seattle, Washington 98119.

Here's just one example of how practical and useful this book is. Under the ways to help the homeless, we found:

ACTION! When walking down the street, rather than giving money, respond with kindness. Try a kind word to bolster their self-confidence and self-worth. Society benefits from their increased self-esteem.

ACTION! Keep a shopping bag in your closet. Every time you go to the grocery, buy something for your shopping bag that can be used by a homeless person. If you get a gift you know you will never use, put it in your shopping bag. Things that you outgrow or do not wear and are not needed by your family, put in the bag. When the bag is full, drop it off at a shelter for the homeless.

ACTION! On your own birthday, buy birthday cards and add a note that reads "To celebrate my birthday, I wanted to give you a gift so that you can have a special day when your birthday arrives." Put some money in the card and distribute to homeless men and women and children.

ACTION! Be a role model to your friends and neighbors. Volunteer at a soup kitchen or food bank. Make it an event for family and friends. Meeting the homeless face to face proves that they're people just like us, just experiencing some bad luck.

ACTION! Support creative projects in your community.

Organize new projects. Street Wise is a newspaper sold in some communities by the homeless. A similar publication is Real Changes. The homeless can get the first ten newspapers free and sell them for one dollar. When they invest that ten dollars in more newspapers they receive forty newspapers for twenty-five cents each and sell them for a profit of seventy-five cents and keep the money. This a well-organized project. Workers sign an employment contract and are licensed by the city. This gives them a step up and a sense of self-worth. If such a program is not in your community, why not help to start one? If it is in your community, buy newspapers and support the homeless that are working.

ACTION! Show your compassion and caring. Start in your own home. Care about your brothers and sisters. Show them love and respect and consideration. Next, become a Big Sister or Big Brother to a needy child in your community. You just may be the one person in their lives who provides the motivation, encouragement—and love—that will help someone face life's challenges without becoming homeless.

Part 7

Coping with Stress-Filled and Embarrassing Moments

*The strongest oak tree of the forest
is not the one that is protected from
the storm and hidden from the sun.
It's the one that stands in the open
where it is compelled to struggle for its existence
against the winds and rains and the scorching sun.*

—Napoleon Hill

13 Embarrassing Moments!

Square your shoulders to the world, be not the kind to quit;
It's not the load that weighs you down
but the way you carry it.

—Author Unknown

IT'S IN YOUR PURSE

One day, after a vigorous workout at her gym, a woman decided to treat herself to an ice-cream cone. Tired and sweaty, wearing her work-out clothes, with her hair pulled haphazardly up in a ponytail, she walked into the ice-cream parlor. There, sitting at a table near the counter, was Paul Newman. Here she was, face-to-face with Paul Newman—handsome film idol and local (as well as international) celebrity—and only having the flu could have made her look worse! The woman cringed at her timing, embarrassed to be seen by someone so famous, looking as she did.

"Don't be nervous," the woman told herself. "Be cool. Be

calm. Be collected. He's just a person who happens to be a movie star—one who happens to be in the same ice-cream parlor as I am. Just be gracious and graceful." So she walked past Mr. Newman, smiled a warm but casual smile and in a friendly voice said, "Hello." Mr. Newman returned her smile, tipped his head and said, "Hello."

Her heart pounding with excitement, she walked to the counter and ordered her ice-cream cone. She paid the man for her cone, took her change, turned and walked out of the ice-cream parlor, smiling again at the movie star as she passed him.

When she reached her car, she breathed a sigh of relief, then looked down at the car keys in her hands and realized she didn't have an ice-cream cone! "Oh, no," she groaned, "I must have left it in the ice-cream rack at the counter—or maybe even in the hands of the clerk behind the counter!" The woman had been so preoccupied with trying to act calm while feeling so nervous, she'd walked out without her ice-cream cone.

"What should I do now?" she wondered, and then decided to just go right back in and get her ice-cream cone. Hopefully, no one would even notice that she had forgotten the cone. Hopefully, it was right there in the rack at the counter, waiting for her. So, the woman took a deep breath, turned around and walked back in the ice-cream parlor. She smiled casually at Mr. Newman and then looked towards the counter.

Paul Newman, knowing what she'd returned for, calmly informed her, "You put it in your purse."

A Word from the Authors

"Putting an ice-cream cone in your purse—in front of someone you'd like to impress—ranks at the top of the 'dumb and dumber' list," said our female teen readers. "Not *even*," said the guys (who shared a great many "war stories"). "I was on a first date with a really cool girl, one I'd finally gotten up the nerve to ask out, only to discover at the restaurant—after our meal when they brought me the bill—that I'd forgotten my wallet!"

"I was trying to be really cool with a girl I wanted to impress," said another. "So I borrowed my mother's new car because it's much nicer than mine. I'd taken the girl to the movies, and afterwards, I discovered I'd locked the keys in the car. I was not about to break into the window with a coat hanger, so by time I found a phone, called AAA and they arrived and got the car unlocked, we'd missed out hooking up with the friends we told we'd meet. At this point I was thinking more about answering to my mother than about being cool. My date wasn't impressed with me or the car."

"I think a girl can understand locking your keys in the car. I had opened a car door for a girl and was helping her out, and slammed the car door on her hand! It broke one of her fingers! Talk about not being impressed!"

"I was introducing a girl to my parents and was so nervous I couldn't remember her name! She just stood there looking at me as though some village was missing its idiot."

Well, at least he remembered his parents' names. Another teen wrote that he wanted to introduce his father to his coach after a game and couldn't remember his dad's name. The stories went on and on and on! For teens, it seems, embarrassing moments are endless.

"At least they seem that way, Mom. Many times, it's those painfully embarrassing moments that stand out in our memory and that can make them seem far worse than perhaps they are. But, regardless of whether they're really as bad as they seem, they can be embarrassing to live through. It makes me wonder why we laugh at someone when they stumble or fall, or trip. Have you ever wondered why we laugh when, in a sense, it's not all that funny? I was at a restaurant recently, sitting at a table fairly close to the hostess stand, when a couple came into the restaurant. The man gestured to the woman he was with that he wanted to take her coat. She handed her coat to the man, he took it and turned to hang it up on the coat rack behind him. In that same instant—because she obviously didn't see the steps in front of her—the woman promptly fell down the stairwell. She bounced, and tumbled and slid down these stairs, crashing in a heap at the bottom. The man—unaware that his lady now lay at the bottom of the stairs—looked around, bewildered that she "evaporated" so suddenly. He looked to the right, and then to the left and upon eyeing the bar area, he rushed to the bar and sat down, perhaps thinking his girl went to the bathroom. You could see that he was a bit baffled, wondering how the girl got away so fast without his knowing it. In the meantime, the girl, now laying at the base of the stairwell, was wondering how she could get up—gracefully—in the long tight dress she was wearing, and how she'd retrieve her heels, one of which lay on the first step, the other heel on the third step. Meanwhile, the hostess was aghast that the woman had fallen, and that her date had nonchalantly 'left the scene of the accident.'

"Mom, the scene unfolded in such split-second timing and was hilarious. I was laughing so hard I thought I was going to wet my pants. But it really *wasn't* funny. The woman skinned her shins so badly in the fall, and had fallen so hard, she required medical attention."

"Maybe we laugh because we can identify, and we are, in a sense, relieved it's not happening to us, Jennifer. Maybe in that moment we see it, we relive it, and now with the incident behind us, we can laugh at it—at ourselves."

As the stories in this chapter assure us, we've all had times when we've suffered humiliation. And, we learn that no matter how tragic at the time, we make it through. Most of us have moments when we want to sink through the floor, or run and hide. But the truth is, those times pass—along with all the uncomfortable feelings they bring with them. So while we don't disappear—though we wish we could—the incident does.

I know that I wanted to disappear on the day of my high school cheerleading tryouts. I found myself standing in the middle of the stage of the high school auditorium, in front of the entire school, with all eyes on me, when the other girls who were supposed to come up on stage with me chickened out at the last moment—without telling me. But it gets even worse. The reason they refused to go on stage with me was because I was wearing the school nerd's letter sweater—which didn't have a letter—only I didn't know it! Eighteen-year-old Tamara Wilson wanted to disappear, too, after making a big deal about her big corsage—when she might as well have been wearing a head of cabbage.

After a painfully embarrassing incident, Ellen Abrams, once dubbed "a bowser," learns you can outgrow an embarrassing moment and that it's not always you who is in the doghouse. The disastrous combination of a tight skirt, a broken zipper and a date with the guy of her dreams teaches Lea Rosen, seventeen, that other people aren't nearly as affected by those embarrassing moments as we think they will be. And surprisingly enough, embarrassment is a good teacher sometimes. Seventeen-year-old Tom McClure has a chance to introduce sports legend Joe Montana at a sports banquet. Worried that he may get there late, Tom speeds to the banquet, being rude to other drivers on the road on the way there. What he doesn't know is that Joe Montana is one of them! The famous football player publicly acknowledges Tom for his "very creative hand signals" and "very explicit directions!" As a result of his embarrassment, Tom became a "much more courteous driver."

While Tom's inability to hold his temper—and his tongue—resulted in his embarrassment, your friend ninety-year-old Elmer Adrian has a different view, saying biting his tongue is "worse than getting stung." Perhaps most important to consider is whether our words or actions hurt others. Whether from reading about the embarrassing moments of others or from having experienced your own, you teens learned that such moments can be the most "tart" of all "taste berries." Yet, they can be used to sweeten life, having taught you not to laugh unfairly at others when they're caught in an embarrassing predicament, nor to do or say those things that will further humiliate them. Overall, tough times can teach us to be compassionate to those we meet throughout our lives—and that's what being a "taste berry" is all about.

The Letter(less) Sweater

"Going steady" was pretty heady stuff in the junior high I attended. This ceremonial dance followed a simple pattern: A boy asked a girl to wear his athletic letter sweater, she accepted, and then she wore it as often as possible around school. This envied exhibition showcased that you were desired by the opposite sex—and probably getting kissed—so there was a lot of attention associated with this ritual for both boys and girls. Of course, it put quite a bit of pressure on the boys to earn the coveted letter sweater. This is one reason so many boys went out for sports in my school—it was the only way you could get one of those status-laden tokens, which were required if you were to become "somebody." It was also necessary if you wanted to go steady with a girl who had already gained a considerable amount of clout because she was considered popular. To be popular and in possession of a letter sweater was really something; it expanded a girl's already great reputation to darn-near nobility.

Of course, if you broke up you had to give the sweater back, which gave the girl a lot of power in the relationship. When Sue Goodell broke up with Jeff Lundgren, she wouldn't return his sweater because she knew that Jeff wanted to give it to Mary Duran. Breaking up could be tricky, too.

While going steady offered mystery and intrigue, if the boy didn't have a letter sweater, your reputation wasn't much above that of your average run-of-the-mill kid. The letter sweater was the thing.

I was really a nobody. I not only wasn't going steady with a guy who had a letter sweater, I didn't even have a boyfriend. This presented me with a real problem when several of my friends and I got the idea to try out for cheerleading. When you tried out for cheerleading, you had to wear a guy's letter sweater up there on stage. Besides being the custom, it was part of the costume. It showed school spirit and advertised that you were going with a guy who was an athlete. In other words, you were a real somebody.

Cheerleading tryouts were held in early spring. By this time of the year, nearly every boy with a letter sweater had found a girl who was willing to wear it. In the event you didn't have a boyfriend and intended to try out for cheerleading, you needed to find a boy who was still in possession of his sweater—and willing to lend it to you. Or you had to ask a girl who wasn't trying out if she would lend you her boyfriend's sweater. All of this got to be very complicated and was in and of itself a test of self-esteem.

I needed to round up a letter sweater to wear for tryouts and began asking around. But alas, everyone, it seemed, was going steady or had loaned out their letter sweaters to one of the many girls trying out for cheerleading. But then, one day, to my surprise—and relief—a newly cleaned and pressed sweater folded carefully in a box directly from the cleaners had been placed in my locker! Someone had come to my rescue. I was thrilled.

There was no bigger social event than when the entire school gathered in the auditorium to vote for the chosen six, those girls who would win the title of "cheerleader." Winning this pageant was quite an honor. If being an athlete and having a letter sweater gave ultimate status to a boy, being selected as a cheerleader brought maximum status to a girl. And the day this was determined was the day of reckoning. All the contestants were anxious. We all wanted to win a coveted spot on next year's squad.

For moral support, each girl sat with her group of friends—all of us scattered throughout the auditorium. When the physical education teacher, who was always in charge of the cheerleading events, called out the numbers assigned to each group of girls trying out, you got up and headed toward the stage. If you were lucky, your little group of friends applauded and stomped their

feet (very loudly, hopefully)—anything to let the rest of the auditorium know that you had groupies. There was an unmistakable
association between the amount of noise made for each contes-
tant and those girls who won.

We were group number seven. When the teacher called out for
our group to go up on stage, my friends pushed me out of my
seat and I nervously headed for the stage. I climbed up the three
steps, anxious every step of the way, and took my place in the
middle; there was to be a girl on each side of me. Then, a girl in
the front row let out a gasp. "Oh my God, she's wearing Alan
Thompson's sweater!"

Alan was the school nerd. Quite simply, he was just too nice a
guy. And too smart. Unfortunately, no one ever told him that in
junior high it wasn't smart to be nice, or nice to be smart. So he
was unanimously chosen to be the school nerd. Alan looked the
part. He had thick black curly hair and a bad hair day every day.
He wore thick glasses, and somewhere in elementary school his
brain had advanced to college-level studies. Besides all that, he
walked like a duck. Poor Alan. There was nothing he could do to
change things. Worse than all this, everyone knew that because
Alan had been the team's water boy and overall gofer for three
years, the coach had given him a sweater (without the letter) as
a token of appreciation, making his sweater less than desirable to
everyone.

I stood there for a moment, watching and waiting for the other
two wannabes to join me. It was soon apparent that no one else
was coming.

At first I thought that maybe I had heard wrong and had gone
up on stage too soon. Perhaps the teacher had called eleven and
not seven; the groups weren't necessarily called in order.
Terrified, I stood there alone in the middle of the big auditorium's stage in front of every one of my schoolmates. And in
Alan-the-Nerd's letterless sweater!

Assuming I was a one-man show, the physical education

teacher called out, "You may begin now." A dead silence fell over the auditorium as they all watched me, wondering what I was going to do. I was so mortified that my feet wouldn't take me off stage, and with suicide unacceptable at the Evangelical Lutheran Church I attended, I had no choice but to do the cheer alone.

You have no idea what it's like to do a cheer that requires three able bodies—totally alone. Nor can you imagine the humiliation I suffered being on a stage alone in front of my peers in Alan-the-Untouchable's letterless sweater. Obviously once the other two girls saw me going up in Alan's sweater, they backed out. Seems I had committed the unpardonable sin—I had touched Alan's sweater, and they would rather have died than be on the same stage with that sweater—the one without the scarlet letter!

How was I to know that everyone would recognize the sweater as belonging to Alan?

I didn't get voted to be cheerleader, but I did make runner-up. In other words, should a cheerleader in our school *die* from yelling cheers, I would fill the vacated slot.

Of course, I begged my parents to let me go and live with my aunt in South America so as not to have to face my classmates ever again, but they said no. And though they allowed me to feign the flu and stay home from school for two days, after that, the flu excuse was used up and they made me go back to school.

How I dreaded facing my classmates! And, I did feel a twinge of embarrassment at having been a part of ridiculing Alan. So I talked to him about it. You can only imagine how surprised I was to discover that Alan hadn't seen the experience in the same way I did at all! True to his style of being unfazed by life's little challenges, Alan laughed and said confidently, "Oh, it was no big thing, really. There were two things that were most important to me: I wanted to have an athletic sweater, and I wanted you to wear it. So when I found out that you needed a sweater to wear at the tryouts, well, my second dream came true. There you were, up front and center stage in front of all the other students

wearing *my* sweater. I was so proud. That was a great day for me
. . . much better than yours, I trust!"

Although he could have chosen to, Alan hadn't experienced
embarrassment or humiliation at all. In fact, as he did in most
trials, Alan had emerged a victor! Alan's measuring stick for success was within. No fanfare, just being Alan. And liking it.

As for me, while that day up on stage didn't necessarily earn
me any new friends, I certainly earned everyone's respect. No
one considered me a wimp or pushover from that day forward,
and, at the end of that school year, my schoolmates voted me
"Most Courageous!" (not that it was any consolation).

Bettie B. Youngs
Adapted from Values from the Heartland

Just Three Leaves

In a magazine I had seen a picture of a large, white, very beautiful flower. A "Casablanca Easter Lily," the magazine called it. It was such an unusual and gorgeous flower, I just knew I had to have a Casablanca Easter Lily as a corsage for the junior-senior prom the following week.

"It's such a special flower, so big and bold. Everyone will notice it!" I said to my boyfriend. I wanted *everything* to be perfect for my prom, and a beautiful corsage is really *the* thing at our school.

"Okay, sounds cool," he said.

The night of the prom, my boyfriend presented me an outrageously large corsage with a gorgeous Easter Lily in the center! My boyfriend was very proud of himself for giving me the flower, a feeling that was surely justified. My parents and little sister ooohed and ahhhed and then began taking pictures. First, my parents took pictures of "the" flower still encased in its plastic container, then of my boyfriend as he was taking the flower out of its plastic shrine, then of me holding the flower—and then comparing it to the size of my hand. Then there were pictures of the flower being pinned on my dress. Because it was a delicate flower, and because it was a large corsage, it took my boyfriend several attempts to pin it on. Once on, Mom took yet another picture, this time of me and "the flower" and then of me and my boyfriend and the flower. "Stand closer to 'the flower,'" she said to him.

When nearly two rolls of film had been taken, I carefully took the flower off, put on my coat, and we left for the restaurant where we were to have dinner. Once there, I was very careful not to damage the flower as I once again put it on in the restaurant, and then took it off as I once again put on my coat to leave. All this was a lot of work, but well worth it because I wanted the flower to be absolutely perfect for the prom. After all, as *the* thing for prom at our school, the flower was a status symbol—not only a mark of your own good taste but also an indication of how much your date cared about you.

I had told *everyone* that my boyfriend was getting me a Casablanca Easter Lily.

When I got to school, I disappeared into the girls' restroom to once again begin the ordeal of putting on "the" flower. When it was finally in place, I emerged from the girls' restroom, proud as I could be! My boyfriend, "the flower" and I were about to begin a wonderful and memorable evening. The lights were dimmed and when the music started, my flower and I joined my boyfriend on the dance floor and the three of us began to dance.

Everyone looked at each other's flower corsages. Of everyone's there, I was certain mine was the most beautiful. Even so, I tried to be very modest. I was careful to stand up straight, chest thrust forward, and tried not to look in the direction of the lily; after all, it spoke for itself. When I did occasionally peek nonchalantly down at my corsage, I saw the beautiful ferns, ribbons and greenery all spraying grandly forth and rested assured my gorgeous Casablanca Easter Lily, though obstructed from my own view, was fittingly framed in its splendor for all other eyes to see.

I was certain that my corsage caught the attention of just about everyone, because nearly all of them said something. "Very interesting!" MaryJane Harriman said, jealous I'm sure. "Hey, great corsage!" Sheila Henry said, and then looked glibly at the pink carnations her boyfriend had given her. "Impressive," Janet Stephenson said, putting her hand to her mouth and acting shocked. "Everyone says I've got to get a closer look at your flower," Cathy Jones announced loudly as she danced nearby. "They say it gets the award for best imagination." Dancing next to me, she confirmed, "Yes, I'll say it does!" Many of the girls just looked and smiled, not knowing what to say.

It was a memorable evening, made sweeter by the fact that I had been the center of attention! It was wonderful.

Finally, the evening just about over, Mr. Thomas, the principal, got up on the stage where the band was preparing to play their last song of the evening and announced, "What a wonderful evening. We are so happy this year's event has been a success. The band is about to play the last song for the evening, so we wish you a safe drive home, and look forward to seeing you in school Monday morning. Just one short announcement. Will whoever dropped their corsage in the girl's restroom take it with you as you leave? We've been holding it since before the band played their first set, thinking someone would claim it." Frowning down at the bloom in his hand, he said, "It's a huge flower, though a very wilted one," and then he held up a bedraggled flower—*my* Casablanca Easter Lily.

I looked down at my elaborate corsage, this time really leaning over to see it. I gently lifted it up on my dress so I could see beneath its "fitting frame" of greenery.

I was mortified at what I saw! To my horror, unbeknown to me, all evening I been wearing a corsage consisting only of ribbons, a spray of ferns and three green leaves (albeit beautiful leaves—only leaves, nonetheless)! My corsage was minus "the flower," and all the while I'd been calling attention to it! I may as well have been wearing a cabbage.

Tamara Wilson, 18

Ellen, the "Bowser"

I was hoping Scott Morrison, a guy I really liked, would ask me to the Homecoming dance at my school. Weeks passed, and though I kept hoping, Scott didn't ask me to the dance. As the day grew closer and Scott still hadn't asked, I realized that he probably had no idea that I was interested in him. We had talked to each other in the one class we had together, but it's not like you can be sure that just because you're being extra cheerful and outgoing, a guy knows that you like him.

I decided if I wanted Scott to ask me to the dance, at the very least I needed to make certain he knew for sure that I was interested in going with him. So, I carefully set out to make sure that word got to Scott. First, I told my friend Michelle that I really wanted to go to the dance with Scott. I knew when I told Michelle that she would instantly gossip and let her friend Darcy know, since Darcy's brother, Jeff, was one of Scott's best friends, and would surely tell him. I didn't want it to sound like I was madly in love or obsessed or anything. So I handled it with as much delicacy as it deserved, or so I thought.

To tell you the truth, I thought Scott was going to ask me because for the next couple of days he kept looking at me whenever I passed by—which I did as often as I could. Of course, I'd smile at him sweetly, anticipating the moment when I was sure he was going to ask. I wanted to give him every opportunity, so I made certain to let him see that I was looking at him, too. I could see it, I knew without a doubt that "word" had reached him, and it looked to me as if he was also interested. I decided he must be a little shy and was working up the nerve to ask me. But I was positive he'd say something soon.

Which he did. The next day. My locker was right around the corner from Scott's, and not too long after I had put out word that I wanted him to ask me to the dance, I heard him and Jeff talking about me. I froze at my locker and strained to hear every word. "Hey, I hear that Ellen Abrams has a thing for you," Jeff said. Then I heard Scott start hooting with laughter and say, "Ellen Abrams, what a bowser—that girl is a dog. I wouldn't take her out on a leash." Just then, he and Jeff walked around the corner and spotted me standing there. When they saw me, Jeff started barking to alert Scott that "Ellen, the bowser" was in sight. My heart had already crashed to my stomach. But now, having heard them refer to me as a dog, I was even more humiliated by their barking.

To put it mildly, Scott Morrison never did ask me to the dance.

I was so embarrassed—to say nothing of having my feelings hurt. It was bad enough to have someone I liked say that about me, but to have him see that I had actually heard it made the humiliation complete.

"Oh, Mom," I wailed, when I got home that day, "I'm so sick of being so tall—taller than all the boys! And I'm tired of being so skinny they call me 'Sticks' and I'm tired of these braces that make me look so ugly!"

My mother said, "Ellen, there will come a day very soon when you will be a swan—you won't always be too tall, too skinny and of course, you won't always wear braces." Still trying to cheer me up, she added, "Honey, what is considered a bad time now may not be next year or in the very near future. You'll see."

She was right. This year I had my braces taken off, and now I'm being complimented on being tall. And no one calls me skinny; instead they say, "Oh, you're so thin," and it's said as a compliment. And a lot of guys are asking me out this year. Guess who had the nerve to be one of them? That's right—Scott Morrison.

I changed my mind about wanting to go out with him a long time ago. It was *very satisfying* to say, "Yeah, right! In your dreams, dog-boy." Scott is the one in the "doghouse" this year.

Ellen Abrams, 16

The *Perfect* Thing to Wear

For as long as I can remember, I had a huge crush on Damon Brunner. It felt like I had waited all my life for him to ask me out. When he finally did, believe me, I wanted to look my very best. I searched my closet for just the right outfit—then tried several on and modeled them for my friends to get their opinion on what looked best. Nothing seemed to look good enough to wear on a date with Damon.

"I don't have anything to wear," I moaned to my best friend, Patricia.

"You can borrow my new flowered skirt!" she volunteered.

I agreed instantly! I knew which skirt she meant, and it was beautiful.

The only thing is, I hadn't taken into consideration that Patricia has smaller hips than I do. Nevertheless, I wiggled into the skirt on the night of my date with Damon Brunner.

Damon walked me to his car and opened the passenger door, and I got in. As soon as I sat down, I knew I was in trouble. Patricia's skirt looked just wonderful on me standing up, but sitting down in it was a disaster. I'd already known the skirt was snug, but when I sat down it made me feel like I couldn't breath. So to make a little more room in the skirt, I sucked in my breath, reached down and pulled out a little roll of skin from my stomach over the top of it. But when we took our seats in the theater, the ultimate fashion disaster struck. All in the same instant I sat down, I heard a ripping sound, felt the breeze of air on my hip, and realized the zipper on the skirt had given way. I held my arms close to my body to try and cover it up. When Damon put his arm around me, I sat there stiff and awkward, my entire focus being on keeping the torn zipper hidden. I was mortified.

Then, things got even worse. We were walking out of the theater—having seen a movie I barely remember since I was so stressed and embarrassed (and short on oxygen, since I couldn't breathe in deeply enough in that tight skirt)—and we ran into some other kids from school. I was sure everyone saw that the skirt I was wearing was so tight that I had actually burst out of its zipper—to say nothing about the way my elbow dug into my hip to try and cover the broken zipper while at the same time to make sure the button didn't pop so the skirt would fall to the floor. All I wanted to do was to get home and hide in my room and recover from the embarrassment of it all.

I was certain that all the girls at school would have a good laugh about me being seen wearing a skirt so tight I was ripping out its seams. I was just as sure it was the end of my chances with Damon Brunner. I hardly slept at all that night.

But you know what? The next morning Damon called to tell me what a good time he had, and he asked me out for the following weekend—just like everything was perfectly great. And no one at school ever mentioned the skirt's tightness or its zipper being broken—with the exception of Patricia whom I'd sworn to secrecy upon promising I'd pay for a new zipper! As embarrassed as I had been, no one else had even noticed. I thought Damon Brunner was the center of the universe until a broken zipper made me feel like all eyes were on me and I was. Like they say, things aren't always as bad as they seem.

Lea Rosen, 17

Introducing Joe Montana

My boyfriend, Tom, and I were going to a special sports awards banquet where he was to introduce a *very* special guest of honor—Joe Montana. At the time, Joe played quarterback for the San Francisco 49ers and had led the team to a Super Bowl win for the second straight year! Plus, he starred in a couple of television commercials.

Tom was ecstatic because he thought introducing Joe Montana was, in his own words, "the equivalent of dying and going to heaven." I mean, it was a big deal. Joe Montana is a star! Tom was sure of other things, too. He was very sure that he didn't want to be late in getting there.

I don't know if it was because the traffic was slow or just seemed slow to him, but Tom was particularly impatient, and practically indignant with other drivers that evening on the way to the sports awards dinner. He must have been very nervous, because from the time we left my house until the time we arrived at the event, my boyfriend "talked" nonstop—but not to me. Everything he said was directed at the other drivers on the road. One of his favorite lines, "C'mon, c'mon, lady! Drive that thing or get off the road!" was used any number of times, as was, "If you aren't going to drive that piece of junk any faster, get out of my way!" I especially found interesting, "The sign says 'yield,' not 'give up,' you jerk!"

But it was more than his mouth that got a good workout that evening. The horn on his car got a special one, too. As did his practice of hand gestures. The drivers he used these on didn't need to be merely in the "wrong" lane or going "below the speed limit." They only needed to be in his line of vision!

Soon we were winding our way through the downtown district where we had to slow down. Once in city traffic, my boyfriend found himself behind yet another slow driver, one who seemed to be making his way according to the written directions he held in his hand. Holding the steering wheel with one hand and the directions in the other, this driver glanced frequently at the paper and then searched for an address or marking around him. For some reason, this particularly irritated my boyfriend, even though the driver was going the speed limit and seemed to be driving safely and disturbing no one. Tom speeded up so that both cars were side by side, as though they were going to drag race (on a fairly narrow street, I might add). Then, at the top of his lungs, Tom yelled, "If you don't know where you're going, get off the #!@* road. You're a danger to everyone."

The poor man said nothing, merely adjusted his sunglasses and continued driving. But even this innocent gesture from the man irked my boyfriend. "Who do think you are, some damn celebrity or something?" Tom yelled. "Get a clue!"

There was no doubt that the man had heard him; Tom was yelling loudly—and the windows were down on both cars! Still, even this harsh appraisal wasn't enough to relieve my boyfriend's frustration. Having shared these "words of wisdom," as my boyfriend sped by the man's car—going well beyond the allotted speed limit—he honked so the man would look in his direction. When the man did, Tom gave the man the finger.

Still, the driver of the other car kept his composure.

With that, Tom sped up, and though we had long since passed the driver in the sunglasses, an irritated Tom resumed his maniacal driving until we reached the posh hotel where the sports awards banquet was being held. We arrived thirty minutes before we expected, and two full hours earlier than the event.

We waited around and finally guests began arriving. Because Tom was introducing the special guest of honor, we were seated at the head table. Everyone took their place, with the exception of the guest speaker—Joe Montana. It wasn't until the person who introduced Tom stepped up to the podium that Joe Montana was escorted to his place on stage. As Tom was getting up from his seat to step to the podium—to introduce a man he idolized so much that he considered introducing Mr. Montana "an equivalent of dying and going to heaven"—Mr. Montana was taking the seat next to where Tom had been sitting. It was in that very moment that my boyfriend realized that the person he had jeered and fingered was the same football hero he was about to introduce—Joe Montana!

Tom quickly made the introduction, then eagerly and meekly sat down.

Joe Montana, always the gentleman, walked to the stage and said, "I would like to thank Tom for such an eloquent introduction and especially recognize him for all the encouragement he gave me on the way here this evening. As I was driving here, I looked up and noticed Tom in the car next to me. What a courteous young man he is. He must have known that I didn't know my way around the city because using a number of very creative hand signals, he gave me some very explicit directions! And when he thought I might not understand hand language, he yelled out, telling me, in no uncertain terms, where to go." Looking Tom in the eyes, Mr. Montana added, "Yes, siree. He's quite the gentleman. And quite the driver, too."

I only dated Tom for about a month after that incident, but I am happy to report that during that time he was a much better driver and far more courteous to other motorists!

Jennifer Leigh Youngs

When I Bite My Tongue

I've been a guinea pig for pain
since back when I was young.
When leveled by a baseball,
a high fast curve that hung.

I've fallen off a ladder
and bounced off every rung.
If there's a bee within a mile,
I wind up getting stung.

I've even fallen off a horse
and landed in the dung.
I got back on with three cracked ribs
and a punctured lung,
but what annihilates me most,
is when I bite my tongue.

Elmer Adrian, 90

More Perfect Than Others

"*She* was as white as a ghost," Aaron announced, pointing at his friend Angeline.

Angeline, her eyes sad, her tone apologetic yet sarcastic, explained, "No one bid on me." Embarrassed all over again, she put a hand to her face, now turning red instead of white, shook her head and added with a sheepish smile, "It's kinda funny now, but it wasn't *then*." Angeline was speaking of her disastrous "Gofer Day" experience.

"You should have seen how you walked to your seat!" Benny jeered, playfully slapping his arm around Angeline's shoulder.

"Whad'ya mean?" she quizzed.

"When you walked to your seat, you stared straight at the floor!" Benny reminded her.

"Yeah, like this," Aaron said, jumping up to mimic her. He hung his head, slumped his shoulders and stared at the floor as he shuffled to his seat. "Then, when you got to your seat, you did this. . . ." Continuing his pantomime, he plopped down, hung his head, and, with a more bleak than mean pout on his face, continued staring at the floor. His arms were crossed high across his chest.

It's a tradition at Jefferson High School that the junior class sponsor what is always considered to be the school's "biggest and best" event—the annual Junior-Senior Spring Prom. What this amounts to is that the eleventh-grade class is responsible for just about every aspect of the prom, from fund-raising to clean-up—and everything in between. On the first school day in October, it's also a custom for the new class of eleventh-grade students to hold a fund-raiser to earn the money necessary to put on the event.

The fund raiser is known as "Gofer Day," an affair where the juniors allow themselves to be auctioned off: They "sell" themselves to members of the senior class for the day. A "gofer" can be purchased for the purpose of doing any task deemed reasonable—such as being hired for the day as a "book caddy" (carrying around a senior's books), or to help clean a locker, return library books, wash a car or any other task a senior class member chooses, within reason, of course.

The auction is held in the school's large auditorium. All seniors and juniors attend, as well as the tenth-graders at the school. Even though they don't get to participate in the bidding, the sophomores are invited so they might "learn the ropes." Next year, it will be their turn to put on an event to raise funds for the prom they sponsor. For them, attending is a "sneak pre-view" of how things are done.

When all tenth, eleventh and twelfth graders have taken their seats in the auditorium, the senior class president, usually sta-tioned at the podium up front, calls out the names—one by one—of each junior. That person then gets up from where he or she is seated in the auditorium, climbs the steps to the stage and stands there—all alone—and the bidding begins. Each indi-vidual student is auctioned off to the "highest bidder."

Like all others before it, this year's fund-raiser started out in a spirit of fun, an event designed to bring the students together in friendship and commerce. Unfortunately, for some students "Gofer Day" turns out to be emotionally painful. For some stu-dents, the time on stage produces "excruciating" moments—waiting and hoping that someone will bid on them, and then hoping that the bid is not a low one. In the eyes of the students—those on stage and in those viewing this event—a high bid is an indication that a particular student is popular; a low bid shows the student is not very popular. Worse yet, it can be seen as indi-cating the student is not liked at all.

Angeline was one of the casualties. She is a beautiful girl with long brown hair and dark brown eyes, and is considered by many of her teachers, as well as those in the community, to be an extraordinarily talented singer.

I was a guest speaker at Jefferson High School two weeks after "Gofer Day," talking about the importance of self-worth and building on the positive in people and how that brings out their best. Several students were more than ready to discuss their feelings about their "Gofer Day" and how, for them, it did anything but bring out their best. Peering at her friends over the rims of her glasses, the lovely seventeen-year-old winced as she confessed in an angelic voice, "I cried." Then, Angeline laughed half-heartedly and accused, "Well, you would *too*, if no one bid on *you*."

"I received the *lowest* bid of all," Aaron consoled. "So it was almost as bad as you. Bringing in the lowest bid was embarrassing to say the least. Insulting. Demeaning. Humiliating. I could go on."

"Yeah, well at least someone was willing to bid on you. *No one* bid on me. *No one!*" Angeline retorted. Their eyes meeting, the friends grew somber, as if digesting their hurt feelings once again.

"Why is it some teens brought high bids and others low bids?" I asked. Without hesitation, Tookie reported, "My older brother is always in trouble. When people hear my last name, they automatically think I'm just the same."

"It's the 'mouth-of-metal.' My braces—look at them," Julie instructed, opening her mouth to bare her teeth. "I can hardly stand to look at my own smile, why would someone else want to?"

"I'm too quiet, too shy," Sarah explained.

Angeline gave out a big sigh and said, "I'm not popular because of my weight."

Searching for something to say—and hoping they might find at least one good thing about the day—I asked, "What did you learn from the experience?"

"That some people are *more* perfect than others!" Angeline answered.

"Well, there you have it!" Aaron announced. "Discrimination is alive and thriving at Jefferson High!"

"I don't think it's fair to mistrust someone just because her brother wasn't trustworthy," Tookie asserted in her own defense.

"And I just don't understand why you should be less popular just because you're overweight," Angeline remarked, the sparkle in her brown eyes dimming. "I mean, I'm a really good singer, and I always get the lead in the choir as well as the plays that need a strong singer, but even so, my talent and good grades aren't enough to make me popular. And it's all because I'm overweight. But what really upsets me is that some of the kids will make snide remarks about my weight, like calling me 'chubs' and stuff. Even when it's coming from friends who are just saying it in fun, it still hurts, even if they smile or laugh when they say it."

"How do you respond to that?" I inquired.

"On days when I'm feeling good, I can take it. But on days when I'm not feeling so great, it makes me cry," she admitted. "What do you think I should do about it?" she asked, her expression intent.

"Well, I think you have a couple of choices," I answered. "You could tell your friends how their comments hurt you, for one. And you can decide how much power you're going to give their words. I mean, what you think about yourself matters too, so if your opinion of yourself is a good one, it can take a little of the sting out of their comments. It helps to remember that we re-create ourselves all the time. The person you see today is not necessarily the you of next year."

Angeline considered my comment and then laughed as she said, "Well, that's true! I know that I'm not the nerd I was in eighth grade!"

"That's what's so wonderful about each day," I said. "We get to start anew. As we learn more about who we'd like to become, we can *re-create* ourselves, each creation moving closer to who we really are. We already hold a picture of that person in our mind. Often we just need to get the outer picture to match the inner picture. It's up to each of us to move closer toward that vision, no one else can do it for us. Try this: Close your eyes and describe to me the Angeline you see in your mind's eye."

Angeline closed her eyes and in a lovely voice, said softly, "Angeline puts a lot of time into training her voice. She's very successful, a great singer and stage actress."

"Sounds good," I remarked. "Tell me more."

She sighed, and continued: "Well, she's beautiful, smart, has a great body. . . ." With those words, Angeline laughed, opened her eyes and said, "Oh, yeah! I can see re-creating myself!" She was quiet for a moment longer before adding, "I need to become who I *really* am."

"You've just put your finger on the real truth," I remarked and then counseled, "The work of life is to grow closer to who we really are, closer to the image of the person we know ourselves to be deep down. Sometimes we have to help others see that person inside, but even if they don't, we can't forget about that person in there. We have to love her and root for her—even when others do not."

With sadness in her voice, Angeline asked, "What about when they're mean to me? Can I re-create that, too?"

"Let's try it," I suggested. "How would you like to see it fixed?" I asked.

"I'd have all the kids in the entire school write me an apology letter!" she answered.

"Okay," I said, and then asked, "What would it say?"

Angeline closed her eyes and sat still for a few moments as she collected her thoughts. Soon a beautiful smile appeared and, as if unfolding an imaginary letter, she then "read" it:

Dear Angeline,
Isn't it nice to know that there are people who admire you not only

for the way you are but for who you are becoming? We think you are a great talent and a good friend. And remember, a bid doesn't reflect your worth. We think you are priceless—and we are embarrassed to admit that no one that day could afford you!

Love,
Everyone at Jefferson High!

Bettie B. Youngs

14

Stress, Moods and Other Tough Stuff

TELL ME "WHY?"

Please God, tell me why
Friends have to die.
It's not fair and it's not right.
Oh God, why that night?

I didn't think life could end so fast.
She was so young but her years didn't last.
Now it's too late to say goodbye.
Please God, tell me, "Why?"

Even if her soul is flying free,
Now her dreams can never be.
Teens aren't supposed to die.
I need an answer, God. Please, tell me, "Why?"

Maybe life isn't what it seems,
And not all teens get their dreams.

I know we're all meant to someday die,
Still God, I have to ask you, "Why?"

Peggy Nunziata, 16

A Word from the Authors

"Mom, adolescence is a time of a million questions like *Am I only the only who feels like I do? Will my complexion ever clear up? Will the boy I like ask me out? How do I get my parents to see my side of things? Will they let me use the car on Saturday night? How can I have more friends? How can I make better grades? Can I afford that terrific new CD? What am I going to do after I graduate? With so many options, what do I really want to do in life—how do I decide what my interests and talents are anyway? Should I go to college? What should I say to my friend who thinks she's pregnant?* Just thinking about these questions makes you realize that not only do you not have all the answers, but also that others (including your own hormones) have as much 'control' or 'say-so' as you do. Besides, this isn't even the extent of your questions—the list goes on and on. There's a problem waiting for you at every turn."

"Jennifer, no one's life is problem-free—at any age—but I do think that teens today are under a great deal of stress, worry far more than we might suspect and wish they were happier."

"Adolescence is such a confusing time, Mom. You're up, you're down. Things are terrific one day and in the pits the next. And, you really don't understand your intense feelings—everything seems so 'do or die.' Also, you don't always know what to do about it, or who to turn to. I think that's why teens everywhere loved the story about Mostly. They understand that, just like Mostly, we all have our moods and would like others to respect that sometimes we just need them to be sensitive and understanding—even gentle with us—as we try to make sense of our lives.

"Many of the problems teens must come to terms with are issues they are confronting for the first time, so it's not like they have the experience to always know the best way to handle things. Sometimes they don't even know what to do at all. For example, when I was in eleventh grade, the mother of a good friend of mine had cancer. My friend was so afraid that her mother would die, and yet, she was also very angry with her mother because her illness overshadowed every aspect of their family's life. Her feelings about her mother and her mother's illness dominated her life. They affected my life, too. I didn't really know what to say to my friend to console her, and she vacillated between defending her mother and being angry with her. No matter what I said, invariably, it was *not* what she wanted to hear at that moment. When we were at her house, I never knew what to say to her mother. So many of the teens we heard from were dealing with confusing and painful times of their own. Like me, they didn't necessarily know what to do or who to turn to."

"These are all very tough, very real issues for teens, Jennifer."

"So you cope the best you can. When you're a teen, sometimes you want to hide and just not have to deal with all the emotional pain—all the hurting. So you just 'drop out' emotionally. It's sort of like sleepwalking—you're not really paying close attention to all the things you're supposed to be doing, like staying on top of your schoolwork and being conscientious about keeping promises and commitments. Sometimes you just feel so lost—and that frustrates you and makes you upset with yourself—that you lash out at your parents or your friends, just because you don't know how to handle it all. Sometimes you argue or pick fights with them (even though they aren't to blame), or you develop an attitude that you know your parents (or teachers) aren't going to stand for, but you just want to see the reaction. In an indirect way, this is just you telling them that you want them to carry the load for a little while. That tactic usually doesn't work."

"Jennifer, when others offer love and understanding, why be angry or 'lash out' at them?"

"Because, Mom, you trust that they're the people who will love you and not leave you at the time when you're feeling your very worst—your most vulnerable and your most unlovable. It's not like you want to take it out on the people you love and trust the most. It's also not as if you can always handle things correctly. Sometimes you realize you're making a mistake, sometimes you don't. Sometimes you 'doctor' your pain by making choices you wouldn't normally make—doing self-destructive things like drinking or taking drugs, hoping these make the pain stop. Sometimes we are embarrassed about what we've done and asking others for help can be a hard thing to do, especially if we are uncertain how they'll respond. It takes a while to realize that we can lean on those we love when we are learning to cope with tough times. We learn that leaning doesn't mean that we aren't strong and responsible. The good news is, as we saw in many of the teen comments in 'A New Boy in My Life'—where many of their opinions were as straightforward and poignant as Helena's—that teens are open and willing to look for loving solutions to tough issues."

Again, we remind you that if you—or a friend—are facing an issue as serious and life-changing as finding out that you are pregnant (or even suspecting that you are) you don't have to sort it out alone. While hurting is a personal "pain" for each of us, we need not go through it alone. Should you find yourself going through a time when the pain just seems too great to handle—rather than suffer alone or resort to doing things that are self-destructive, confide in an adult you trust.

In this chapter, you will meet other teens who are dealing with tough challenges and learn how they are working through them. Interestingly, not all teens see only a down side to the tough issues of life. Many teens found a bittersweet "taste berry" in their pain and said, "It's the pain that got my attention." They saw it as an important signal: they needed to take better care of themselves.

"Mom, when we do this, when we take better care of ourselves, we lighten the load a bit. I know I don't take things as seriously, things aren't so 'do-or-die' as they seemed in high school. Back then, when I was upset with anyone, or something didn't turn out the way I wanted it to, the problem just seemed so catastrophic, so never-ending."

"What do you think is the reason for this change?"

"Well, for one thing, I've gained a little perspective, and for another, I've learned at least a couple of skills to repair 'the leak in the boat.' Do you remember the story about the leak in the boat?"

"No, I don't believe I do."

"It goes like this: There was a woman standing on a shore who saw a man in a rowboat, frantically alternating between rowing the boat and bailing water out of it. 'If you don't bring that boat ashore and repair the leak,' the woman yelled, 'you're going to drown!' 'Can't you see, lady?' the man shouted back. 'I don't have time to fix the leak! I'm too busy bailing out water.'"

"It makes a good point, Jennifer. As the story shows, it's important to find the leak in time, before it gets really big! Sometimes we get so embroiled in the problem that we focus on it long after it's productive to do so—often to the point where it's counterproductive—instead of moving on and working toward finding a solution."

"It's taken a long time for me to learn many of those 'boat repair' skills. And, unfortunately, by making some poor decisions, I've actually caused some of the holes myself. But I keep reminding myself of what I tell teens and their parents: You can learn from your mistakes."

The teens we heard from agreed with Jennifer. Hindsight enabled many teens to see that some very good lessons came from their mistakes—even though it didn't feel like anything good could come from them when they were in the middle of their problems. Like the man in the boat, we are often just caught up in continuing to row furiously away, unable to get anywhere and taking on more and more water.

A first step toward "fixing our boat" is gaining perspective—stepping back, taking a deep breath and looking at the entire picture, not just pieces of it. In the story "Miss Alpo," there's a community rumor that a woman eats dog food. But the whole rumor was based on only a small piece of the picture. "The Lovers' Fight" is another good example of how perspective can change the whole picture. Driving behind a car with two people in it, I thought the couple was having an argument, while Jennifer thought they were two lovers engaged in a romantic conversation. But when we looked at the two people from a different angle, we were surprised to discover that we were both completely wrong.

A second step toward "fixing the boat" is taking the time to think about the consequences of the decisions you're making. It takes discipline to stop simply reacting on impulse and, instead, to honestly "get a handle" on the situation. It's important to weigh the consequences. In "The Gun Wasn't Even Loaded," Shawn McLaughlin, seventeen, wished he had considered the consequences before he took his father's gun to school. Shawn learned that although the gun wasn't loaded, the potential for disaster was! In the end, Shawn was the one who had to suffer the disastrous consequences, which included his ending up in juvenile hall.

Another step toward "fixing the boat" is making a decision to "get back in charge" when things first begin to get out of control. When Rob Lawson, fifteen, hit the snooze button instead of getting ready for school, not only did he find himself running late, but because he had to ask his dad to give him a ride, he had the stress of his dad being upset with him. Now being late for school resulted in an "unexcused" slip, and so his first-hour teacher didn't allow him to make up the quiz he missed. Those were valuable missed points, and resulted in his being so upset that he found himself making one poor choice after another. Rob realized the effects of his stress and decided to stop the cycle, and not allow a series of small setbacks to snowball into an avalanche of stress.

If you're having a hard time managing your day-to-day stresses, there are practical steps you can take to help you gain stress-management skills. You can make a to-do list, so you're clear about what you need to do and by when, or you can keep a calendar or day-planner where you list all your projects, appointments, assignments and their due dates. Take classes on time- and stress-management. Make sure you rest and eat properly. As basic as this sounds, feeling your best physically will help reduce stress, help you think more clearly and give you the energy you need to manage your time and activities the most efficiently. You should turn to friends and family to whom you can talk openly about any struggles you are having coping with daily stress.

As we said earlier, on those days when everything about our life seems bleak, if we give ourselves permission to be extra good to ourselves (get enough rest, eat properly, exercise to be fit and to release tension) and reach out to those whom we know will offer support and understanding, then we can use the difficult experience to help us gain perspective. If we do this, the experience will help us become stronger and wiser. It also helps us develop compassion for others. Again, this is how we each become a better "taste berry" to others—and to ourselves.

Mostly

In Del Mar, California, there is a quaint little specialty pet supply store by the name of Petland, where a big kitty spends his days. He's a very beautiful cat with a thick coat of glossy-white fur that's sprinkled with patches of orange and black tufts. This is capped off with a pure-white face, set off by a teeny-tiny nose that is entirely midnight black. He's a very proud-looking kitty, and I suspect he is. He's also a bit standoffish, preferring to observe customers rather than interact with them. Nevertheless, many customers, especially children, cannot resist petting him. Though I've seen him on a number of occasions while in the store, he was always asleep, so I hadn't disturbed him.

One day while in the store, I observed a father and his two children, who, when they noticed the cat (who lay asleep) hurried over to stroke him. Startled when the first little hand clumsily landed on his back, the surprised cat hissed defensively at the child. Momentarily frightened, the youngster jumped back, and then stood silent. But this didn't deter his brother. Without hesitation, he, too, reached over to stroke the cat. Like his brother before him, it was the exuberant and innocent pat of a child, his touch uncensored and untrained in being careful and gentle. Once again, the cat disapproved. He hissed again, and then shuffled around in the little nest atop the little perch he was in, turning his body from the comfortable position he was in to one more active and alert.

"What's the matter with you?" the father demanded brusquely, and at the same time placed his hand squarely on the cat's head, no doubt intending to stroke the animal. This infuriated the cat even more. Now beside himself, the cat's meow sounded anxious. It was easy to see that he'd like these interlopers to leave him alone. It worked. Making a few off-handed remarks about the "unfriendly" and "unsociable" cat, the father and his two sons went on about their business of browsing in the store.

I have two cats of my own, both of whom love attention and affection—but like most cats, they prefer to be the one to let you know when they want to be petted. Knowing this, I walked over and stood quietly by the cat, just observing him for a moment. He observed me right back. Then I began talking gently to him, basically to calm him and so he could tell by the tone of my voice that he needn't be fearful of me. "Hi, kitty," I said in a soothing tone. "You look like a sweetheart to me. Surely you must like being stroked." On and on I gibbered, waiting for him to relax before finally asking, "Won't you let me touch you?"

Slowly I put my hand out for him to smell, then raised it ever so slowly above his head, with the intention of then rubbing him. Before I could lower my hand to lovingly connect, the cat beat me to it, raising his head with friendly purpose to make contact with my hand. "Aha!" I exclaimed. "You do like to be touched!" And with that, I gently stroked the beautiful cat.

Unbeknownst to me, the store owner, a friendly, helpful man who takes his cat with him to work each day, had been observing. "Pick him up," he invited. "I can see he'd like that."

"Is he usually this sensitive to people petting him?" I inquired.

"Mostly," the store owner replied. "Go ahead. Pick him up."

So I did. I lifted the large cat from his perch and down into my arms. It was then that I discovered the cat had only three legs! "What happened?" I asked the owner, now standing beside me.

"There is no particular story as to how he lost his back left leg," the man said, "he simply was born without it. The vet told me that perhaps because the nerve endings are so close to the surface, the missing leg pains him, and so he's overly sensitive. Sometimes customers think that he's a cantankerous kitty, but the assumption is . . ." the man searched for the right word and looking at the kitty, chuckled and then finished his sentence with, "only mostly correct."

"So does he like people, or just tolerate them?" I asked.

"I think he likes them—mostly," he said, laughing good-naturedly before adding, "Though I think the area around his missing leg sometimes hurts him, especially when people handle him roughly, or pet him without advance warning, like the young unsuspecting children did today."

"So, what's this kitty's name?" I asked, now stroking the purring cat.

"Mostly," the man said, smiling.

"Mostly?" I asked, wondering if I had heard the man correctly. "Mostly?"

"Mmhmm," he replied.

"How did he get a name like Mostly?"

"Well," the man replied thoughtfully, "He's a kitty that didn't come with all his parts, but mostly he did! He doesn't always like to be touched, but mostly he does. So, we call him Mostly!"

Now feeling safe and secure, there was nothing "mostly" about the cat's desire to be stroked. Basking in the attention, and liking it, Mostly purred and leaned his head into my hands demanding to be stroked.

Perhaps Mostly reacted as most of us do when others impose themselves on us without first asking or warning—and sometimes, even when we object. It was clear to see that Mostly had his reasons, as we all do, for our moods. Respecting "his reasons" was the key to making a friend of him. And, just like most people, when Mostly found I was going to be sensitive to his moods—and his right to have them—he became my friend.

Bettie B. Youngs

The New Boy in My Life

There is a new boy in my life. He's just across the room, sleeping. Though he is younger than me, I've never been so in love. I've been in love lots of times, but this is different. I am sure I will always be in love with Ruben. He's real, and our love is real, though sometimes when it's quiet and the house is still, I drift off and become lost in this place in my imagination. There I see myself being carefree, going to college, working part-time, dancing and partying the weekends away. I see myself wearing the "in" clothes and driving a car of my own. I see myself looking forward to new and exciting things to do and places to go. I see myself dating some great guy. It's a fantasy place that will never be because of the new boy in my life.

In a crib across the room lies my new love, my sleeping baby boy.

Finding out I was pregnant at the age of seventeen was the most traumatic news I've ever received in my whole life. In my heart, I knew I was pregnant before I ever took a pregnancy test, but having the results come back positive was my worst nightmare confirmed.

I had always thought if I ever got pregnant, I'd get an abortion for sure. Having a baby while being a teenager would be unreal and something I would never want. I enjoyed time with my friends; late nights out dancing; being able to sleep in on weekend mornings; and having no worries besides an exam at school, or what to wear for a big date. Besides, I thought it could never happen to me.

But it did.

Suddenly, I noticed every pregnant woman, whether she was four months pregnant or nine. I noticed every single baby stroller in the vicinity. Both images were nerve-wracking. My first thoughts were to schedule an abortion immediately. But on the second wave of anxiety, I saw myself holding my baby. Or reading to my little child, or walking hand in hand down the street with her. Or sitting across the table in a restaurant with my teenager, like my mother and I do. At those times, I'd think of what I would name my baby.

These images often collided with each other, leaving me confused and filled with an overwhelming, anxious self-doubt. One moment I thought, "I can't have a baby!" and the next, "I want my baby." The back and forth and back and forth of my seesaw of emotions produced an endless and crazed agony. And it made me realize that even if I ended my pregnancy, I would never be the same again. Just being pregnant was a life-altering experience. With or without the baby, I would never be the same.

That I was pregnant filled my every waking moment and overshadowed the importance of everything else—friendships, grades, the upcoming prom I had so looked forward to attending.

My boyfriend stopped seeing me the instant I told him I was pregnant. He ran the other way. I guess he found that was easier than facing the consequences of pregnancy. Sometimes I wished I could have done just that—ignore and forget. But I couldn't; I was the one carrying a life within me. On some days, I wanted to do what he did. Other days I was so angry, I wanted to just pound him into the sand. I told him the pregnancy was also his responsibility, at least financially. He said, "No, it takes two to decide they want to have sex. I never wanted a kid. You let yourself get pregnant. It was never part of what I wanted." And so I faced my decision knowing that if I kept the baby I'd be doing it alone, that my baby's father would not help me in any way.

Making the decision to keep my baby was the hardest and most altering decision I have ever made. I actually made an appointment to have an abortion, but I never went. In the end, I just couldn't go through with it. So, I finally told my mother that I was pregnant and wanted to keep the baby. We talked and cried and had harsh words. And then she did what she always does: she supported me in my decision.

Then a new phase began: I was to become a statistic, a single teenage mother.

It was hard to stay positive when I was pregnant. Even with my mother's support, I felt so alone. Being pregnant, taking care of myself, coping with myself became a full-time job. It was a very trying time. Physically I was hungry and exhausted all the time. And my emotions—always erratic—ruled me. At times, I felt full of love and happiness for everyone and everything. At other times, I was filled with feelings of anger and hostility for everyone and everything. Sometimes I just felt very sober—and alone. I cried a lot.

Throughout my entire pregnancy, I questioned if I had made the right decision. And every day of it, I questioned if I had the strength to see it through. I longed for problems of my past; now they seemed so trivial and minute. I wished I was simply in an argument with my mother over curfew, or with my boyfriend because he wasn't on time for a date. I would gladly exchange my new problems for the old ones! But there's no way to be half-pregnant. I simply had to cope. And so I struggled from day to day—for nine long months.

Before I was pregnant, I valued my friends over my family. My parents are divorced. I'm the youngest of four. During my pregnancy, it was somehow very important to me to have a relationship with each of them. A good relationship with my mother became an important priority—and a bridge to my new reality. I stopped seeing her as "police of rules" and, instead, as someone who possessed information I was suddenly interested in. I needed to know if all the ways I questioned myself, from my health to the daily games my mind played on me, to my uncertainty and even fear of going through childbirth was normal or not. My mother quickly became a teacher—and a solid friend.

My doctor did a sonogram, a picture of the baby inside you,

like an X-ray—only better. On the day that I first saw this image of my baby, I called my father for the first time in two years. Before that, it was he who telephoned and me who rolled my eyes and begged my mother to tell him I was too busy to take his call. We talked for a long time. It felt nice to be close to an adult male, someone who cared for me no matter what.

Though I wanted a good relationship with my two sisters, it didn't turn out that way. I now found that being with them only made me feel bad about what I was missing out on—and wished I wasn't. It was just too difficult to watch them living the life I thought I had been heading for; going to work, shopping for a special outfit for a big date or a special party, searching for a bigger and better apartment because a raise from a job was in the works. They were extra kind to me and asked me a lot of questions about what it was like to be pregnant. And they were very sure that they intended not to get pregnant before marriage. Even talking about boys wasn't as exciting as it used to be because I was feeling bitter toward the father of my baby, and being pregnant didn't make me the most sought-after date! Hearing about my sisters' escapades only made me feel down on myself.

My relationship with my older brother changed too. He is twenty-seven and in love with a woman who is twenty-six. They have *plans*—plans for saving for a nice wedding, for a home, for traveling together before having children. Plans that, in his words, call for the "responsible planning of children." I got the message; it stung.

It was my family, more than anyone else—especially my mom—that helped me get through those nine months. I came to realize that family comes first and means the most. I now value my true friends—those who stuck with me through all my moods. Fair-weather friends had to go. But of course, I didn't have to tell them to go; many left on their own accord.

The day I turned eighteen, I was seven months pregnant. The

day I was "legally an adult" didn't feel like I thought it would. First of all, there was no all-night wild party for me. I was a tired, seven-months-pregnant person sipping water! And though I was eighteen, I felt anything but grown-up and independent. In fact, I felt as if I were a child who wanted—and needed—to cuddle up in the arms of my parents. Or my boyfriend. Better yet, my husband and father of my child.

Going from being pregnant to holding a baby in my arms and actually becoming a mother produced the biggest change of all. I can't sugar-coat my story in describing my son. He's a little thing who cries a lot, frowns a lot and always *needs*. He needs constant care and attention. There is no such thing as an easy day. Tending to his needs leaves me tired, harried and feeling frazzled. Sometimes I resent him because he's so much work, and I don't have time for my friends. I sometimes resent that where once I spent money for makeup and getting my nails done, now I buy baby formula and diapers instead. The money I once saved for a special outfit is now saved for things my baby needs. Currently I'm saving for a jumper-swing, a piece of baby furniture that will come in handy as I try to keep him quiet and soothed long enough for me to get my homework done. I want to graduate from high school. I have four months to go.

But I don't want to resent him, so I remind myself that my son is helpless and innocent and that he didn't ask for his circumstance: He is an outcome of *my* doing. It makes me feel better to tell myself that he is a gift, that there's a reason why he was brought into my life.

There are other changes. When I look in the mirror, I see someone totally different than just months ago. I see what others do not see. Like others who see me, I still see a youthful face, but I now see a face far more experienced than I care to be, someone who *feels* far older than her years. I find it strange that the face in my mirror is also the face of a mother. Others tell me I have smiling, friendly, pretty eyes; I see them as tired from worry. But they are also eyes that have never smiled so much, smiled every time I see my baby. My body, the once-lithe form that all too quickly accepted its ability to grow life inside, cannot hide its loss of innocence. Though it may not be noticeable to others, it is to me: My hips are wider, and my waist and rib cage are larger than before. The angle and form of my breasts have changed. Mine are more than just a part of my physical beauty; now they feed an infant. The mouth that hungered for the kisses from my boyfriend now hungers to kiss the infant baby boy I love. And where once it uttered "I," it now says "we." The appearance of my nose remains unchanged, but new smells arouse my senses. Where once my nose so readily took in the scent of my boyfriend's cologne, now it takes in the scent of a baby's skin—and stands guard to alert me to his soured stomach or dirty diapers.

My ears look the same, but they aren't. Where once they listened for the phone to ring, now they wait for different tones— like the regular breathing of an infant in the middle of the night, or for his cries for food or comfort. I no longer fuss over the chipping of my once-salon-manicured nails, no longer concerned with their uniformed length nor intrigued with the latest color. Nothing, it seems, remains unchanged. Even my dreams for the future have changed from "me and mine," to "him and his" and "ours."

But there are other changes too, more positive ones, even if they are challenging. I never thought it was possible to love someone so deeply. But I do. I would do anything for my son. Not a moment goes by that I do not think of him or do for him. For sure, he is the most beautiful creature in this world, with ten tiny fingers and ten tiny toes, a little upturned nose, delicate lips and beautiful, brown, sparkling eyes. Though he needs me, he also loves me. It's a feeling that registers deep within me. It's a feeling that has left me changed, altered forever. One I never want to live without.

Still, I worry all the time. I'm only eighteen and I worry about my future, and that of my son's. I worry that I'll have to put my dreams on hold in order to provide for him. And I worry that I may not be able to provide for him. I worry what the effects will be for him not having a father who loves and wants him. I worry if I can be patient enough to be a good mother: I have a child to raise; a little person who needs to learn how to become a good person. I know I have to be strong and hope I can.

I still want to be a carefree teenager. Sometimes I want to just run from the house and not return home. Sometimes I dream that I'm back in time fourteen months ago, and making a different decision. But I'm a mother of this little boy now, a little boy who smiles at me with twinkling eyes. In his eyes, I see my future—a future that has arrived. So though I'd like to dance the night away in some great place with my friends, I can't. I must get some sleep. I have a long-standing date with the new boy in my life—and he's counting on me. And when I doubt myself, I need only look into his face and see his smile and his twinkling eyes, and I know the choice between dancing the night away and time with friends has been made for me.

My life is not going to be easy, but the new boy in my life can count on me. And I will not run away; I will be his love—his taste-berry love—for always.

Helena Moreno, 18

I'm the Baby's Father

I've often thought about how it's never up to the father to decide what's going to happen when it affects his life, too. That doesn't seem fair to me.

My best buddy's girlfriend decided to have an abortion and he didn't have any say in the matter. He still can't get it out of his mind. As far as he's concerned, he lost a child—and his parents lost a grandchild. He's very upset about it, and I understand completely.

It just seems one-sided that making a decision about having an abortion is always considered a girl's right and hers alone.

Just because my friend didn't want to get married to his girlfriend at seventeen didn't mean he didn't want to be his child's father. No one asked how his parents felt about it either.

I can understand that my buddy's girlfriend was probably scared and really thought her decision not to have the baby was the best one possible, but I wish she would have thought about how many lives her decision was affecting. If she had, maybe she would have realized that the decision might not be hers alone to make. It even seems to me that it would be easier to make that kind of decision with someone you once felt close to.

Rob Stephenson, 17

A Horrific Experience

My choice was the opposite of Helena's, so I know what she means when she says even if she didn't have the baby she'd never be the same. Just the experience of having been pregnant means that you can never be the same. An abortion can't change that fact.

Six months ago, I had an abortion. It is the most horrific experience I've ever been through. I can't put it out of my mind. Sometimes when I see a baby or when I'm missing mine, I wonder what my child would have looked like and what kind of a person she would have been, especially when she grew up. Would she have been someone who invented a cure for a terrible disease, or someone very ordinary? Or, would she have been someone who went to prison for doing something bad?

Sometimes when I see a baby, my heart aches and I feel terrible for what I've done. Always, always I wonder if I made the right decision to have an abortion. I never question my decision to have unprotected sex. It was the most stupid, irresponsible and hurtful thing I could have ever done.

Now when I hear people talk about facing an unwanted pregnancy, my whole heart goes out to them. If only they could feel what my heart feels now that I've done what I've done, they could make a better, wiser choice.

Trisha Cartland, 16

I Think She's Selfish

I just wonder if Helena's decision to keep her baby was the best one. After all, what kind of life can a teenager give a baby? It's not like having an abortion or keeping the baby are the only options. There are so many people who want to adopt a child. My aunt can't have kids of her own, and she and her husband have tried for two years to adopt and still haven't been able to.

There are so many couples who want a child to love and care for—great couples, who aren't kids and who have great lives together. After reading Helena's story, I realize more clearly how important it is to make certain to prevent such a situation from happening in the first place. But, if my girlfriend ever became pregnant, I would advise her to put the baby up for adoption rather than have an abortion.

I see adoption as a very compassionate answer—and the most unselfish one.

Jake Lempke, 15

An Abortion at Fifteen

I had an abortion when I was fifteen. So when I got pregnant again at sixteen, I knew it wasn't as easy a decision to make as some people think. This time, my boyfriend and I wanted to keep the baby, but still I was scared. Luckily we have a lot of friends. So we all got together, and I asked them for their opinions. We all talked about whether or not I should keep the baby. Then we voted on it. And that's how I made the final decision.

I had the baby four months ago. Though my boyfriend and I aren't together any longer, his parents like the baby and watch him much of the time. I'm not sure if I'm all that ready to be a parent because I like to have time for my friends, but luckily for me, my mother and ex-boyfriend's parents like being grandparents. Still, sometimes when I date a boy, I wished that I didn't have to explain to him that I also have a child.

Being a parent is a lot more complicated than you may think— even if your parents are helping you care for your baby until you get it together.

Lisa Brown, 16

Just Because I Say I Love You . . .

I think too many girls in high school think that just because a guy tells her that he loves her, it means she's found the person she is going to marry. That's not realistic.

Most guys fall in love for the first time in ninth grade and think only about that one girl. But that's the last time that sort of thinking goes on. After your first heartbreak, a guy may be in love time and time again, but he has no thoughts about marriage—not in high school. From that point on, it's not even something that crosses his mind. I mean, just because I tell a girl "I love you" doesn't mean I want her to pick out a china pattern! I mean, let's just be frank. Most high school romances do not end up in marriage!

Shane Wiggins, 17

Picking Up the Pieces

When I was in ninth grade, a boy I was sure I was in love with started dating my best friend. Just like that. One day he was walking me to my locker; and the next day, he was walking my very best friend to her locker. "We're not going together anymore!" he announced, and in the same breath added, "I'm going with Tammy now."

I didn't know how to "fix it." I didn't know what to think or how to feel. Should I be mad at him? Angry with my best friend? How should I explain it to my friends?

I was clear about one thing: I hurt all over. No one, not even my friends or parents really knew how deeply I was hurting. I didn't want to go to school. I didn't want to go to soccer practice. I didn't want to do anything. I just wanted to be alone. I didn't want to talk with anyone about it—certainly not my parents.

Not that it stopped them from asking. Noting that I was upset at just about everyone and everything, Mom asked, "Would you like to talk about what's bothering you?"

"No!" I cried.

"Talking can make it better," Mom reminded me.

"It's just about my stupid best friend. I'll be okay," I said, hoping I didn't have to explain any more.

She didn't ask again, no doubt assuming that I'd tell her about it when I was ready. In the meantime, my parents were extra kind and tried to give me the space I needed; like a couple of times they allowed me to eat dinner in my room rather than coming to the dinner table.

After about a week or so of my still being tearful, my mother stepped up her inspection of the issue. "I can see you are suffering over this," she said. "I think we should talk about it."

"Oh, Mom," I cried. "It hurts too much to talk about it!"

"Yes, honey," she soothed, "I can see that you are hurting."

"Why does it hurt so much?" I asked.

"Pain is God's way of saying your heart is broken."

"I don't need God to tell me my heart is broken," I cried. "I just need him to fix it."

"Well," my mother counseled tenderly, "better give him all the pieces. God can't fix your broken heart if you don't give all the pieces to him."

I'll always remember those beautiful words: "God can't fix a broken heart if you don't give him all the pieces."

Jennifer Leigh Youngs

The Lovers' Fight

On our way to the airport, my daughter and I found ourselves traveling behind a car with two very animated passengers inside of it.

On the passenger side, a woman pressed herself against the door on her side of the car, practically leaning out the window. It appeared to me that she was rejecting whatever the driver—who was visibly upset—was saying. Her husband shook his head from side-to-side, shaking his fist in the air, and from time to time he bobbed his head in the direction of his wife, as if to punctuate his tirade. Observing them made me uneasy. I took note of the fact that my daughter was gazing intently in their direction. Trying to lighten the impact of witnessing such conflict, I teased, "Think they're just arguing over whose turn it is to cook dinner?"

My daughter, nineteen at the time, looked at me in total amazement. "Why would you assume they're arguing, Mother?" she chided. "They are lovers! These two aren't wasting time arguing over whose turn it is to cook dinner!"

Surprised and interested in this completely different viewpoint, I asked, "Lovers? How do you figure that?"

"Well, just look at them, Mom," she directed. "The guy's girlfriend is resting against the door on her side of the car because she's got her legs stretched out on the seat. When he's not making a point, he's probably rubbing her feet. And look how happy they are. The boyfriend is using his hands to express himself passionately, and he keeps moving his head from side to side, always in her direction, as if he's just drawn towards her. They're probably planning something wonderful, or discussing the fun of some trip they just got back from—or maybe even sharing something funny about their friends."

"Sorry, Jennifer, I just don't see it that way," I said.

Jennifer advised, "Keep an open mind, Mom."

"Let's check it out," I suggested.

"Okay," she said. So sure she was right about the two people in the car in front of us, Jennifer wagered, "Whoever is wrong has to cook dinner."

So sure I was right, I willingly conceded. "Deal!" I said.

Curious to solve the mystery of whose perception was accurate, as we stopped at the stop sign where they were turning right and we were turning left, Jennifer and I made certain to get a better look. My "husband and wife" and Jennifer's "boyfriend and girlfriend" were, in fact, two men! The driver wore his hair short, the passenger wore his shoulder length. They were eating and laughing. Just two regular guys, together at lunch hour, coming or going somewhere, enjoying each other's company, maybe telling jokes or discussing a movie they had seen!

We had both been wrong about their relationship, though Jen had no doubt been right about one thing: These two probably weren't wasting time arguing over whose turn it was to cook dinner! As Jennifer said, "It just goes to show you, things aren't always what they seem!"

Then she informed me, "So, I guess we're eating out!"

Bettie B. Youngs

Miss "Alpo"

When I was a young girl, I heard a rumor that an older woman, who lived in the same town I did, was so poor that all she could afford to eat was dog food. This sounded illogical to me (and very unappealing), until one day, while in the grocery store with my mother, I saw her at the check-out counter with nothing more than two bags of dog food in her grocery cart. "Aha!" I thought, "The rumor must be true!"

The woman lived on the outskirts of town in a large two-story house that sat back from the street. Two other buildings sat on her property: a shed of some sort and a small barn or hay loft. Perhaps at one time her property had been a farm. Now it was encased by blocks and blocks of houses on all sides—she had her own farm in the city.

Because the woman mostly kept to herself and was rarely out and about except for her trips to the grocery store, no one seemed to know too much about her other than that she had two grown children, both of whom lived in other cities. Many said that her name was Ida, but we kids called her "Miss Alpo"— Alpo being the brand of dog food frequently seen in her grocery cart. We thought our nickname for her was original and, of course, very, very funny. When our school bus passed Ida's home on the way to our school each morning and afternoon, we rivaled to be the first to say something clever about Miss Alpo. "Wonder what Miss Alpo is having for lunch today?" someone would gibe. The comment was greeted by a chorus of giggles— and yet another comment.

One day, having missed the bus because I had been late to class and had to stay after school to make up the time, I was walking home from school and passed by Miss Alpo's house. As I neared her property, I heard the whimpering of what sounded like a small dog. Then I saw the puppy—a very cute little brown- and black-speckled basset hound. Delighted to see the small animal, I called, "Hi, puppy!" Suddenly, not just one puppy but a whole litter of little spotted basset hounds came loping to the wire gate to view the passerby, tripping over one another's long floppy ears as each clamored to get there first. Seeing me, they yipped and moaned in anticipation, frantically wagging their little tails.

Unable to resist a closer look at the puppies, I hurried over. The puppies struggled to get closer to me, pouncing and tumbling over each other. The ones in front were now standing on their hind legs, their plump little bodies leaned taunt against the wire gate so as to be as close to me as possible. Like the pup who greeted me, the others looked to be about one or two months old. As I stood with my fingers poked through the wire fence to enjoy their affectionate licks, I was startled by a woman's voice.

"Hello there!" There, in the middle of her yard, in a large, old wooden chair, sat Miss Alpo bottle-feeding a teeny tiny puppy. Next to her lay a mother basset, feeding a litter of newborns.

"Seems they like you!" she called in a friendly voice, nodding her head in the direction of the puppies. At the sound of her voice, the puppies turned to face her. When she looked toward me, they turned and looked at me also. This they did alternately, gazing expectantly from her to me, from me to her, perhaps trying to decide to whom to pledge their allegiance—on the one hand, devoted caretaker, on the other, exciting new smaller person.

"Want to give me a hand feeding them? One of my two female bassets had her puppies today and this little guy here," she motioned with her chin to the one she was holding, "is not quite sure if he has the strength to make it. I'm trying to convince him that life is wonderful, and he should give it a chance. But, I've been holding the little guy and trying to get some food in him for nearly two hours. Oh, by the way, my name is Idalene," she announced. "Some call me Ida, though I prefer Idalene." Then, motioning in the direction of the begging puppies she added, "As you can see, that 'tribe' is hungry. It's past their feeding time!" Smiling, she shook her head fondly at the lively litter. "They're sure growing fast," she remarked. "All of those are sold. Next week they'll be old enough to go to their new homes. I'm sure going to miss them, but as you can see, I've got a new family of pups to raise. Anyway, if you just lift that top latch the gate will open. In the corner of that first shed, you'll find a bag of Alpo. The bag is small, so you shouldn't have any trouble carrying it. I'd tell you where their bowls are, but I won't need to. As soon as they see you holding the bag of food, they'll run straight to their food bowls!" Laughing, she advised, "Just follow them!" She turned her concentration back to the newborn pup she held.

"Miss Alpo"—or rather, Idalene—raised basset hounds!

Having fallen in love with the puppies that day—and having a drastic change of opinion about what the woman was doing with the dog food she purchased—I visited her frequently after that, sometimes just to play with the puppies. It wasn't long before we became good friends. In the process of visiting and helping her with the puppies, I became quite attached to that one little puppy who she'd been coaxing to take a chance at life the day we first met.

Several months later, on my birthday to be exact, Idalene presented me with a gift—that teeny tiny little pup she had so carefully and lovingly convinced to make a go at life. Now it was a plump, rambunctious, playful and very healthy puppy. She named him Chance because she said, "Not only does every living being deserve a chance," but also because she was "glad he decided to give life a chance."

That puppy became one of the most remarkable and devoted pets I ever had the pleasure of raising—no doubt because of the woman's abiding love for her animals, and all the special affection, attention and love she had given him. Maybe my own pleasure and devotion in raising that puppy was greater because every time I looked at him, I was reminded of how mistaken I had been about the woman. Coming from her, my puppy's name seemed perfect to me, too. After all, she taught me everyone deserves a chance. And thinking back on the way I'd been so quick to judge her, I was really glad I'd been given the chance to find out who she really was.

We kids had been so wrong about "Miss Alpo." She wasn't what she seemed at all. She wasn't a destitute woman living on dog food. She raised puppies, and bought them dog food.

From time to time, especially when things in my own life get especially stressful, I think about "Miss Alpo." Seeing her in the store with dog food in her cart didn't mean she took it home to eat it herself. It helps to have all the pieces of information in order to see the whole picture. When you have all the pieces, sometimes it changes the way you see things—and sometimes it even changes the entire picture.

Jennifer Leigh Youngs

You Snooze, You Lose!

Last Wednesday, I set my alarm for seven o'clock in the morning, just like I always do. But I'd gone to bed a little later than usual, so when it went off, I rolled over and hit the snooze button, thinking I'd catch five more minutes of sleep before I got up. For some reason, the snooze alarm didn't go off. When I looked over and saw that it was 7:45, I couldn't believe it!

Since I was running late, I skipped breakfast (and feeding my dog Samson), and I didn't make my bed or straighten up my room—even though it's part of the "house rules."

I ran as fast as I could to catch the bus, but even so, I missed it. Luckily for me, my father hadn't left for work yet, so I asked him for a ride to school. He wasn't too happy about it because it meant he would be late for an appointment he had set up. So he was annoyed at me, especially since it was the second time in two weeks that I had missed the bus. We rode to school in dead silence.

By the time I got to school, the five-minute bell had already rung, so I had to go to the office to get a late-pass before I could be admitted to class. That's when I remembered that I hadn't asked my father to write a note for my being late. He'd been in such a bad mood, and I knew this was especially directed at me, so I decided there was no way I could call him now. Besides, he was sure to be in his meeting.

So, there I was, sitting out first hour in the principal's office. Things were really starting to snowball—but it was only the beginning. Since I was absent from my first-hour class, I missed my science test. My teacher said I couldn't make up the test since I had an unexcused absence. The reason this really upset me was because I needed that test to bring up my grade-point average in order to stay eligible for the tennis team. I'm captain of the team, and being removed because of low grades would be really embarrassing. Besides, my dad promised to pay half on a car for me if my grades improved by the end of this semester. So I started thinking about not being able to buy a car, and I got even more upset.

Then, when I went to my locker to get my books for my second-hour class, I discovered my math book was missing—but only after I searched for it like crazy—yanking everything out of my locker, piling it all on the ground and stuffing it all back in. It seems, by mistake, my lockermate, Barney Johnson, had picked up my book instead of his own. By this time, I was frantic. I hadn't turned in my math assignment the day before, and Mr. Cohen warned me not to let it happen again. Naturally, my overdue math paper was in the book Barney had, and I had no idea where he could be. So, rather than face the teacher, I decided the best thing to do was to skip math class.

The math teacher took attendance, and because I wasn't reported on the absence list the vice-principal called my mother at work to tell her that I wasn't in school. (I'm not the type of kid whose parents usually get these kind of calls.)

Finally, the bell rang and I went off to third-hour class. When I got there my friends, who were just kidding around, teased me about my whereabouts during second hour. But by this time, I was in no mood for their humor and I was really rude to them. "Why don't you just worry about yourself," I snapped, then snarled, "Who do you think you are, a truant officer?" Being upset with my friends always makes me feel uneasy, even on the best of days—on a day like this one, it felt even worse.

I was standing in the lunch line when I noticed Barney Johnson. "Hey, Johnson! You took my math book, you idiot!" I called out. Barney, who wasn't having such a hot day either, yelled back, "Get off my back, you jerk!" Already at the end of my rope, I shoved Barney against the wall. My fist was raised ready to hit him when who should appear—the vice-principal!

Surprised to see me, he ordered me to get away from Barney.

Then he told me about the call he made earlier to my mother. "You'll need to come with me," he commanded.

Feeling really frustrated, I replied, "Not right now, I don't. I'm hungry and I need to eat. Even prisoners have rights!" For me to say I "said" this to him may be playing it down. I think I may have shouted it—at the vice-principal. You can imagine how this tactic went over.

As he led me to the office, all I could think about was what the vice-principal had in mind for me. I was also worried about the phone call he'd made to my mother. Knowing my mother had been told that I wasn't in school made me feel even more stressed out. I knew she was going to call my father and tell him, too. I asked if I could use the phone in the office to call my mom, but I was reminded that students aren't permitted to use the office phone. Since I wasn't allowed to leave the office because I was in trouble for fighting, I wasn't able to make a call from the hall pay phone, either.

Finally, at three-fifteen, the school day was over. What a nightmare—and the day still wasn't over for me. I still had to go home and face my parents.

Deciding that honesty was the best policy on this one—and not having the energy to make things sound any less disastrous than they were, I just told my parents the whole story. And you know what? They were really cool about it.

"Sounds like your day was tough, all right," my dad said after I told him about it.

"Let's get you some dinner and talk about what you might've done to make it less difficult," my mom suggested.

When I went to bed that night, they brought me in another alarm clock. "Here, the snooze alarm works on this one," my dad said. "But I guess I don't have to remind *you* anymore that when you snooze, you lose."

Rob Lawson, 15

The Gun Wasn't Even Loaded

I've never been much of an athlete. Even so, I decided to try out for the football team. My older brother had been such a football star in high school that it seemed like the thing to do. But I wasn't very good. Unfortunately, a lot of guys felt the need to remind me. It's not very fun to be the source of great entertainment to the "jocks" who made the team—even though I'm sure my clumsy throws were hilarious. And I did cause a good share of my own bruises, including a sprained wrist, just by tripping over my own feet!

But then the guys took to calling me names in the halls—like "sissy," "sweetie," "nerdo" and a lot of other names. There was nothing good-natured about their comments.

I tried ignoring them. Then I tried not to let it bother me. Then I tried to tolerate them. But they kept it up, and wouldn't let up. I really thought about slugging each of them, but they were so much bigger than I was, I decided that would be asking for a trip to the emergency room—for myself! I asked them to stop. Of course they didn't. I think it made it worse: They stepped up their crusade of name-calling, and added tripping me whenever I walked by any of them, as well as a few "playful" punches that landed anywhere between the top of my head to my stomach. And it wasn't as if I could beat them up—I'd get slaughtered.

That's when I came up with this plan: I'd take my stepfather's gun to school with me, and the next time they started in on me, I'd flash it in front of them. It's not like I was really going to use the gun—it wasn't even loaded. But I knew it would really scare them, and I figured then they would leave me alone.

I was at my locker one day when a couple of guys from the team came by. When they saw me, they heckled me and just about the time one of them reached out to hit me on the top of my head with his history book, I lifted up my shirt so they'd see the gun in my waistband. Then I told them in no uncertain terms that they'd better back off for good—or else. It seemed to work because they took one look at the gun and left. I was relieved and thought, "Okay, so I'm getting a little respect! This is good."

But word traveled fast. Next thing I knew, I was hauled out of class and into the principal's office, where the cops came and carted me off to the sheriff's substation.

They called my mom at the bank where she's the vice president, and after she posted five thousand dollars bail, I was booked and released to her. Needless to say, I was in big trouble: at home, at school and with the law. And I was worried. This was a far bigger issue than having the guys at school think I was a nerd. I felt terrible that this was also a blow to my parents, and I kept thinking about ending up in juvenile hall—being locked up with some of those guys would be much worse than facing the football stars at school. I couldn't sleep. Every night I'd lay awake thinking how much trouble I had gotten myself into. So the night before I was supposed to go to court, I sneaked out my bedroom window and ran away.

Boy, was that dumb! I ended up at my older brother's apartment with his two roommates. My brother was out of town on a ski trip, so I told his roommates I was mad at my parents and asked them to please not tell them I was there—which they had no problem lying about when my parents called my brother's place to ask if they'd seen me. Well, it was a bad deal because since I didn't appear in court when I was supposed to, my mother lost the bail she posted. Then I just knew that I really couldn't go home.

Everything seemed to get worse and worse from there on out; everything I did turned into a disaster. Which doesn't at all fit the "good kid" reputation I had before all this. Everybody—my neighbors, teachers, the other kids, *everyone*—thought of me as a trustworthy, responsible, considerate, nice, easygoing guy. Neighbors trusted me with the keys to their houses when they went on vacations (so that I could pick up their mail, feed their pets, water their flowers). They hired me for odd jobs and yard care. I got good grades, and got along well with both my mother and my stepfather. Now, here I was in this mess that even the biggest school troublemakers couldn't have imagined being in.

Strangely enough, as much as I wanted things to get better, things went from bad to worse. I just kept digging myself in deeper and deeper. Every decision I made turned out to be the wrong one and made matters worse. Now I can see that every one of those decisions was based on getting out of the problem I was in at that moment, without thinking of any of the long-term consequences of my actions. Not once did I just stop and try to gain perspective. If I had, the situation wouldn't have gotten so far out of hand. My mother says that eventually one learns to see that no matter how bad life gets, there is always "light at the end of the tunnel."

I'm back in school now, and trying to stay out of trouble. I'm on two years' probation, so it's important that I not screw up my life even more. That's my goal. I know I can do it. I can see "the light at the end of the tunnel."

Shawn McLaughlin, 17

My Struggle with Drugs

When I was fifteen, I started using drugs—mostly because I was hanging around with some friends who were using them. One drug led to my using another, and pretty soon I was doing a lot of drugs. I stopped hanging out with my "straight" friends and began only hanging out with friends who were "using" as much as I was. They were usually older than me. A lot of them didn't go to school, and many of them didn't have jobs, either. They just hung out all day and did as much drugs as they could.

At the time, this all seemed really cool to me. With this crowd I began to use harder and harder drugs—even though it was beginning to scare me. One thing led to another, and pretty soon I was seriously hooked.

Both of my parents always taught me the importance of taking care of myself—including choosing to live drug-free. I used anyway, and continued even when I knew that my health was suffering.

Using drugs messed up my life in a lot of ways. My grades went from average to bad to failing. Then, because I felt like a failure, I'd try not to think about it. Drugs helped me run away from facing things, like my grades and my parents. Then I began to stay away from home, sometimes for a day or two—or three—at a time. That led to me and Mom fighting all the time.

After a while, she told me that if I was going to be a "druggy," I had to leave, which was fine by me. Every kid using drugs wants to get "permission" to leave the house and crash at a friend's place. It's very easy to find a place to stay if you're a good-looking girl.

Mom had tried everything she knew to help me get straight. Even though my mother had resigned herself to the fact that I needed to "reach bottom"—to make a decision that I wasn't going to do drugs any longer—she didn't want me to live away from home. She wanted me to stop using drugs and get healthy, not just leave home because she had a rule of no drugs—or else. But what could she do? I had made a choice to do what I wanted to do, which at that time was to do drugs.

My life went on like this for months and months. Until one day, Mom said she woke up in the middle of the night and just knew that I needed help. She said she just knew in her heart that I needed rescuing, and that she could no longer just wait for a day when I would turn my life around on my own.

My mother is very resourceful. She found me! One Thursday at two o'clock in the morning, she drove to where I was staying. Even though she was scared and didn't know what she was walking into, she came into the rented house where I was hanging out at the time. I was there with five of my "friends," all of us really wasted from doing drugs.

My mother knew from looking at me that I needed medical help. Good thing, too, because I was really messed up. Though she looked calm on the outside, Mom has told me since then that she was terrified. I guess the friends I was with, all of us, looked pretty dangerous. I know that I was really out of it. I can only imagine how difficult it must have been for my mother to see me in the condition I was in. I mean, here I was, her daughter, once an okay student and athlete, now looking lifeless, stoned out of my mind.

I saw the pictures that were taken of me when I was in the emergency room. They were pretty scary looking.

When I look at those pictures now, it still scares me. So it must have been especially terrible for her. What courage she had! And to take me with her! I mean, it's not like I was happy to see her and so happy to be taken from my friends and my addiction that I skipped to her car and went merrily on home with her! Because my mother had come to what I thought was my private hide-away, and there I was with my "cool" friends, all of us high and happy about it, and now a parent—mine—was standing in their living room—no doubt judging them as terrible people—I was more than upset about her being there.

When my mother tells the story, she says I was "hostile," and I don't doubt that I was.

Because I was in no condition to walk, let alone be reasoned with, my mother didn't even try to force me to leave. Instead, she calmly announced that she was staying until I decided to come home with her! The standoff between the two of us lasted almost the rest of the night—what was left of it. As the drugs began to wear off, and when I got so tired I would have done anything to get some sleep, I finally gave in and we went home together.

Over the next few days, my mother really set in motion one million plans—all designed to get me some help. She got a drug "intervention" to take place. This is where the people dearest to you come together and, along with a drug counselor, try to convince you that they're fearful that you may kill yourself—or hurt someone else (like in a car accident)—if you continue doing drugs.

As Mom had hoped, it worked. I agreed to go for help at a drug rehab center. Even when I was released, Mom continued to help me get my life back together. And that's what I'm up to now, living in a healthy way, day-by-day, one day at a time—rather than the day-by-day failing I had been doing.

Mom says it was the "most harrowing experience" of her life. I am so lucky she loves me and believed that with help I would break free of drugs and get my life together. It took a lot of courage for my mother to do what she did.

Whenever life seems tough, and I wish I didn't have to feel what I was feeling, I think about getting high. But only for a moment. What keeps me from relapsing is thinking of my mother's courage. It helps me be strong. I know if she could do all she did for me, face all she faced, I can get through whatever I'm going through without drugs. I'm very grateful for my mother's love and loyalty. I think one of the greatest examples of courage I've ever seen is what my mother did for me.

I credit her with saving my life. Because of what she did for me, she is the most courageous person I know.

Next to her, I am the most courageous person I know.

Every day of my life I struggle to stay drug-free. And that's exactly what it is. A struggle.

So if you aren't using drugs, don't. If you are, go to your parents. Even if they yell at you—which they probably will—go to them anyway. When they're done being mad that you're slowly killing yourself because of doing drugs, they'll help you get well.

Gianne Warren, 16

A Capacity to Mend

Each of us begins with a garment
of different weave and design,
which in time's passage
becomes worn, washed, wrinkled,
stained, stretched, shrunk,
faded, frazzled, fragmented
and hung up.
That's the way it is my friends.

But we are equipped with a capacity to mend
and with a colorful variety of patches.
It's up to us whether we wind up
tattered, tangled, torn and tossed,
Or become a pleasing example
of patchwork artistry.
It's a choice.
And that's the way it is my friends.

Elmer Adrian, 90

Permissions *(continued from page iv)*

What I'd Like to Tell You—If I Could, by Bettie B. Youngs. Reprinted with permission by publisher Health Communications, Inc., Deerfield Beach, Florida, from *Gifts of the Heart* by Bettie B. Youngs, Ph.D., Ed.D. ©1996 Bettie B. Youngs, Ph.D., Ed.D. Adapted from the story "The Blue Ribbon."

Love Is Everywhere, by Bettie B. Youngs. Reprinted with permission by publisher Health Communications, Inc., Deerfield Beach, Florida, from *Taste-Berry Tales* by Bettie B. Youngs, Ph.D., Ed.D. ©1998 Bettie B. Youngs, Ph.D., Ed.D.

The Pickle Fork, by Priscilla Dunn. Reprinted with permission by Cyndie De Neve, editor, *North County Times,* May 10, 1998.

To My Teenager, by M. Joye, ©1984 Blue Mountain Arts, Inc. All rights reserved. Reprinted by permission of Blue Mountain Arts.

Secretly, I Changed My Name, by Hanoch McCarty. Reprinted with permission by publisher Health Communications, Inc., Deerfield Beach, Florida, from *A 4th Course of Chicken Soup for the Soul* by Jack Canfield, Mark Victor Hansen, Hanoch McCarty and Meladee McCarty. ©1997 Jack Canfield, Mark Victor Hansen, Hanoch McCarty and Meladee McCarty. Adapted from the story "What's in a Name?"

The Greatest Love of All (Footprints), excerpted from *Footprints, the True Story Behind the Poem That Inspired Millions,* by Margaret Fishback Powers ©1993. (HarperCollins). Reprinted with permission.

Equal Pay for Equal Worth, by Bettie B. Youngs. Reprinted with permission by publisher Health Communications, Inc., Deerfield Beach, Florida, from *Gifts of the Heart* by Bettie B. Youngs, Ph.D., Ed.D. ©1996 Bettie B. Youngs, Ph.D., Ed.D.

I Have to Live with Myself and So . . . , 52 Simple Ways to Encourage Others and *You! Yes, You!* Excerpted from *I CAN Ignite the Community Spirit: 301 Ways to Turn Caring into Action,* by Joy J. Golliver and Ruth Hayes-Arista. ©1997 Joy J. Golliver and Ruth Hayes-Arista. To order call 1-800-254-ICAN. Reprinted with permission.

The Three-Legged Cheetah, by Bettie B. Youngs. Reprinted with permission by publisher Health Communications, Inc., Deerfield Beach, Florida, from *Taste-Berry Tales* by Bettie B. Youngs, Ph.D., Ed.D. ©1998 Bettie B. Youngs, Ph.D., Ed.D. Adapted from the story "The Gift of Subira."

Kevin Got "Lucky," by Bettie B. Youngs. Reprinted with permission by publisher Health Communications, Inc., Deerfield Beach, Florida, from *Gifts of the Heart* by Bettie B. Youngs, Ph.D., Ed.D. ©1996 Bettie B. Youngs, Ph.D., Ed.D. Adapted from the story "Just Lucky."

About the Authors

Bettie B. Youngs, Ph.D., Ed.D., is a professional speaker and the internationally renowned author of sixteen books translated into twenty-nine languages. She is a former Teacher of the Year, university professor and executive director of the Phoenix Foundation. Currently, she is president of Professional Development, Inc. She is a long-acknowledged expert on teens and has frequently appeared on *NBC Nightly News*, CNN, *Oprah* and *Geraldo*. *USA Today*, the *Washington Post*, *Redbook*, *McCall's*, *Working Woman*, *Family Circle*, *Parents Magazine*, *Better Homes & Gardens*, *Woman's Day* and the National Association for Secondary School Principals (NASSP) have all recognized her work. Her acclaimed books include *Safeguarding Your Teenager from the Dragons of Life; How to Develop Self-Esteem in Your Child; Stress and Your Child: Helping Kids Cope with the Strains and Pressures of Life; You and Self-Esteem: A Book for Young People; Taste-Berry Tales; Gifts of the Heart;* and the award-winning *Values from the Heartland*. Dr. Youngs is the author of a number of video-cassette programs for Sybervision and Nightingale/Conant and the coauthor of the nationally acclaimed *Parents on Board*, a video-based training program to help schools and parents work together to increase student achievement.

Jennifer Leigh Youngs, twenty-four, is a speaker and workshop presenter for teens and parents nationwide. She is the author of *A Stress-Management Guide for Young People* and the co-author of *Goal-Setting Skills for Young Adults* and *Problem-Solving Skills for Children*. Jennifer is a former Miss Teen California finalist and a Rotary International Goodwill Ambassador and

Exchange Scholar. She serves on a number of advisory boards for teens including the National Advisory Board for Caboodles International. Her interests focus on the well-being of teens. "I'd like to be happy, to live my life around those things that seem meaningful to me, and I'd especially like those who meet me—even if for a brief moment—to feel they met a friend," she says.

To contact Bettie Youngs or Jennifer Leigh Youngs, write to:

Bettie B. Youngs & Associates
Box 2588
Del Mar, CA 92014

Other HCI Titles from Bettie B. Youngs

Gifts of the Heart

These 27 inspiring "parables" show us that it is often how we choose to handle a situation—not the situation itself—that infuses our lives with new meaning. These real life lessons—often passed on in subtle ways during "defining moments"—are genuine, potent and precious.

Code #4193 • $12.95

Values from the Heartland

Bettie B. Youngs shares her memories of growing up in America's heartland with loving detail - a rich tapestry that allows us to share in the warmth and balance of a principle-centered life.

Code #3359 • $11.95

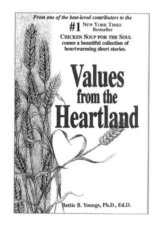

Taste-Berry® Tales

25 poignant short stories of real-life people who make a difference in the lives of others. These individuals, by their example, show us how to use the events of daily life to improve the world we live in and the lives of others with whom we share it.

Code #5475 • $11.95

Bestselling Chicken Soup for Teens

Collect all three of the *Chicken Soup for the Teenage Soul* volumes. Bestselling stories from teens on learning to embraced life, becoming the person you can be, being happy with who you are and loving yourself.

Code #4630—$12.95

Code #6161—$12.95

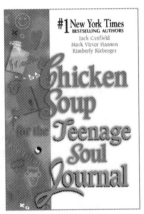

Code #6374—$12.95

More from the *Chicken Soup for the Soul®* Series

#6161—$12.95

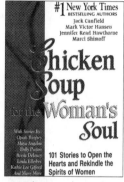

#4150—$12.95

#6218—$12.95

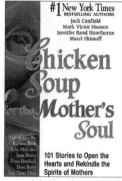

#4606—$12.95

Chicken Soup for the Soul® Series

Each one of these inspiring *New York Times* bestsellers brings you exceptional stories, tales and verses guaranteed to lift your spirits, soothe your soul and warm your heart! A perfect gift for anyone you love, including yourself!

A 5th Portion of Chicken Soup for the Soul, #5432—$12.95
A 4th Course of Chicken Soup for the Soul, #4592—$12.95
A 3rd Serving of Chicken Soup for the Soul, #3790—$12.95
A 2nd Helping of Chicken Soup for the Soul, #3316—$12.95
Chicken Soup for the Soul, #262X—$12.95

#1 New York Times
BESTSELLING AUTHORS

Jack Canfield
Mark Victor Hansen
Mark & Chrissy Donnelly
and
Barbara De Angelis, Ph.D.

Chicken Soup for the Couple's Soul

With Stories By:
Paul Reiser
Marianne Williamson
Deepak Chopra
George Burns
Joan Wester Anderson
Charlton Heston
And Many More

Inspirational Stories About
Love and Relationships

Chicken Soup for the Couple's Soul

Whether single, married or separated, everyone wants to find
and keep this elusive thing called "love." Bestselling author
and foremost relationship expert Barbara De Angelis teams
up as a co-author of *Chicken Soup for the Couple's Soul,* a
collection of heartwarming stories about how real people
discovered true love with the person of their dreams. A
sweet spoonful of this enchanting Chicken Soup collection
will warm the hearts of romantic readers everywhere.
Code #6463 Paperback • $12.95